Against the Closet

Against the Closet

BLACK

POLITICAL

LONGING

AND THE

EROTICS

OF RACE

Aliyyah I. Abdur-Rahman

DUKE UNIVERSITY PRESS

DURHAM AND LONDON   2012

© 2012 Duke University Press
All rights reserved
Printed in the United States
of America on acid-free paper ♾
Designed by Amy Ruth Buchanan
Typeset in Quadraat and Quadraat
Sans by Keystone Typesetting, Inc.
Library of Congress Cataloging-
in-Publication Data appear on the
last printed page of this book.

TO ISA

Contents

Acknowledgments

The successful publication of any scholarship is a collaborative endeavor. An undertaking as extensive and time- and energy-consuming as researching and writing a manuscript and developing it with sufficient refinement to publish it requires the cooperative effort and dedication of a very large group of people. I have had since graduate school the very best group of people—those who have taken all that is at their disposal to give license and direction for others, for me, to grow.

It is with utmost gratitude that I thank, first and foremost, my two dissertation advisers at New York University (NYU): Elizabeth McHenry and Phillip Brian Harper. Absolutely central to my own development have been their mentorship, standard of excellence, and continuous support. All of my successes to this point are a testament to their generosity, intellectual rigor, exemplary professionalism, and genuine dedication. And no less to Ross Posnock, Steven Kruger, and José Muñoz, the other members of my dissertation committee, I owe sincerest, eternal gratitude. This book is born of the critical conversations their graduate classes engaged. In its earliest incarnation as a dissertation, this book benefited tremendously from their support. Over the years, they read numerous drafts, offered critical feedback, and pushed me to refine and rethink my propositions. Their classes and their individual conversations provided some of the richest material for the work this book undertakes. I am grateful to other professors at NYU who took an interest in me and assisted me greatly in terms of scholarship, funding, and professional preparation: Carolyn Dinshaw, Lisa Duggan, John Maynard, Hal Momma, Cyrus R. K. Patell, and G. Gabrielle Starr.

Since graduate school and throughout my career, I have been blessed to receive financial support for research. This project has benefited from fellowships awarded by the Ford Foundation, the Mellon Foundation, the Woodrow Wilson Foundation, the American Association of University Women, and the

Dean's Offices of NYU and Brandeis University. I am convinced that without this funding, coming always at critical moments in the development of this manuscript, I would not have completed it. In the last stages of revising the manuscript, I had the benefit of spending a semester as a visiting scholar at the University of California, Berkeley. I owe the book's existence and its final arrival in print to these various institutions.

For their scholarship, without which mine would not be possible; for the most illuminating conversations of my career; for familiarizing themselves with my work and pushing me to make it better; for reminding me always of the real-world stakes of any scholarly undertaking; for generous mentorship and genuine friendship, I am most grateful to Houston Baker, Rich Blint, Jennifer Brody, Kimberly Juanita Brown, Michele Elam, Nadia Ellis, Sharon Holland, Abdul JanMohamed, Koritha Mitchell, Joycelyn Moody, Robert Reid-Pharr, Leigh Raiford, Riche D. Richardson, Hortense Spillers, and Salamishah Tillet. At Brandeis University I have found a true institutional and intellectual home. I am most fortunate to have as colleagues in the English Department and as personal friends Ulka Anjaria, John Burt, Mary Campbell, Billy Flesch, Michael Gilmore, Caren Irr, Tom King, Sue Lanser, Paul Morrison, John Plotz, Laura Quinney, Dave Sherman, Dawn Skorczewski, Faith Smith, and Ramie Targoff. And no less to Lydia Fash, I am grateful for exquisite research assistance and countless delightful moments on campus. For the past few years, I have also enjoyed the camaraderie and intellectual support of a magnificent group of black women scholars in the New England area. I am grateful to the members of the New England Black Scholars Collective: Sandy Alexander, Nicole Aljoe, Alisa Braithwaite, Soyica Diggs-Colbert, Régine Jean-Charles, Stephanie Larrieux, Monica White Ndounou, and Sam Vasquez. Not only are these women some of the most brilliant, *badass* upcoming scholars in the field of black cultural studies, but they are also the best models of how to thrive in this profession with personal integrity and abiding friendship.

Mere words cannot express my gratitude to Ken Wissoker. Since our first, fortuitous meeting at the Modern Language Association's annual convention some years ago, he has been a generous supporter and a visionary, seeing in my promising idea what this book could be and needed to become. I am grateful as well to the two anonymous readers whose incisive thinking and guidance proved to be essential to realizing the best version of this book. I am grateful to Leigh Barnwell at Duke University Press for her timely and generous support throughout the publication process. An earlier version of the first chapter, "'The Strangest Freaks of Despotism': Queer Sexuality in Antebellum African American Slave Narratives," appeared in *African American Review*

40, no. 2 (Summer 2006). I am grateful for permission to reprint. I am also grateful to the *Faulkner Journal* for granting me permission to reprint in my second chapter portions of the earlier essay "White Disavowal, Black Enfranchisement, and the Homoerotic in William Faulkner's *Light in August*," which originally appeared in *Faulkner Journal* 22, nos. 1–2 (Fall 2006–Spring 2007), copyright 2007 by the University of Central Florida.

I am eternally grateful to the many "loving others" who comprise my life and my self. I am indebted to numerous friends—too many to name here—for support and care throughout the long and arduous process of writing and publishing this book. I am convinced that the book would not be here if not for all of those late-night phone calls, midafternoon teas, and well-timed embraces. I have a huge family, composed of fourteen siblings and a huge extended family. I owe all to them: my parents, Inshirah and Mujahid Abdur-Rahman, and my sisters, brothers, aunts, uncles, nieces, nephews, cousins. For my entire life, they have been my main sources of love, confidence, and courage. I have found in my Muslim parents the best models of personhood. They are for me the truest exemplars of love, steadfastness, generosity, integrity, and wisdom. And while I do not expect that the subject of this book will resonate completely with them, I am confident that its commitment to social justice will.

And finally, to Isa, the beautiful child and ingenious soul I have the distinct honor of calling my son, I dedicate this book. Arriving shortly before I began graduate school, Isa has been with me for what feels like my whole adult life, massaging into being the things I like best about myself. Isa is my engine, my reason, and the person whose thriving is tied most inextricably and tenderly to my own. I wrote this book for him, and I offer it now in the hope that it may be a small contribution to making the world in which he grows up better.

Introduction

AGAINST THE CLOSET

Racial Logic and the Bodily Basis/Biases of Sexual Identity

[The] erotic . . . [is] our deepest knowledge, a power that, unlike other spheres of power, we all have access to and that can lessen the threat of our individual difference.
—Gina Dent, *Black Popular Culture*

I envision a politics where one's relation to power, and not some homogenized identity, is privileged in determining one's political comrades. I am talking about a politics where the nonnormative and marginal position of punks, bulldaggers, and welfare queens, for example, is the basis for progressive transformative coalition work.
—Cathy J. Cohen, "Punks, Bulldaggers, and Welfare Queens"

Gayness . . . exist[s] under the mask(s) of blackness.
—Sharon Patricia Holland, *Raising the Dead*

Like many researchers of African American identity and U.S. expressive culture, I had hoped to produce a straightforward examination of blackness—an abstract racial designation as elemental and vital as blood, as socially formative as nationhood. I wanted to trace the making and meaning of a racial identity that is clearly mere theorization, ideological innovation, and yet terribly potent in its ability to make its meaning manifest in the "real" world through myriad denigrating social, material, and psychological effects on millions of black Americans. I wanted to explore blackness's essence, its fungibility, its nothingness, and the sheer weight of its possession. But for so many reasons I found this to be an impossible task, especially without bringing to bear on racialized blackness a broad conception and application of "queerness," or transgressive sexual theorization—for not only does sexuality fundamentally underlie racial logics, but, more to the point, racial identity is itself conceived, regulated, and disciplined through sexuality—through sexual practices, violations, and norms.

A consideration of Harriet Jacobs's *Incidents in the Life of a Slave Girl* is illuminative here, demonstrating the relevance of the erotic or the sexual—the sexually normative, the sexually abusive, the sexually divergent or defiant—to the creation of race and to the acquisition and maintenance of power. Although her narrative is ostensibly one of slavery, Jacobs presents her experiences in and escape from bondage as a tale of sexual pursuit, sexual harassment, sexual compromise, and sexual freedom. For her, incidents of sexual abuse serve as both metonym and metaphor for the lived experience of American slavery. While it is becoming increasingly commonplace to locate the emergence of codified sexuality in reified notions of gender and sexual difference, Jacobs's text demonstrates the interimbrication of racial and sexual ideologies in the making and maneuvering of exclusionary political and social apparatuses. *Incidents* also makes clear that, as early as the antebellum period, African American writers, spokespeople, and cultural producers sought to narrate the struggles of black life, revise dominant ideologies of racial difference, and agitate for personal and collective liberation through an appeal to sexuality. As Jacobs's narrative exemplifies, depictions of rape, of coerced concubinage, of forced reproduction—of bereft, sexually abused black girls— serve as truly apt metaphors for the violence and violation of embodied black slavery. There is power in the erotic, and in sexual non-normativity, to narrate a world—or, more specifically, to narrate the world of particular marginalized, minoritarian subjects and to remake it.

In the U.S. cultural imaginary it is quite nearly impossible to separate ideas about race from ideas about sexuality. As Michel Foucault famously put it, sexuality is a "dense transfer point for relations of power."[1] In the United States, the ideological regimes that disqualify black people from participating fully in American civic and political culture exploit heteronormativity as the index of both inclusion and exclusion. Because sexuality, as Ellen Ross and Rayna Rapp posit, "both generates wider social relations and is refracted through the prism of society," sexuality serves as a useful lens for investigating the constructions and contradictions of power relations organized around multiple axes of difference, including gender, class, and especially race.[2]

Taking, then, Jacobs's literary, liberatory deployment of transgressive sexual representation as fundamental to the development of African American forms of literary expression, political intervention, and cultural self-fashioning, this book advances a new architecture of race in which race operates *as erotics*—that is, part destiny, part desire. Accordingly, this book asks: what would it mean for racial embodiment and experience if, instead of belonging to the realm of the external, the phenotypical, the material and instead of heavy-handedly fueling the operative forces of compulsory interpellation, race moved inward and operated for the racialized subject primarily from an internal site of instinct, impulse, intuition, longing? What, furthermore, might be the productive effects of representations of deviant sexualities on African American cultural identity, and might these representations inform an emancipatory political project that undergirds an entire literary tradition?

Guided by a logic of investigative inquiry, though not necessarily of resolute finding, *Against the Closet* analyzes African American literary and cultural production of different epochs to analyze the ways in which black writers have deployed constructions of transgressive sexuality tropologically to challenge popular theories of identity, pathology, national belonging, and racial difference in American culture. This book reads genres from the slave narrative to science fiction and such authors as Harriet Jacobs, Pauline Hopkins, William Faulkner, James Baldwin, and Octavia Butler alongside and against contemporary queer, feminist, and critical race theory to illuminate how race, politics, and sexuality intersect in the social and racial ordering of U.S. culture and in the making of African American literature and expressive culture. A fundamentally irrational force, sexuality has the power to wrest individuals from their ideological investments and thus to begin to level the playing field of human interactions, despite existing social asymmetries. This study attends to the liberationist impulses and disruptive impacts underwriting representations of sexual deviance and alternative domesticities in black cultural productions, even as it historicizes pivotal moments at which ideologies of sexual normalcy and sexual pathology have supported racism and the unfair distribution of rights and resources in American society.

My primary goal in this book is to undertake and to advance a radical reconsideration of the dominant scholarship on black American literary engagements with sexuality—one in which homosexuality, lynching, interracial love, sadomasochism, and incest are understood principally as tropes that gain currency in African American literature and expressive culture of different historical periods. Treating in each chapter a different form of sexual aberrance across a range of texts, I show that the depiction of sadomasochism, or incest, or any other expression of "perversity" is a deliberate utilization of the metaphorics of sexuality that, when read closely and particularly,

(1) speaks to the psychodynamics of particular racial injuries, (2) exemplifies or explodes generic conventions in popular literary and expressive forms, and (3) illuminates the exigencies of African American social life and political aspiration during specific historical periods. Less to make a claim about the linear development of a representational structure than to produce a lucid and rigorous study, my analysis proceeds chronologically. I identify four critical periods in African American experience: slavery, post-Reconstruction, civil rights and black power, and the post-civil rights era, tracking the emergence of a specific sexual trope in African American literature that works to represent and remedy the unique challenges of that moment.

Specifically, during slavery, under a totalizing regime of domination, sadomasochism figures prominently in African American writing to represent the internal operations of slavery and its sadistic social and performative requirements. Sadomasochism refers in my analysis to slavery's "sadistic" institutional protocols and what I read as their "masochistic" textual reproduction in slave narratives. As such, sadomasochism both dramatizes the despair of stolen personhood and presents strategies for redefining agency and autonomy. During the post-Reconstruction era, lynching emerged as a powerful trope for figuring the solidification of whiteness through state-sanctioned racism and extralegal forms of racial terrorism. Lynching exposed, even as it perpetuated, the charade of black emancipation. During the civil rights era, literary representations of interracial romance presented idealized versions of interracial cooperation and anticipated the tranquil domestic space of a racially unified nation. The turn to black homoerotic love in the late era of black power, specifically in the work of James Baldwin, imagines a self-sustaining black community that can accommodate difference, an avowal of black humanity and political solidarity that does not require racial proscription. Finally, in the late twentieth century, incest appears repeatedly in the writing of prominent black female authors. Literary depictions of incest speak to racism's profound and incessant injuries to black women and children, epitomizing the disintegration of the black family under the pressures of the legislative retrenchment of civil rights, reinvigorated black patriarchy, dwindling communal supports, negligible economic resources, and urban decay.

This study is indebted to black feminist literary criticism. Ann duCille, Hazel Carby, Claudia Tate, and Frances Smith Foster are notable scholars of nineteenth-century black women's writing. It was their pioneering work that first posited black literary constructions of erotic desires as allegories for political desires, domestic spaces as instantiations of social and racial relations. For more than twenty years, the scholarship advanced by these scholars

—and most recently by Candice Jenkins—has emphasized heteronormativity under the rubric of (domestic, cultural) respectability as the primary analytic for reading the imaginative deployment of sexuality in black American literary products. Bringing to bear theories and histories of sexuality and black queer studies, *Against the Closet* makes the case that a strident distrust and disavowal of heteronormativity—as a regulatory ideal, an elusive construct, a dangerous component of hegemony—underlie the African American literary tradition, even as it recognizes the anxious efforts of black cultural workers to refigure blackness as (hetero)normative so that black Americans could enter the cultural mainstream and enjoy the full benefits of unqualified citizenship. Beginning in the mid-nineteenth century and proceeding to traverse the entire twentieth century, this book shows that it is within constructions of sexual perversions that we find the most searing, astute illustrations and indictments of race-based inequality in the United States. Charting the long history of black American letters, my study unfolds to illuminate the potential of transgressive erotics to constitute a representational structure that expresses the longings of African Americans to achieve individual and collective freedom. The very utility of this representational apparatus, evident in the long history of black American political resistance via textual production, is its repeated challenge to hegemonic whiteness's attempt to fasten to black people sexual and racial pathology, along with the negations of personal worth, human capacity, and rights-bearing citizenship that such pathologies both imply and secure.

By engaging black feminist historiography, queer theory, and critical race theory, I hope to dislodge queer studies a bit from its primary disciplinary location in gender studies and to resituate it more firmly within the study of race or, more specifically, in the history of African American articulations of identity formation, expressive culture, and political resistance. *Against the Closet* joins a growing cadre of studies dedicated to the exploration of sexuality and race that have emerged between the late 1990s and the current millennium, moving ultimately, however, in a different direction.[3] While many scholars of sexuality and African American studies readily acknowledge the coterminous invention and regulation of codified racial and sexual identities, the interrelation of these categories within the symbolic system of cultural signification has not been recognized in the main. For me, simply historicizing the intersection of race and sexuality does not exhaust the critical and political potential of their alliance. My goal in this book is thus to move beyond the mere historicization or redemption of same-gender sexuality in the African American context. The analyses taken up in the various chapters of this book do not centralize same-gender eroticism as their exclusive focus per se. Neither am I invested in solidifying racialized queerness *as* identity; rather, this book examines modern epistemologies of sexuality to distill their specific implications and sociopolitical utility for racial blackness, for black cultural expression, and for ongoing attempts at black freedom. My goal is to harness the insurrectionary potential of an expanded, reformulated queer theory in the service of a radical and collaborative politics of race.

Notably, sexuality is crucial in *Against the Closet* for its many operations: as a constitutive element of identity, as a source of pleasure, as an organizing principle in the allocation of power, as a disciplinary practice or methodology, and as a liberatory political enterprise. The centrality of sexuality to this book's development and execution is owed finally to three basic tenets that undergird its focus and, for me, operate at the level of fact: (1) that race is the most important factor in the formation of (both individual and national) identity in the United States;[4] (2) that sexuality is a crucial component of racial difference;[5] and (3) that the creation and representation of difference in general is both a fundamental crisis in U.S. literary and cultural production and a vital instrument in the development of U.S. political practice. *Against the Closet* pursues a deep and wide-ranging examination of African American articulations and tropological deployments of sexual transgression toward manifestly political ends. Accordingly, I look unflinchingly at a range of non-normative sexual practices—including those that are enabling and those that are violating—to uncover not an erotics of liberation but a politics of liberation rendered in sexual terms in African American expressive culture.

The queer subject of this study is not exclusively, or necessarily even, the woman-loving woman or the man-loving man of our common understanding, although the lesbian and the male homosexual delineate and concretize in useful ways the genealogy, epistemology, and iconography of queerness in the U.S. cultural context with which this study is preoccupied. To be clear, the queer subject here is not defined wholly by sexual or identity practices and politics.[6] My queer subject is drawn from the various characters I encounter in the texts that I read throughout this book: the gang-raped black girl, the infantilized black man, the pedophile, the unwed teenage mother, the extraterrestrial, the castrated victim of lynching, the gun-toting revolutionary, the victim of domestic violence, the religious fanatic, the incest survivor, the lynch mob, the slave. In other words, the queer subject of this book inhabits social (and sometimes sexual) margins, throwing into crisis and into relief our most precious and pervasive ideations of the normative, along with the ideological, economic, and political apparatuses in which the violences of normativity operate.[7] This book emphasizes the ways in which dominant ideologies of racial difference and divergent sexuality function, usually in combination, in the service of a racially stratified and asymmetric social sphere. More important, it demonstrates the ways in which depictions of sexual deviance constitute in African American literature and expressive culture a recurrent, usable, emancipatory representational apparatus.

Sexuality and Race

For the better part of the past two centuries, both ordinary and specialized knowledge regimes have characterized black people as maladaptive social and sexual deviants. This characterization has justified the devastating and unrelenting marginalization of African Americans.[8] Because black identity establishes and exposes the limits of whiteness as identity category and ideological apparatus, the myth of black social and sexual deviance has also made black people, black suffering, and black cultural expression objects of intense interest and longing in the culture at large. To be sure, African Americans have been relegated to a lowly social status from the earliest arrivals on American shores; however, that status had been based in part on enslavement and not race alone. Ideologies of racial blackness, replete with predominantly negative beliefs about it, came to full fruition during the post-Reconstruction era, when segregation was institutionalized, minstrelsy gained in popularity all over the country, an emergent advertising industry profited primarily from derogatory stereotyped images of black people, and lynchings occurred nearly every week for three decades. According to historians of sexuality and scholars of African American studies, the development of discrete sexual categories in the late nineteenth century coincided with the discursive and legislative deployment of racial blackness to support coercive regimes of race-based social stratification between citizens. The linkage between the invention of blackness and that of alternative sexualities was cemented through the popular sciences of the late nineteenth century, including anthropology, psychology, and sexology, which established and circulated discourses of sexuality and race via similar, if not identical, ideologies about identity, normalcy, and pathology. These discourses of racial and sexual pathology contributed significantly to juridical measures (ranging from antimiscegenation laws to legal segregation) and acts of racial terrorism (such as lynching) that prevented black Americans from accessing the full entitlements of citizenship.

At the turn of the twentieth century, African American identity was biologically determined and legally constrained. It was defined primarily in relation to a set of anatomical markers of difference, including facial features, skin color, hair textures, and genitalia. Popular discourses and legislative processes that served to mark African American bodies as racially distinct also served to limit black participation in political and civic life. In 1877, the U.S. troops left the South as the government turned to the reunification of the fractured union after the Civil War. This period, generally called post-Reconstruction, was one of the bleakest in African American history. William Gleason summarizes, "Where Afro-Americans had expected first-class citizenship, they were offered [instead] segregation, discrimination, exploitation, and contempt. . . . [This historical moment] marked the nadir in the quest for equal rights."[9] To reunify the country after the Civil War, the government conceded to the South, granting most states the sovereignty to preserve or to develop racist legislation in every area of political and social life, including voting procedures, property laws, miscegenation laws, and hiring practices. In 1883, the Civil Rights Act of 1875, which prohibited discrimination against black people in public facilities, was overturned by the Supreme Court. One decade later, in 1896, the ruling in Plessy v. Ferguson allowed states to provide separate accommodations for white and black people in transportation and other public facilities. By legalizing the race-based division of public spaces, the Supreme Court mandated the physical separation of the races in the South.

Grace Elizabeth Hale argues that the racially volatile era of early-twentieth-century American culture inaugurated the racially tinged era of the spectacle.[10] Examining the emergence of the advertising industry, the popularity of minstrelsy, and the frequency of spectacle lynchings, she argues that new modes of production within capitalism enabled racial stereotypes to become firmly entrenched in the popular imagination. The railroad, cinema, and photography provided the means of disseminating negative images of African Americans quickly, and, unlike in earlier historical periods, these images were primarily photographic or cinematographic. For example, photographs of charred, dismembered, lynched black bodies that appeared in national newspapers helped to create and sustain the belief that black Americans were less than human, unqualified for full citizenship, and unworthy of full integration within the body politic. Furthermore, the "spectacle" itself granted authority to the onlooker to remain concealed and unnamed, even as she or he defined the "object" or "objects" in view. This relationship takes on particular significance in terms of racial placement when we consider that in early-twentieth-century visual culture, the spectator was generally presumed to be white, and the spectacle was generally black. Concretized in the era of the spectacle, language (or concepts) and visibility operate together to produce racial categories and to locate individuals within them. Even before raced individuals are stereotyped and evacuated of their internal lives and personal differences, they are noted and named because of their visibility. Since the early era of the spectacle, U.S. culture has depended in part on a "regime of looking."[11]

The late nineteenth century is widely regarded as the period that saw the proliferation of discourses relating to sexuality, as well as its rigid regulation. In this moment, taxonomies of sexual desire and behavior found a visual supplement—if not a corollary—in representations of racial difference that were enacted and enforced by legal statutes, pseudoscientific studies, and commodity culture. While it is generally recognized that sexual pathologies characterized by insatiability and excess (such as rape, cross-racial desire, and incest) have long contributed to the construction of blackness, what I intend to make evident here is the extent to which the very notion of racialized sexual pathology depended on emerging discourses of homosexuality.[12] Amid the cultural hysteria of the late nineteenth century around tracking, policing, and codifying racial difference, juridical processes and the pseudoscientific discourses labored to make sexual alterity visible—first by naming it and then by locating it on the body—and relied on racial concepts to do so. In this moment, homosexuality was transformed from a set of preferred sexual behaviors to the basis of an emergent identity, and, like race, its deviance was thought traceable to and interpretable on the body. "Homosexuality [was] a condition of, and therefore an identity of particular bodies," writes Siobhan Somerville, echoing Foucault's famous quip, "the homosexual was now a species."[13] Even when covert or left undeclared, sexual difference was signaled (in cinema and advertising, for example) through the visual register of representative difference between the races. It is important to keep in mind that, despite taken-for-granted assumptions about (homo)sexual identity (including undertheorized notions of the closet) that posit the invisibility of sexual difference, historical evidence suggests that the initiatory classification of sexual aberrance incorporated a logic of racial and corporeal identity by which to make it visible. Transgressive sexuality was subject to and defined by a set of conventions related to appearance, particularly in the arena of race, by which to make it known.

Judicial prohibitions against homosexuality, demonstrated by the widely publicized trials of Alice Mitchell and Oscar Wilde, necessitated readily available bodily representations of the homosexual in culture. The same modes of production within capitalism that helped to lodge racial stereotypes in the cultural imagination, particularly the press, scientific journals, photography, and cinema, disseminated imagistic representations of the "sexual pervert," as well. Under the "regime of looking," the semiotics of dress, behavior, reputation, and bodily appearance became crucial for determining the (sexual and racial) identities of individuals.[14] Once visible, non-normative sexuality was subject to the social exclusion, ridicule, and regulation that go hand in hand with corporeal demarcation. As Somerville astutely summarizes, "Those whose bodies were culturally marked as nonnormative lost their claim to the same rights as those whose racial or sexual reputation invested them with cultural legitimacy."[15] Efforts to police sexual divergence when it emerged in the late nineteenth century included marking and defining it so that it could be outlawed, its borders secured.

In the United States, the outlaw, the criminal, is made intelligible, and notorious, by referencing blackness. Biological determinism—the belief that certain bodies are mentally inferior, socially inadequate, and predisposed to criminality and, moreover, that these conditions are legible on these bodies—was prevalent in nineteenth-century scientific discourse and evident in state practice. Evolutionary theory, sexology, and eugenics provided both justification and fuel for the racist practices of legal segregation at home and U.S. imperialism abroad.[16] Both homosexuality, in its association with sodomy, and black sexuality, in its association with insatiability and excess, were believed to be inappropriate, maladapted, and underdeveloped (read: primitive) expressions of sexual desire. The entwinement of illicit sexuality and a predilection for other forms of social deviance was promulgated by scientific investigations that alleged that the size and shape of genitalia predetermined both illicit sexual and violent propensities. As Lisa Duggan notes, media coverage of sex crimes generally furnished sexologists with case studies.[17] Sciences that treated human anatomy as a legible text worked to concretize racial and sexual difference through comparative studies of the brains and sexual organs of black and white people. For example, black men were (and in some cases still are) popularly believed to have larger genitals than white men, and this corroborates their characterization as beastly, brutal, sexually rapacious, and dangerous. Because women are generally accorded the status of "the body" in culture and are imagined as the repositories of sex (sexual desire and sexual activity), sexologists focused primarily on women's bodies and sexual behavior to arrive at conclusions about sexual attitudes, behavior, and identities in the culture at large.[18] Black women were (and still are) believed to be sexually insatiable and irresponsible, immoral, and incapable of both decency and delicacy. This characterization springs from a number of sources: the pervasiveness of rape and concubinage during slavery, which itself guaranteed that black women could not fulfill the dictates of modesty and chastity; enduring disproportionately high numbers of out-of-wedlock births in black families since Reconstruction; the continued exploitation of the sexualized black female body in popular culture throughout the twentieth century; black women's traditional labor outside the domestic sphere; and black women's historical interrogation of and resistance to the norms of marriage and patriarchy.[19] Sexologists and medical scientists alleged that supposed genital irregularities (e.g., enlarged labia or an elongated clitoris) that predisposed white lesbians and prostitutes to sexual deviance were standard features of black women's sexual organs.[20]

Sander Gilman traces meticulously the development of theories about genital irregularities and illicit sexual behavior of (white) lesbians and prostitutes that referenced and reinforced existing theories of black female genital malformation. He suggests that the prostitute was believed to be "an atavistic form of humanity whose 'primitive' nature [could] be observed in the form of her genitalia"—or, in other words, in the anomalous labia that are said to be a standard feature of the black woman's genitalia. He reveals the common conception to be that "the primitive is the black, and the qualities of blackness, or at least of the black female, are those of the prostitute."[21] In discussing lesbian sexuality, he suggests the same: sexologists believed that "the overdevelopment of the labia . . . [led] to those 'excesses' which are called 'lesbian love,'" and he concludes that "the concupiscence of the black is thus associated also with the sexuality of the lesbian."[22] It is important to note that Gilman is not simply identifying a casual, observable association among white lesbianism, white prostitution, and black female sexuality but, rather, positing a causal, meaningful one. The criminalization of lesbianism and prostitution was effected in part through sexologists' claim of their bodily and behavioral kinship with black women, the archetypes of sexual deviance.

To further illustrate the interconnection of the pseudoscientific investigations of female bodies and the deployment of racial concepts to interpret sexual behavior, I refer to a passage taken from the book *Sexual Racism*. The sociologist Charles Herbert Stember attempted in the late 1970s to produce a hierarchy of physical beauty and sexual desirability based on racial differences. His work is reminiscent of Havelock Ellis's, and it is relevant here because, although it belongs to the area designated social sciences and not sexology per se, it incorporates and activates a similar logic found in sexology studies: it purports to determine sexual behavior and explain sexual object choice by reading the anatomies of women through the lens of racial difference. Here, as elsewhere in this chapter, I show the confluence of racial thought in the late nineteenth-century sexologists' and late twentieth-century sociologists' accounts of sexual difference. Stember writes:

It would seem that the man's focus on the beauty of a woman's face occurs because it has a broad symbolic meaning—that in some way stands for the woman herself, in a way that the rest of her body does not. What it must convey to be attractive it seems is the opposite of what exists in the lower part of her body—"dirt" in its widest sense: excretion, bodily odors, and the general character of the genital-urinary-excretive areas. . . . Any hint given in the all-important upper part of the woman that there lurks in the lower part an odiferous, slimy, dark, wet organ in between her legs, or to be precise, between her organs of excretion, tends in a very important sense to render her less attractive sexually. We have seemingly split our image of the woman into polarized extremes of upper and lower parts. Her physical "attractiveness" in a real sense is based on her facial features diverging as far as possible from anything suggesting the genital area and its adjacent organs of excretion. She must look, smell, and feel like the antithesis of anything suggesting dirt, sex, sin or "animal" attributes.[23]

Theorizing about why white women are deemed more attractive in general among both white and black men, Stember proposes that white women are more attractive because in Western culture women's sexual desirability is indexed by a representative disjuncture between the female face and female sexual organs.

Explaining how this cultural standard determines black women's inability to qualify as attractive, Stember continues:

The notion that facial features must be perceived as "antigenital" throws light on the criteria of female beauty found to have such widespread currency. It serves to explain the existence of a hierarchy of female beauty in which the black woman appears at the lower end. It is not alone her skin color . . . conceivably associated with the color of excrement, but her thick lips and wide nostrils, suggesting the vulva itself. The hair of the black woman as well is in its texture much like pubic hair, and carries the same association. The black woman, in other words, projects in her face, hair, and skin—her upper half—the explicit image of her lower half.[24]

According to Stember, a woman's face—and presumably her overall physical appearance—should not conjure an awareness of the "odiferous, slimy, dark, wet organ in between her legs" lest she lose the ability to arouse the sexual appetites of men. The disdain for the female body and genitalia is sufficiently virulent and self-evident here as to not warrant, I think, any additional comment. Two other things, however, do strike me as noteworthy. First, regardless of the woman's face and its capacity to distract attention from her genitalia, her genitalia are presumably the ultimate object of men's sexual interest and a definitive site of sexual intercourse. It is useful, then, to consider the extent to which cultural narratives of sexual arousal and sexual activity *depend* on the associations Stember denigrates—namely, the intimation of something hidden, as in the "lower" unseen part of the woman's body, and (or as) the fantasy of the dark, or the black. The very "dirt" or darkness that Stember associates with female genitalia in his explanation of its failure to attract men's sexual interest is precisely what makes female *and* black bodies (and particularly black female bodies) the culturally designated repositories for sexual ideology, fantasy, and activity. Numerous eroticisms traffic in tantalization of the dark, the unseen, the hidden, the down-low.

Second, in the discussion of black women's faces, Stember postulates that the upper part of black women reflects and discloses their blatant, lower sexual parts. Black women are wholly genitalized, visualized here as manifestly sexual and debased. Stember, however, does not describe any particular black woman's face to substantiate his claims. Instead, he refers to readily available caricatures of black faces in general. The associations of brown skin with excrement and curly hair textures with pubic hair are neither causal nor self-evident, although Stember's regard for them as "conceivable" has the effect of naturalizing them. Those similes derive from and have gained currency in racist lore, particularly prevalent in slavery and later in popular (consumer) culture. Important also, in Stember's formulation, the racial characteristics associated with whiteness (i.e., straightness of hair, narrowness of nose) are sufficient to mitigate the association of the white woman with overt sexuality. Blackness itself, then, serves as the signifier of sexual activity—transgressive or otherwise.

To add another dimension: theories of homosexuality share with common conceptions of black sexuality a central focus on asses, on anality—or, as Sigmund Freud would have us believe, a crude psychosexual, psychosocial underdevelopment—and improperly (per)formed gender. In *Three Essays on the Theory of Sexuality*, Freud famously cast homosexuality as an expression of mental illness, as arrested development at or regression to an early stage on the path to "healthy" adult sexuality and, by extension, sociality. Notably, the so-called primitive psychic mechanisms that centralize anal sexuality in the homosexual in Freud's (il)logic have also been used to define generally the sexuality of the black. Here I allude, on one hand, to Freud's and Havelock Ellis's claim that homosexuality is more prevalent among people of color.[25] Freud wrote, "Inversion is remarkably widespread among many savage and primitive races."[26] Ellis wrote, "Looking at the phenomena generally, so far as they have been recorded among various lower races, we seem bound to recognize that there is a widespread natural instinct impelling men toward homosexual relationships."[27] Ellis goes as far as to record, "Inversion is extremely prevalent among the American negroes [sic], far more prevalent among them than among the white people of any nation."[28] Here my second contention becomes clear: in early psychoanalysis and sexuality studies, instead of simply indicating individual perversion or maladaptation to the social and sexual requirements of adult maturation, anal sexuality takes on a cultural resonance, indicating the primitivity and perverse propensies of embodied racial subjects in general.[29]

In the collective cultural imagination, notions of an ass-centered or generally anal sexuality haunt even heterosexual desiring and coupling between black people. The purported anality of blacks' sexual desire is everywhere evident in contemporary popular culture and visual culture.[30] In movies and music videos, young black women are frequently depicted as having large asses, while young black men are frequently depicted in hot pursuit of them. Instead of being regarded as a secondary sexual organ, black women's asses have been treated for the past century as the main focus of (black) men's sexual interest, the supposed effect of a cumulative and widespread racial and cultural retardation. The historical Western fascination with black women's asses is, of course, evident in the enduring iconicity of the Hottentot Venus.[31] Linking the medical theories of black sexuality to nineteenth-century aesthetic practices, Gilman illustrates the ways in which black women's butts, represented by the Hottentot Venus, captured the white imagination: "When the Victorians saw the female black, they saw her in terms of her buttocks and saw represented by the buttocks all the anomalies of her genitalia. . . . This fascination with the uniqueness of the sexual part of the black focuses on the buttocks over and over again. . . . The presence of the exaggerated buttocks points to the other, hidden signs, both physical and temperamental, of the black female."[32] It is important to note here that black women's sexuality symbolized in nineteenth-century scientific discourses only the excesses of white women's sexuality, whereas it figured black women's and men's sexuality as a whole. In other words, the enormity of black women's asses purportedly revealed the primitive (read: anal) sexuality of black people generally. Again, this anality marks a regressive sexuality that, while not exclusively evocative of homosexuality, is nonetheless queer.

Finally, Freud contended that anal sexuality, when properly regulated by the phallic system, is diverted into the pursuit of wealth—the generation of "valuable" material—or mastery over capital. Under the theorization that the sublimation of anality precipitates capitalist accumulation, black men's inability to procure sufficient capital for the secure economic provision (and patriarchal ordering) of their families would seem to reveal a lingering (infantile) anality, or, rather, the failure of full anal effacement under the phallic order in the African American context. Dominant psychoanalytic discourses that seek to explain social and subjective development via early psychosexual maturation present the black and the queer as similarly underdeveloped. Repurposing those pseudoscientific discourses of the late nineteenth century, sociologists throughout much of the twentieth century have blamed African American existence at the bottom rung of the social scale for the production of sexual and gender noncomformity in the black American context.[33] Ultimately, beginning in the nineteenth century and continuing throughout the twentieth century, racial difference has provided the landscape and the logic for defining and delineating the pathological from the normal in both the sexual and social arenas in U.S. culture.

Gender and Race

Because a primary objective of *Against the Closet* is to understand the significance of sexual logics in the solidification of race as a most meaningful social category (one especially determinative of the material lives of masses of black people living in the United States), this section delves further into sociological discourses of the twentieth century. Unlike psychoanalytic and sexological discourses of the nineteenth century, which emphasized sexual desire and behavior, sociological discourses of the twentieth century foreground gender. In other words, the strongest queer resonance in black sexual and familial arrangements results less from the supposed anatomical excesses and behavioral perversions of black sexuality than from the common characterization of black people as gender-noncompliant—a debased, impoverished, dysfunctional nation of butchy black women and sissified black men. It is important to note that unwantedness is a defining characteristic of marginalized experience, or, in explicit racial terms, what Patricia Hill Collins calls "social blackness."[34] Circuits of desire are particularly meaningful in the African American context because desirability, both in social and political contexts and in cultural production, is a crucial part of ascribing individual and communal value to blackness. Moreover, desirability in the realm of the social is a key factor in determining who gets recognized in the body of the citizenry and who may thereby access the entitlements of citizenship and the resources of the state. In

what follows, I read closely Daniel Patrick Moynihan's The Negro Family to elucidate the repercussions of sociological theories of black non-heteronormativity
on contemporary black material and political life.

In 1965, Moynihan published The Negro Family, the notoriously controversial
Moynihan report, which solidified the conceptualization of black American gender, sexual, and familial arrangements instead of structural oppression as the
basis for black Americans' poverty. A trained sociologist, the assistant secretary
of labor, and one of the chief architects of Lyndon B. Johnson's Great Society
Program, Moynihan produced The Negro Family as a document to support Johnson's War on Poverty policies. In the report, Moynihan grappled with the conundrum of continued generational poverty in black urban communities despite
gains in civil liberties, access to education and employment, and a growing black
middle class. Moynihan found that, although African Americans had made notable progress collectively, single parenthood, joblessness, crime, and other manifestations of poverty continued to rise. Using data from the Bureau of Labor
Statistics and from several U.S. Censuses, he attempted to address this dilemma
and to rectify welfare policies that served only households headed by single
parents. Moynihan recognized that policies that denied welfare benefits to families in which fathers remained present perpetuated one of slavery's most deleterious legacies: the removal of black men from, and the decentralization of the
father function in, black families. Unfortunately, Moynihan soon veered from
his original contention to theorize a "tangle of pathology" in black families that
was "the principal source of the most aberrant, inadequate, or antisocial behavior that did not establish, but now serves to perpetuate the cycle of poverty
and deprivation."[35]

Overall, Moynihan's text hinges on common conceptions of the perverse
sexuality and gender inadequacy of black men and women. (In)famously, he
postulates, "At the heart of the deterioration of the fabric of Negro society is
the deterioration of the Negro family. It is the fundamental source of the weakness of the Negro community at present. . . . Unless this damage is repaired, all
effort to end discrimination and poverty and injustice will come to little."[36]
Through a series of maneuvers, Moynihan denies the centrality of structural
racism in the perpetuation of poverty in urban black communities, and he
denies ultimately the extent to which racism itself undermines the cohesion
and sustainability of black family life. As Roderick Ferguson so aptly contends, "While racist prejudice might be irrational, there were objective differences that prevented black achievement. For the sociologist, African American
familial arrangements and their nonheteronormative disfigurements spawned
those differences."[37] Moynihan's hypothesis minimizes the effects of discrim-

ination in employment, disparities in educational opportunity, housing segregation, and the general psychic toll of racism and its attendant material effects on black Americans. Moreover, as his report diverges from its initial objective of arguing for increased access to needed resources for poor black families, it becomes a study of black sexuality—or, more specifically, the negative relation between the sexual practices, patterns, prerogatives in black communities and the failure of black people to achieve social equity and economic parity with white Americans. To cite an illustrative example, Moynihan analyzes criminal tendencies in youth and claims that the primary determinant of criminal behavior in young people is the inability to delay gratification. He writes, "Children who hunger for immediate gratification are more prone to delinquency, along with other less social behavior. . . . Inability to delay gratification is a crucial factor in immature, criminal, and neurotic behavior."[38] Moynihan predictably proceeds to explain that delayed gratification is acquired in homes in which the father is present and functional, presumably by virtue of children's subjection to operant paternal regulation. The implication here is that children bred in households headed by women will develop criminal propensities. Notably, Moynihan simply overlooks the sociopolitical and material factors that contribute to criminal behavior, emphasizing instead the misdirection and mismanagement of desire. In sundry lists, graphs, and statistics, he presents a bleak picture of black life in which premature mothering, out-of-wedlock births, and desertion by husbands dog potentially functional black families.

Since much of the backlash, and criticism, of Moynihan's report has focused on his pathologization of single black mothers, it is useful to attend to his depiction of black men and its wider gender implications and effects on black families and communities. In essence, Moynihan casts black men as infantalized patriarchs who are too lazy, criminal, or intellectually deficient to serve as responsible heads of black families. An illustration: high unemployment rates for black men, which Moynihan blames for their frequent desertion of families, is not caused by workplace discrimination in his account but by black men's overall masculine inadequacy. This characterization is most clearly evident in Moynihan's discussion of the U.S. military and its benefit to black families in the form of stable employment, educational benefits, and character development. The logic goes something like this: black men would have jobs if they served their country, were proper citizens, were real men. In Moynihan's assessment, the armed forces are "the only experience open to the Negro American in which he is treated as an equal: not as a Negro equal to a white, but as one man equal to another man in a world where the category 'Negro' and 'white' do not exist. . . . a world away from women, a world run by strong men of unquestioned authority, where discipline, if harsh, is nonetheless orderly and predictable, and rewards, if limited, are granted on the basis of performance."[39] Disregarding all racial disparities in the U.S. military, Moynihan presents it as an alternative, if not the ultimate, well-run patriarchal household. Ferguson summarizes this maneuver succinctly: "The Moynihan Report cast racial exclusion as fundamentally feminizing. If exclusion is the trace of feminization, then equality can only be won by recovering the hetero-patriarchal loss suffered under racism."[40] Deploying the language of paternal rule—authority, discipline, reward—Moynihan suggests that the military can counter the effects of infantilization resulting from excessive maternal leniency and paternal disregard in the black household. Citing their frequent failure on "objective tests and standards," however, Moynihan contends that black men are frequently rejected from the armed forces, unable to serve because of their low intelligence rates and inadequate masculinity.[41] In other words, the presumed inferiority of black men undermines their best chance to achieve gender normativity in any social context. In a rather unexpected twist of logic, Moynihan concludes, "How this group of Americans chooses to run its affairs, take advantage of its opportunities, or fail to do so is none of this nation's business."[42] No longer advocating social programs to alleviate deleterious conditions in impoverished black communities, he encourages the nation to abdicate all responsibility for this group of sexual and gender miscreants. What begins as an impassioned plea on behalf of African Americans whose lives and life chances have been shortchanged by racism becomes a treatise on the characterological and cultural maladaptation of African Americans in the related realms of sex, gender, reproduction, and familial organization.

William Connolly describes identity formation among citizen-subjects: "identity is established in relation to a series of differences that have become socially recognized. These differences are essential to its being. If they did not coexist as differences, it would not exist in its distinctness and solidity. . . . Identity requires difference in order to be, and it converts difference into otherness in order to secure its own self-certainty."[43] This explanation of identity is key to understanding the construction and preservation of whiteness through a dialectal relationship of simultaneous acknowledgement and repudiation of both racial and sexual others. It is my contention that both blackness and queerness are used to shore up whiteness; both function as its exiled and abased excesses. Both blackness and homosexuality pose a threat to whiteness in that each impedes the continuous propagation of white generations and violates the unity and integrity of the white family as the basic unit of capital acquisition and consolidation in the American political economy.[44]

Furthermore, both blackness and queerness disrupt the symbolic systems of the English language and of cultural signification generally. With the word for biological sex serving as the word for gender performance and the word for sexual object choice, a system of heterosexual desire and activity is organized and naturalized as the only possible outcome of "sex" itself. Anything "queer" —that is, non-heteronormative—is rendered illegitimate and excluded from the symbolic system. "Forced into the margins of a symbolic system that refuses it, the homosexual can only impinge upon the heterosexualized center, not as a coherent 'I,' but only negatively as a figure of excess or absence."[45] Homosexuality is relegated to the space outside normativity and intelligibility. Defined always in the negative, it becomes that which heterosexuality is not. Moreover, it becomes the so-called deviance against which heterosexuality is defined and legitimated.

Blackness functions similarly in relation to whiteness. It is the exiled, the negated, the outside-of-the-black–white-binary that brings whiteness into being and delineates its contours. As Robert Reid-Pharr argues, "The Black has been conceptualized as the inchoate, irrational non-subject."[46] In the American cultural imaginary, the figure of the black is the abjected, contaminated, and chaotic opposite of the white. Understood historically, in the nascent American Republic composed of dislocated Europeans from varied countries, blackness provides the delineating contours for the emergence and consolidation of whiteness as a necessary component of (individual and national) identity and as the basis for group claims to privileges as both coherent subjects and New World citizens. Wahneema Lubiano states the case plainly in the introduction to *The House That Race Built*: "the basic character of the United States not only harbor[s], but depend[s] upon, a profound violation of the spirit of democracy, and that fundamental violation is racism."[47] Originally a slave, an "irrational non-subject," the figure of the black delineates the contours and produces the inevitable failure of an archaic, propertied, masculine whiteness. Here the formerly enslaved, marginally enfranchised, "irrational non-subject"—the abject—threatens the very basis of the white citizen-subject's coherence and social entitlement and provides a potent lens for rethinking and reorganizing the sociopolitical schema, with incumbent considerations of culture and class. Such critical rethinking and political reorganizing is the work taken up in the pages of *Against the Closet*.

The Steps Ahead

A crucial foundation of the work undertaken here is my belief that new epistemologies and key revisions within domains of knowledge that have emerged in the fields of queer and feminist studies over the past two decades have much to contribute to the understanding of race. *Against the Closet* proceeds from the belief that there are genuine ideological, sociopolitical, and material advantages to using black feminist theory, queer articulation, and political mobilization in concert with histories and theories of race. Such a critical maneuver supports the development of a progressive methodology that anchors politics in various identificatory practices and, more importantly, that anchors identifications in political exigency. Further, by linking theories of sexual nonnormativity to matters of race, and by understanding how sexual alterity has historically underwritten constructions of blackness, we are able to perceive the political instrumentality of transgressive erotics in black American cultural production.

Chapter 1, " 'The Strangest Freaks of Despotism': Queer Sexuality in Antebellum African American Slave Narratives," argues that the generalized consensus among scholars of sexuality that sexual taxonomies emerged in the late nineteenth century should be reconsidered. Continuing my work of tying the invention of aberrant sexualities to already operant racial logics and racist institutions, I explore the period and the practice of embodied black slavery as the pivotal axes around which early ideologies of sexual difference coalesced and cohered. The brutal enslavement of black people; their legal definition as three-fifths human; and the social, economic, and legislative practices of slavery influenced U.S. cultural notions of the citizen, the person, and the heterosexual, as well. The ungendering of African Americans in slavery marks a representational structure that resurfaces in later theories of sexual inversion. Chapter 1 also demonstrates the sophistication with which early African American writers harnessed the representational power of transgressive (specifically, sadomasochistic and homoerotic) sexuality in support of their efforts to abolish American slavery. I argue that the authors of slave narratives concede to race-based notions of sexual criminality by showing the sexual depravity of white masters, not of enslaved black people.

Chapter 2, "Iconographies of Gang Rape: Or, Black Enfranchisement, White Disavowal, and the (Homo)erotics of Lynching," reads representations of lynching in the post-Reconstruction period. It treats *Contending Forces* by Pauline Hopkins and *Light in August* by William Faulkner alongside and against each other. Although Faulkner is not a black American writer, I have chosen to include him in the chapter on post-Reconstruction black literature because of my sense of his rightful inclusion in the African American literary canon. As a writer who both assimilated and influenced many features of twentieth-century African American writing, Faulkner expanded commonplace notions of race writing. The importance of this critical observation is not to be overlooked, as African American writing does not emerge in a cultural and literary vacuum but engages always intertextually with dominant writerly practices and output. Moreover, as a brilliant purveyor of American history in racial terms and as a great aesthetician in the realm of literary production, Faulkner is key to my study of narrative stylization, particularly as it is inflected by racial iconography and sexual non-normativity.

This chapter illuminates the ways in which imaginative depictions of lynching function to call our attention to the proliferation of lynching as the white communal effort to fix racial hierarchies in the absence of slavery's organization and operational logic. In other words, lynching functions as a disavowal of black humanity and as a will to whiteness in the post-Emancipation period. To address the issue of racial indeterminacy in Hopkins and Faulkner, I open chapter 2 by making the case that miscegenation speaks to the general (bi)cultural and political status of African Americans in the post-Reconstruction period as endowed with citizenship rights, on one hand, but bound by pseudo-slave Southern codes, on the other. To underscore the effect that representing lynching has on formal aspects of the novel, I demonstrate that scenes of lynching haunt and upset narratives of sexual normalcy in both black and white literary contexts. Hopkins's *Contending Forces*, for instance, situates the lynching of black men alongside the rape of black women, thereby subverting the conventional marriage plot of early black fiction. Faulkner's *Light in August* depicts lynching as a gruesome, sexually charged cross-racial encounter meant to recover an already imperiled white masculinity but that, in its very homoerotic enthrallment, puts white masculinity into further crisis. By emphasizing the rape–lynch alliance in Hopkins and the homoerotic underpinnings of lynching in Faulkner, my hope is that chapter 2 will further our understanding of lynching as a kind of racialized gang rape, a profound expression of communal sexual perversion—specifically, one in which the victim of lynching is gruesomely violated for the psychic satisfaction of a whole host of participants and spectators.

Such a project as this would not be complete without a chapter on James Baldwin, the visionary twentieth-century author, political spokesperson, philosopher, and prophet of his people. Chapter 3, "Desire and Treason in Mid-Twentieth-Century Political Protest Fiction," situates Baldwin along with Ann

Petry in relation to the mid- to late-twentieth-century civil rights struggle to understand how, from abolition to Black Power, theories about sexual propriety, heteronormative family, and empowered masculinity have informed the development of political programs in the black, and larger American, community. Opening with an analysis of Petry's final novel, The Narrows, I explore the synechdochic operation of cross-racial romance in African American fiction to measure racial progress since the post-Reconstruction era and to highlight remaining social and economic barriers to integration. Baldwin's novel Another Country instantiates his ideological alignment with and political investment in the goals of the Civil Rights Movement. Through depictions of pained, longstanding interpersonal relationships that confront and even cross racial, sexual, and class boundaries, Another Country advocates a historical reckoning that would enable egalitarian cooperation—and possibly even reconciliation—between racial groups that contentiously inhabit the same country. Baldwin's final novel, Just Above My Head, promotes among African Americans the practices of self-love, interdependence, and self-determination, principles that, I argue, are rooted in Black Power philosophies. In moving from the North to the South and to Europe and back, Baldwin attempts to document and decry America's exclusionist, and even exterminationist, policies with regard to African Americans and the devastating (psychic and material) effects of these policies on black people. Chapter 3 contends, ultimately, that Baldwin depicts (and links) the black esthete and the homosexual as figures of cultural reformation, as those who most embody and influence the journey toward personal freedom and widespread social and political reform in both the Civil Rights and Black Power eras.

Chapter 4, "Recovering the Little Black Girl: Incest and Black American Textuality," continues my critique of racial prescription by analyzing representations of incest in the late-twentieth-century writing of black female authors. Considering an array of late-twentieth-century texts, including Imago, the last novel of Octavia Butler's Xenogenesis series, Sapphire's Push, Toni Morrison's The Bluest Eye, and Gayle Jones's Corregidora, chapter 4 illustrates how ideologies of black motherhood and girlhood that arose during slavery to excuse rampant rape and the forced removal of black children from their mothers find their contemporary correlates in stereotypes of the welfare queen and the unwed teenage mother.[48] I focus on these figures to highlight the impacts of Civil Rights retrenchment and the waning popularity of a largely masculinist black nationalist agenda on black families in the late twentieth century. In other words, by emphasizing the hierarchy of familial relations obtaining in father–daughter incest, as well as the failure of Civil Rights legislation and refigured patriarchy under black nationalism to produce meaningful improvement in African American lives in U.S. inner cities, I critique phallocentric racial struggle and refute the nuclear, heteronormative model of family as a requirement for black social advancement. I show, moreover, the incredible utility—and versatility—of the incest narrative, on one hand, to critique society for its egregious neglect of black women and girls, and, on the other hand, to offer progressive paradigms for (racial) survival after conquest.

Against the Closet is characterized by an ambitious and productive unwieldiness. Its historical reach stretches across two centuries; it deploys varied and, at times, seemingly oppositional methodologies to read African American experience and expressive response; and it attempts to unearth a radical strain of sexual representation in African American literature generally. Despite its chronology, this is not a historical study that traces the linear rise and fall of a creative, politically engaged literary enterprise. Rather, it presents a series of snapshots that show the consistent deployment of one. The intellectual and political aims compelling, propelling this study are neither self-evident nor uncomplicatedly consistent. I am at once beholden to identity politics, particularly for their force of mobilization under the rubric of social justice, even as I am highly skeptical of taxonomies of difference and various nationalisms. This book cannot be categorized according to strict disciplinary boundaries or one discursive regime. I fruitfully engage the domains of African American studies, psychoanalysis, sociology, queer theory, and gender studies. I, moreover, use a performative theory of blackness that recognizes its ability to serve as a signifier that accumulates different meanings in different cultural and literary contexts and to carry a whole host of assumptions. This project might be best described, then, as an aggregate study, gathering smaller historically and textually discreet examinations into a composite whole.

As literature has operated historically as the main vehicle of African American political struggle and public self-fashioning, Against the Closet is at its core a study of black American writing. I examine the ways in which African American writers have explored and attempted to come to terms with difficult notions of identity, sexuality, and racial difference by both representing and challenging them within fictive worlds. In reading literature produced at different historical moments, my goal is to illuminate how literary constructions of sexuality demonstrate aesthetic innovations to the literary form and reflect transformations in the social and political character of the United States. In each text under consideration, I investigate whether representations of racially inflected sexual transgressions necessarily lead to ruptures in literary conventions or whether established literary forms have the tenacity to impede those disruptions.

Emphasizing the racialization of transgressive sexuality and sociality, this book proceeds with the understanding of race's primary function as an ideological enterprise that, on one hand, supports socioeconomic and political stratification and, on the other hand, provides a most potent means to resist it. Although I do attend to issues of defining and categorizing sexual desire and sexual practice, my point is not to determine whether a figure or sexual arrangement can be properly labeled "queer." What I argue instead is that ideas about sexuality derive from and contribute to racial ideologies. My aim in this book is to assess and explain the imaginative purposes of representing sexual difference in (mainly) black American fiction to show how particular representations affect—that is, sustain or undermine—existent beliefs about race.

1

"THE STRANGEST FREAKS OF DESPOTISM"

Queer Sexuality in Antebellum African American Slave Narratives

The full enjoyment of the slave as a thing depended upon the unbounded authority and totalizing consumption of the body in its myriad capacities."
—Saidiya Hartman, *Scenes of Subjection*

In a well-known passage from Zora Neale Hurston's *Their Eyes Were Watching God*, the elderly ex-slave Nanny attempts to explain to Janie, her adolescent and newly sexually awakened granddaughter, the plight of African American women and families under slavery to emphasize the necessary, corrective force of sexual repression within nascent free black communities. Nanny wants Janie to understand why the benefits of Janie's financially stable, virtually asexual marriage to a man three times her age outweigh the prospects of a romantic union and sexual gratification with a man Janie likes. Nanny tells Janie, "Us colored folks is branches without roots and that makes things come around in queer ways."[1] What Nanny's pronouncement means is that slavery had the effect of corrupting and contorting the most basic familial relationships. Not only did the institution deny slaves basic claims to familial, spousal, and hereditary bonds, it also insidiously assaulted their sexuality, robbing them of the basic rights of bodily autonomy and sexual choice.[2] Through Nanny, Hurston describes this violating, soul-shattering feature of slavery and its cumulative generational effects on black identity formation even after slavery's formal abolition as "queer."

This chapter reads literary renderings of black enslavement as founding articulations of a plausible connection between the institutionalization of sexual violence and racial subordination in slavery and modern theories of sexual difference. Tracing certain modern epistemologies of sexuality to the era *before* the late nineteenth century—their acknowledged moment of formal entrance into the ideological order—I suggest that representations of sexual perversity under conditions of enslavement have contributed to notions of sexual alterity and to the ideologies by which aberrant sexual practices were named, domesticated, and policed in the first decades of the twentieth century. In other words, what I intend to demonstrate in this chapter is that the era, institution, and literary representation of slavery helped to shape emergent models of sexual difference. The entwinement of violent racial separatism, sexual regulation, and the discursive production of bodily difference characteristic of the late nineteenth century may be usefully traced back to the institutional patterns of slavery and to the theories of black inferiority promulgated by its proponents and practitioners.

The critical questions pursued in this chapter include: How did the enslaved address the proliferation of nonconformist sexual behavior and attitudes under a depraved institution in which the enslaved body was exploited to fulfill the desires of both slaveholding and non-slaveholding white people? How did both public avowals and literary representations of sexual nonconformity on the plantation serve to curtail the rampant abuse of slaves and further the cause of abolition? And, finally, how did writers of slave narratives subvert existing discursive and narrative modes to describe experiences of such horrific magnitude and deep personal pain that the experiences defied both cultural conventions around what could be said publicly and the language in which to say them at all? I read Frederick Douglass's *Narrative of the Life of Frederick Douglass* and Harriet Jacobs's *Incidents in the Life of a Slave Girl* to show the linkage of slavery, sexual nonconformity, and social order in the antebellum period. As canonical exemplars of the slave narrative form, Douglass's *Narrative* and Jacobs's *Incidents* not only demonstrate the material history of slavery but also manifest the power of literature to shape the cultural construction of identity, fantasy, and ideology. That the written testimonies of Frederick Douglass and Harriet Jacobs grapple at all with the relation of non-heteronormative sexual practices to (sexual *and* racial) identity formation suggests that we may productively extend modern theorizations of sexual identity to an earlier historical moment and locate them, at least partially, in the sexual deviance and sexual violence of the slave plantation.[3] This chapter's main contention is that the brutal enslavement of black people, their legal definition as three-fifths human, and the social, economic, and legislative practices of slavery helped to influence and to institute cultural constructions not only of whiteness but also of the person, the citizen, the normal, and the heterosexual. Despite the importance of late-nineteenth-century medical and legal discourses, which founded theories of sexual perversion and its punitive consequences, racial slavery provided the background—and the testing ground—for the emergence and articulation of those theories.

The specific linkage of homosexuality and blackness in the eighteenth century and nineteenth can be traced not only to the obfuscation, or obliteration, of gender roles in slavery with regard to enslaved persons but also to the widely held belief by Europeans that black sexuality in Africa was so libidinous, so unregulated, so wanton that African men not only kept as many wives as they wanted but there also existed "men in women's apparel, whom they [kept] among their wives."[4] As Winthrop Jordan and George Fredrickson have noted, Europeans' beliefs about black sexuality developed out of their first contact with Africans in the sixteenth century and seventeenth. Upon arriving on African shores and encountering Africans who wore clothing befitting the hot climate and who had polygamous marriages, Europeans formulated the notion that Africans were sexual savages who had not undergone the disciplining regulation that civilization entails.[5] These ideas were further promulgated by scientific investigations in the nineteenth century that alleged that black people had abnormally large genitals and that the size and shape of their genitalia predetermined their illicit sexual propensities.[6] While it would oversimplify the case to suggest that homosexuality encompasses all forms of sexual deviance, the specific resonance of homosexuality within blackness can be traced in part to the belief in slavery that, as descendents of Ham, black people were doomed to generational enslavement precisely for the historical crimes of incest and homosexuality. The unrestrained sexuality of black people was thought to extend beyond promiscuous heterosexuality, by which I mean a rapacious sexual appetite for the appropriate objects of sexual desire (members of the opposite sex but of the same racial group), to include sexual violence, interracial wanting, bestiality, and homosexuality. In other words, racial blackness was believed (throughout slavery and since) to evince, and to engender in others, an entire range of sexual perversities.

Despite the mediated production of slave narratives and their conformity to generic conventions and audiences' expectations, slave narratives remain useful sources of data on the internal operations of slavery and its harrowing personal and communal effects. Noting that slave narratives document the inner workings of slavery in ways that the official records do not, I use slave narratives for their dual function as both historical documents and a literary genre. To engage theories, as well as the history, of the production of sexuality, this chapter emphasizes the ways in which two slave narratives that have amassed significant cultural capital authorize a particular set of historical race relations and embody and influence sexual ideology. My main effort here is to demonstrate that complex figurations of eroticism and domination narrativized in canonical slave testimonies mark an emerging representational structure that may be traced in modern epistemologies of racial and sexual identity. I read pivotal scenes in Douglass's *Narrative* and Jacobs's *Incidents* to illustrate how literary constructions of sexuality function as tropes, both politically and imaginatively, to reveal heinous institutional practices within slavery and to decry its personal abuses. As the experiences of human bodies are so intimately connected to individual psyches and to the life of communities, the accounts that slaves provided about the myriad ways in which their bodies were hideously and repeatedly violated became apt metaphors for revealing the gruesome and violent nature of American slavery itself.

I begin by explaining the historical and representational processes by which slaves came to embody various forms of sexual deviance. I read Frederick Douglass's *Narrative* to illustrate the overall linkage between enslavement and sexual criminality. Exposing domination and same-sex eroticism as the undeclared basis for heterosexuality and sexual normalization in both enslavement and developing theories of sexual inversion, the chapter moves into the analysis of a much overlooked scene in Jacobs's *Incidents*—one in which a male slave, Luke, undergoes extensive sexual abuse by his male master. In reading selections from Douglass's *Narrative* and Jacobs's *Incidents*, my aim ultimately is to point to the ways in which authors of slave narratives acknowledged the notion that sexual criminality was a racial characteristic but subverted this belief by exposing the sexual perversity not of enslaved black people but of white slaveowners.

The Trope of Silence

My analysis of slave narratives dwells within their sites of omission. To glean rounded, unabashed accounts of the sexual and reproductive lives of slaves from the reports they have left, it is important to interpret sites of suggestive silence and scenes of acknowledged discursive or representational impossibility. Alluding to the position of slaves and their rampant sexual abuse on the plantation, Saidiya Hartman writes, "Blacks were envisioned fundamentally as vehicles for white enjoyment, in all its sundry and unspeakable expressions."[7] I want to focus on the rhetorical moves Hartman makes in this statement, for I think that some attention to them provides a useful way to introduce in general the focus of this section: the imposition of silence on slaves and their strategic appropriation and management of silence as a discursive measure and as a method for resisting enslavement.

According to the edicts of American slavery, the fundamental status of the black was that of a mindless, will-less, completely abject *object* to be employed, enjoyed, consumed, or eradicated according to the master's will. It was the *thingness* of the slave that made her silence requisite, for her silence corroborated her status as commodity and possession and as non-reasoning object who was socially animate only through the will and wishes of the whites around her. Silence effectively excised the slave from the human family, pushing her firmly and permanently beyond the realm of the civic, the civil, and the socially recognizable. Silence, further, affirmed the slave's powerlessness to change her condition. Without recourse to language to decry slavery's fundamental injury to her personhood, the slave could neither effectively resist enslavement nor name its innumerable, intrinsic abuses. To coerce slaves into silence, into a condition of perpetual, quiet acquiescence to their enslavement, a number of legal statutes and plantation codes had to be adopted; slaves' silence was secured through a range of heinous practices, from the use of instruments of torture that prevented the slave's physical use of her tongue to laws mandating illiteracy and legal codes that denied slaves the basic right to give legal testimony against whites who unduly harmed, exploited, and violated them.[8]

Slaves, of course, resisted these strictures and used their abilities to communicate, to witness, and to record in defiance of the institution. In the early nineteenth century, when slavery's endurance as an American institution depended in part on the outcome of a hotly contested national debate, the slave's voice was particularly potent, for it affirmed the sentience and rationality of the black person. Speech announced the self-willed interior that the process and patterns of enslavement worked to deny, negate, or completely annihilate, but could not. William Andrews posits that the ability of slaves to use language in defense of their humanity and to document their experiences in public records was important for two reasons: "first, language [was] assumed to signify the subject and hence to ratify the slave narrator's humanity as well as his authority. Second, white bigotry and fear presumably [could] not withstand the onslaught of the truth feelingly represented in the simple personal history of the former slave."[9] The oral and written narratives of slaves provided evidence that slaves, that all black people, were rational human beings. With the indisputable evidence of personal experience, the enslaved argued most convincingly against the institution that had reduced them to the level of chattel.

But there are, of course, limits to speech. The language in which slaves communicated and testified belonged first and foremost to those who had enslaved them. Moreover, many aspects of enslavement simply defied telling. Specifically, slaves had to contend with the incontrovertible and nonnegotiable fact of regular and severe bodily damage, which not only characterized their enslavement but also compelled their compliance with it. Physical pain—the pain of constant and excessive toil, of starvation, of rape and routine physical torture—falls outside the domain of language and therefore could never be represented in words alone.[10] Slaves could not express linguistically the entire content of their lives, because pain, which constituted so much of it, is ultimately unrepresentable. Slaves incorporated and managed silence as a trope and narrative technique to call attention to what language could not directly relate. In their oral and written reports of life under the regime of slavery, they conjoined suggestive silence to speech to maximize the discursive (or expressive) and political impact of their testimony.

Returning to the statement "Blacks were envisioned fundamentally as vehicles for white enjoyment, in all its sundry and unspeakable expressions," Hartman asserts that, according to the logics and mandates of slavery, slaves were commodities to be exploited in whatever ways proved pleasing and beneficial to owners. Hartman clearly refers, at least in part, to sexual use; this is signaled initially by her use of the word "sundry," which connotes activities that are richly varied and beyond the scope of formal or immediately identifiable expectation. Instead of then listing directly the numerous services slaves were obligated to provide their masters, however, she characterizes the extremity, barbarity, and depravity of some of those services by deeming them "unspeakable." Instead of approximating slaves' experience by attempting to render it in particular, concrete, ghastly details, Hartman goes a step further and demonstrates that the many uses to which black bodies were put during slavery defy linguistic (and perhaps all forms of) representation. She uses suggestive silence, or the pronouncement of impossible disclosure, as a figurative device to be decoded, or as a trope.

This rhetorical strategy is common in representing slavery and particularly in representing the sexual dimensions of slavery. Even contemporary black female writers who reinvigorate the slave narrative form to provide more complete accounts of slave life at times use the trope of silence or impossible disclosure to get at the sexual violence at the heart of slaves' experience. One example from acclaimed recent black fiction is the ominous and undisclosed "lowest yet" sexual experiences of Toni Morrison's character Ella in *Beloved*. Ella proclaims to have seen it all: slave torture, slave mutilation, slave rape, and slave murder. But none of these horrendous and, unfortunately, commonplace atrocities on the plantation compare to the repeated sexual torments she suffered as the enslaved captive of a white man and his son.[11] The hint of wounding that is the "lowest yet"—that is essentially unsaid and *unsayable*—has the same effect as Hartman's allusion to the "sundry and unspeakable" desires of slaveholding whites. Both phrases activate and depend on the listener's or reader's (erotic) imaginary. This is fitting for two reasons. First, slaves' bodies *were* subject to the full range of sexual practices that can be fantasized or imagined at all; their bodies were susceptible to *all possible* violations. And second, some of these experiences were in fact too horrific, grotesque, and traumatic to be captured in language.

Strategic, suggestive silences function in slave narratives as a mechanism for implicating readers in scenes of masked sexual violence by turning them on, so to speak, in order to turn them off. Moments of voluntary omission in passages dealing with sexual violence invite the reader's own musings or imagings of perversion and sexual debasement. In this way, suggestive silences arouse readers to a conscious experience of their own most repressed and illicit sexual desires by inviting speculation in the form of erotic fantasy. This is followed immediately by the reader's disgust and outrage at her own phantasmic brutality or perversity. In other words, when the reader finds herself imagining, and being terrorized or even tantalized by, thoughts of sexual deviance that range from the most commonplace and innocuous to the most socially prohibited and injurious, she is prompted to revulsion and indignation that may initially be directed inward but are then transferred to the perpetrator of the (mainly unspecified) sexual crimes in the narrative so that readerly complicity is disavowed.

To give an example of how this process might occur, I cite the report given by a slave woman about the doubly burdensome agricultural and sexual labor required of female slaves. She laments, "A nigger 'oman couldn't help herself, fo' she had to do what de marster say. Ef he come to de field whar de women workin' an' tell gal to come on, she had to go. He would take one down in de woods an' use her all de time he wanted to, den send her on back to work. Times nigger 'omen had chillum for de marster an' his sons and some times it was fo' de ovah seer."[12] To illustrate her complaint, the speaker does not relate a specific incident that has happened to her, or to a woman in her family, or even to a woman who is known on the plantation or in her community. She speaks in general terms, emphasizing not particular injuries to a specific woman but the commonness of these injuries to all slave women. Slave women were, in the main, made to toil in the fields all day beside slave men and endured the added burden of reproductive labor and sexual exploitation.[13] The violence of sexual assault is occluded and yet insinuated in the speaker's declaration that the master used slave women "all de time he wanted to" before sending them "back to work." Omitted from the speaker's statement is that the master not only used slave women *whenever* he wanted to but also *however* he wanted to. Omitted also is a description of the master's specific sexual practices: his particular methods for enjoying slave women, the numbers he used at a time, their ages, whether different slave women were partnered or pregnant at their time of use, the injuries some women sustained as a result of his use, and, most important, the emotional impact on slave women of being raped repeatedly by slave masters and overseers. To get at the sexual practices alluded to in this passage, the reader must work through her own erotic imaginary. The interpretation of "use . . . all de time he wanted to" is necessarily tied to the reader's own fantasies or desires of what precisely constitutes absolute and unbounded sexual "use." The interpretive labor required to derive meaning from such a statement risks the (implicitly nineteenth-century white female) reader's own psychic comfort because it provokes fantasies of sexual assault and thereby prompts an alliance with antislavery politics as a way to disassociate from the sexual perversions that precipitate and permeate enslavement— and that to some extent are the reader's own.

In addition, sites of voluntary omission within slave testimonies are notable sources of meaning in that, operative as a trope, silence is capable of both supplanting and supplementing discourse. Michel Foucault explains, "Silence itself—the things one declines to say, or is forbidden to name, the discretion that is required between different speakers—is less the absolute limit of discourse, the other side from which it is separated by a strict boundary, than an element that functions alongside the things said, with them and in relation to them within over-all strategies."[14] Foucault proposes that silence and voluntary omission do not necessarily signify the breach or absence of speech and communication. Instead, the interplay between what is said and how and what is omitted and why exposes the hierarchies that organize the speakers and their respective social locations. "There is no binary division to be made between what one says and what one does not say," he insists. "[Instead,] we must try to determine the different ways of not saying such things, how those who can and those who cannot speak of them are distributed, which type of discourse is authorized, or which form of discretion is required of them in either case. There is not one but many silences, and they are an integral part of the strategies that underlie and permeate discourses."[15] Strategic silence is a powerful rhetorical device for conjuring what is indirectly referenced or merely insinuated, because silence is itself an element or particular mode of communication. Moreover, silence can be a powerful form of resistance when used by those who are marginalized and oppressed in defense against those whose domination is assisted and legitimized through language.

Because the sexual dimension of slave life was cloaked in a veil of silence created and protected by slave statutes and repressive cultural conventions, slaves, particularly women, had to negotiate prohibitions on their speech to provide potent and enduring testimony against the institution of slavery. They did this in part by assigning to their readers the task of grappling with meanings engendered by their well-placed, strategic, and voluntary refusals to speak at all in certain moments.

U.S. Slavery and the History of Sexuality

Much recent scholarship in sexuality studies has tended to treat the late nineteenth century as the critical juncture at which sexual definitions emerged, coalescing in the oppositional figures of the homosexual and the heterosexual. Foucault, arguably the most influential theorist on the cultural production of sexualities, suggests that although religious, economic, judicial, and medical methods for tracking, categorizing, and punishing non-(re)productive sexualities had existed in the West since the eighteenth century, it was in the late nineteenth century that "peripheral sexualities entailed an *incorporation of perversions* and a new *specification of individuals.*"[16] Medical, pedagogical, psychoanalytic, and judicial discourses around sexuality proliferated in this era, bringing with them new modes of naming and classifying individuals according to their illicit sexual tastes and behaviors. People whose sexual inclinations fell outside the heteronormative model were now identified as, for example, auto-monosexualists, pedophiles, and homosexuals. These identities were named, and thereby invented, in the late nineteenth century. No longer were sexual perversities things one engaged in; they became the criteria for determining what one *was*.

Alluding to the importance of scientific racism to grounding models of sexual difference, David Halperin postulates, "All scientific inquiries into the aetiology of sexual orientation . . . spring from a more or less implicit theory of sexual races, from the notion that there exist broad general divisions between types of human beings corresponding, respectively, to those who make a homosexual and those who make a heterosexual sexual object choice." He proposes that the rac(ial)ist roots of sexual definitions must be uncovered: "when the sexual racism underlying such inquiries is more plainly exposed, their rationale will suffer proportionately."[17] Halperin recognizes here that sexual ideologies, like racial theories, function to classify individuals for the purpose of organizing the social sphere. He also reveals that sexuality determines many beliefs about different races. At the turn of the twentieth century, beliefs about the deviant and excessive sexuality of black people led to the myth of the black male rapist, to Jim Crow legislation, and to lynching as the punishment for black men who supposedly raped white women. Prohibitions against interracial marriage and against homosexuality supported the ascendancy of whiteness (and the propagation of white generations) at the precise moment of the nation's reunification after the Civil War, westward expansion, increased immigration of non-white peoples into the United States, and the enfranchisement of African Americans.[18] Compulsory heterosexuality in the late nineteenth century helped to shore up a whiteness that was being assaulted by the increased presence of non-white peoples in the national polis at the level of putative parity.

Of course, sexual practices on the slave plantation and, specifically, sexual violence—understood not only always as a form of sexual deviance but central to the very definition of it—established whiteness as the requisite racial category for heteronormative qualification even before slavery's formal end.[19] In her study of racism, Elisabeth Young-Bruehl postulates that racist attitudes in the United States are rooted in embodied black slavery and in the despotic practices and psychic processes engendered by its organization, its emphasis on the purity and preservation of the white family, and its systematic obliteration of the slave's autonomy, identity, and sexuality. She writes, "The 'others,' either as domestics or slaves or as a fantasized part of the prejudiced person's household, are love and hate objects in the loving and hating of whom no bans on incest or on rivalry are violated. . . . They are needed alive, so they can be loved like mammies, prostituted or raped like whores, sexually mutilated, beaten, deprived of their power, crippled, emasculated—and in all instances kept in their places."[20] The instrumentality of black slaves to the domestic organization and financial maintenance of the plantation expanded the white family to include auxiliary people onto whom familial rivalries and incestuous desires were projected. White familial dramas were in this way safely experienced and directly enacted. The distinction between black and white women on the plantation grounded heteronormativity and secured its association with whiteness and with capitalist accumulation. Ideologies of white womanhood were articulable and meaningful only in relation to slave women's experience: forced physical labor, "natal alienation," reproductive exploitation, necessary dependence on extrafamilial networks, enforced prostitution, enslavement.[21] The differential positions held by black and white women were essential to the structure and economy of plantations because they determined the heritage and inheritance of all children born on the plantation. As a sexual imperative based on the proper choice of sexual object, heteronormativity outlawed interracial sexuality between white women and black men and assigned white women the responsibility of reproducing in monogamous marriages white heirs, or more white masters. Hazel Carby posits that the fact that the slave followed the condition of the mother "necessitated the raising of protective barriers, ideological and institutional, around the form of the white mother whose progeny were heirs to the economic, social, and political interests in the maintenance of the slave system."[22] Under the regime of slavery, the racial category of the mother determined the status of the child: children of white women were born to the master class; children born to slave women became enslaved. The routine rape of black women increased the wealth of slaveowners and solidified an enduring association of forbidden sexuality, sexual violence, and blackness.

I turn now to Frederick Douglass's *Narrative of the Life of Frederick Douglass, An American Slave*, to examine an initial black literary rendering of the interrelation of race, rape, and identity under the regime of slavery. Douglass's narrative has been widely regarded as the archetypal slave narrative, representing with the eloquent authority of an intelligent and defiant ex-slave the innumerable atrocities that characterized slave life as well as the journey slaves had to undertake on the path to freedom. Analyzing the opening of Douglass's narrative, Hartman states, "The passage through the blood-stained gate is the inaugural moment in the formation of the enslaved. In this regard it is *the primal scene*."[23] Hartman's comments refer specifically to the beating of Aunt Hester, which concludes Douglass's first chapter. Hartman suggests that Douglass's representation of the physical torture of slaves not only reveals the brute, coercive force of slavery but also demonstrates the extent to which slaves' status was secured and made legible through susceptibility to that force. As Douglass himself describes:

> I have often been awakened at the dawn of day by the most heart-rending shrieks of an own aunt of mine, whom [the master] used to tie up to a joist, and whip upon her naked back till she was literally covered with blood. No words, no tears, no prayers, from his gory victim, seemed to move his iron heart from its bloody purpose. . . . I remember the first time I ever witnessed this horrible exhibition. I was quite a child, but I well remember it. . . . It struck me with awful force. It was the blood-stained gate, the entrance to the hell of slavery, through which I was about to pass.[24]

According to Hartman, the "blood-stained gate" through which Douglass and other black people passed to become slaves was the whipping post. My suggestion is that, as a metaphorical image for female genitalia ravaged by violation and childbirth, the "blood-stained gate" refers also to the institutional pattern of slave rape. It was not simply the whipping post but the violence, the illegitimacy, and the inchoateness of rape that produced the body, the status, and the (non)identity of the slave.

That Aunt Hester's beating is not just a violent whipping but also a forced penetration is made evident in the details that Douglass provides about the first beating he witnessed. Aunt Hester's beauty is initially described: Douglass calls her "a woman of noble form, and of graceful proportions, having very few equals, and fewer superiors, in personal appearance, among the colored or white women of our neighborhood." He informs us that the offense for which Aunt Hester is savagely beaten is her alleged romantic involvement with a male slave named Ned Kelly. After the master discovered her in Ned Kelly's company,

> he took her into the kitchen, and stripped her from neck to waist, leaving her neck, shoulders, and back, entirely naked. He then told her to cross her hands, calling her at the same time a d—d b—h. After crossing her hands, he tied them with a strong rope, and led her to a stool under a large hook in the joist, put in for the purpose. He made her get upon the stool, and tied her hands to the hook. She now stood fair for his infernal purpose. Her arms were stretched up at their full length, so that she stood upon the ends of her toes.[25]

Key words signal the sexual underpinnings of the gruesome exchange. Aunt Hester stands "fair for [the master's] infernal purpose." She is, in other words, vulnerable and defenseless against his sexual assault. Douglass continues, "He then said to her, 'Now, you d—d b—h, I'll learn you how to disobey my orders!' and after rolling up his sleeves, he commenced to lay on the heavy cowskin, and soon the warm, red blood (amid heart-rending shrieks from her, and horrid oaths from him) came dripping to the floor."[26] The beating performs the standard disciplinary function of breaking the slave's will through humiliation and torture. The repeated blows to Aunt Hester's body (in this beating and in subsequent ones) cause her to become disfigured in a way intended to lessen her desirability to other men and, ultimately, to destroy her confidence as an agent in her own (sexual) life. The master calls Aunt Hester debased names that intimate sexual familiarity and coercion. His rolling up his sleeves demonstrates the need for some disrobing to perform his violent act, as well as the brutal force he exerts while engaged in it. The cowskin serves as a phallic replacement, and Aunt Hester's bleeding and shrieking demonstrate the terrible loss of both sexual purity and her sexual choice in the matter. As Douglass lost his mother to her daily toil as a slave and her consequent early death, Aunt Hester is a main source of maternal nurturance for him and serves in this instance as a metonymic substitute for his biological mother. The primal scene for individuals is their parents' copulation, imagined by the on-looking child as a violent struggle in which the mother is abused by the father. For Douglass, the primal scene is one of actual physical and sexual violence. In the scene depicting Aunt Hester, Douglass witnesses, and conjures for his readers, his own originary moment: the interracial rape of which he was born.[27]

As I will explain in greater detail, the relation of interracial rape to the formation of the slave is for Douglass threefold. First, widespread institu-tional rape necessitated matrilineal genealogies. Second, offending fathers were absent and did not bestow social legitimacy or a proper legacy to their offspring. Third, brute force and sexual violence not only characterized slave life but brought it literally into being. As such, the slave was not simply the product of sexual criminality but its very incarnation.

The absence and anonymity of Douglass's father affirms his birth not into human community but into chattel slavery. In tracing his genealogy, Douglass laments that he knows neither his date of birth nor the identity of his father. Noting that white children on the plantation knew their birthdays, Douglass acknowledges that the circumstances surrounding a person's birth announce her membership in a specific social network and in the human family in general. The circumstances of Douglass's birth—specifically, what is not known about it—make him and, he believes, all slaves akin to horses and other chattel on the plantation. "The whisper that my master was my father, may or may not be true," Douglass declares, "and . . . it is of but little consequence to my purpose whilst the fact remains, in all its glaring odiousness, that slave-holders have ordained, and by law established, that the children of slave women shall in all cases follow the condition of their mothers; and this is done too obviously to administer to their own lusts, and make a gratification of their wicked desires profitable as well as pleasurable; for by this cunning arrange-ment, the slaveholder, in cases not a few, sustains to his slaves the double relation of master and father."[28] Slavery was a matrilineal system. It was the centrality of black women to establishing kinship and heritage that deter-mined Douglass's status—inhuman, illegitimate, slave. Hortense Spillers de-scribes the enslaved black woman as the "principal point of passage between the human and the non-human world. Her issue became the focus of a cunning difference—visually, psychologically, ontologically—as the route by which the dominant modes decided the distinction between the self and 'other.' "[29] Early-nineteenth-century culture was racist and patriarchal. Traceable heritage and the inheritance of family name, status, property, wealth, and citizenship were determined by white fathers. Douglass decries his position as a male child born to a white father and therefore rightful heir to wealth, property, and the entitlements of citizenship but robbed of his just inheritance because he was born to a black woman whose status decided his own.[30]

Douglass is finally outraged that he was conceived, as were the overwhelming number of slaves, through the gruesome ritual of rape. The violence that produced black bodies in slavery not only typified their lives under its regime but also ousted them from the domain of human and intelligible beings, of those capable of regulation and worthy of recognition in an established social schema. Strict heterosexuality in the context of monogamous marriage was reserved for members of the master class. Sexual mores and plantation sexual practices of the early nineteenth century supported the social order of slavery.

Race and Rape

For centuries, slavery has been popularly referred to as "the peculiar institution." While I will not go so far as to posit that "peculiar" in this designation connotes all that is meant by "queer" as it is used in the current academic and activist lexicon to refer to non-heteronormative sexuality and identity, I do think it is important to recognize the synonymity of these two terms to grasp fully what the designation "peculiar" reveals about the sexual arrangements and, therefore, the larger social infrastructure of the institution. The Oxford English Dictionary defines "peculiar" as both an adjective and a noun. As an adjective, "peculiar" denotes specificity and unorthodoxy. As a noun, it denotes property or possession. In the seventeenth century and eighteenth, mistresses and concubines were commonly referred to as "peculiars," connoting that they were themselves sexual property, existing in uneasy relation to dominant sexual norms. Extending this logic, we may understand slaves as their masters' "peculiars." Thus, on one hand, slavery's peculiarity was directly related to its continuance in the South in the mid-nineteenth century after it had been abolished in most Northern states. It was an odd, distinctive, regional socioeconomic system that was increasingly problematic, morally and politically, to the Union as a whole. It was also a system whose internal operations were increasingly denied or veiled by those who benefited from its propagation. On the other hand, slavery was peculiar in a sense more directly associated with the economies of desire and sexuality in that it provided a cover under which aberrant sexuality flourished. Under the system of slavery, nonconformist sexual attitudes and behavior found flagrant expression unlike anywhere else in culture. In the eighteenth century and nineteenth, the plantation and the slave quarter became the definitive locales for the practice and proliferation of outlaw sexual behavior. The institution granted to all whites— slaveholders and non-slaveholders—the full-fledged, legal right and unchecked personal authority to exploit, consume, and destroy the slave's psyche and body in whatever ways they chose. This arrangement inevitably engendered, even as it concealed, all manner of sexual perversion.

Scholars including Winthrop Jordan, George Fredrickson, Angela Davis, and Robyn Wiegman, have noted that the promulgation of the myth of the black male rapist is rooted in slavery as a phantasmal projection of the white male/master rapist. Jordan writes, "The image of the sexually aggressive Negro was rooted . . . firmly in deep strata of irrationality. For it is apparent that white men projected their own desires onto Negroes: their own passion for Negro women was not fully acceptable to society or the self and hence not readily admissible. Sexual desires could be effectively denied and the accompanying anxiety and guilt in some measure assuaged, however, by imputing them to others. It is not we, but others, who are guilty. It is not we who lust, but they."[31] He goes on to describe the methods by which black men accused of raping white women were punished: the penalty for black men's sexual encounters with white women was either castration or execution. The criminality of sexual violence was conflated with interracial sex, as both were considered debased and inappropriate expressions of sexual desire. The castration of black men for rape and for desiring women of a different race was an egregious and extreme result of white men's projecting their interracial desires and sexual violence onto subjugated slaves. It is important to note that castration was also the punishment for "grave sexual offenses such as sodomy, bestiality . . . [and] incest" in some states, such as Pennsylvania, and applied to free blacks and white men, as well.[32] The deviance of sexual violence, interracial desire, and homoeroticism was linked in the cultural imagination not only because all were taboo sexual behaviors but because all warranted the same judicial penalty: castration, itself a punitive act that produces the queer subjectivity it is designed to curb.

Early theories of homosexuality centered on sexual inversion, or malformed gender. David Halperin, Jonathan Ned Katz, and other historians of sexuality trace the invention of the homosexual in the late nineteenth century to the model of the sexual invert, the person who, as Katz describes, "Wore the clothes and hairstyle, undertook the work . . . , performed the sexual acts and felt the emotions of the 'other' sex."[33] Halperin states that homosexuals were initially believed to be sexual inverts, people who pathologically "reversed, or inverted, their proper sex-roles by adapting a masculine or feminine style at variance with what was deemed natural and appropriate to their anatomical sex."[34] While, on one hand, racial slavery allowed for the full exploitation of black bodies in slavery in whatever gendered capacity, it simultaneously—and paradoxically—disallowed distinctions in gender among black people. Enslaved black men were feminized by virtue of their subjugation as slaves, the regularity with which many were castrated, and the denial of their patriarchal and citizenship rights. Enslaved black women were masculinized by virtue of their backbreaking labor on par with black men and their being denied male protection and provision. Spillers describes the process of "ungendering" in slavery as rendering slaves "neuterbound."[35] The slave's body was rendered "neuter" in that, despite the slave's anatomical referent, as a non-person she or he did not register gender legibly according to established paradigms of masculinity or femininity. The conditions of enslavement and its obliteration of families disallowed enslaved men and women from fulfilling normative gender requirements and helped to create a class of people whose emblematization foreshadows the representational logic underwriting the figure of the sexual invert or the "sexually reversed" person in later decades.

More than simply a condition of black women's experience under slavery, rape serves as a useful paradigm for assessing and describing the position and experience of black people in total under slavery's brutal regime. As Katz describes the sexual invert's participation in the sex acts of the other gender, Spillers refers to the "pansexual potential" of the slave that is caused by gender failure resulting from dehumanization and enslavement. Spillers's formulation speaks not to slaves' roaming and unspecified erotic urges but to their complete vulnerability to any number of invasions by both men and women of the master class; it comments on the condition of black people in slavery as thoroughly socially and sexually abject. In this way, Spillers corroborates Jordan, who summarizes adroitly, "Sexually, as well as in every other way, Negroes were utterly subordinated. White men extended their dominance over their Negroes to the bed, where the sex act itself served as a ritualistic enactment of the daily pattern of social dominance."[36] Spillers's description of the slave's "pansexual potential" alludes to rape as a significant event in the formation of the enslaved in that it situates slaves within relations of power along sexual, gendered, and racial lines. Abdul R. JanMohamed also describes this process, asserting that "rape is simultaneously the metonymy of the process of oppressive racist control . . . and a metaphor for the construction of the racialized subject. Regardless of gender, the racialized subject is always already constructed as a "raped" subject. . . . Rape thus subsumes the totality of force relations on the racial border, which is in fact always a sexual border."[37] The vulnerability of all enslaved black people to nearly every conceivable violation produced a collective 'raped' subjectivity. Again, given that the first theories of homosexuality centered on sexual inversion, or malformed gender, and given the association of blackness with sexual violence and victimhood, it is reasonable to assert that representations of black men and women under conditions of enslavement have influenced configurations of (homo)sexual abjection in later decades.

Luke

Although critical discussions of *Incidents in the Life of a Slave Girl* have tended to focus on Linda Brent's sexuality and struggle for sexual autonomy, I read it here to illustrate the linkage of sexual abuse, homoeroticism, and racial dominance in the early nineteenth century. Harriet Jacobs indicts slavery for its total consumption and commodification of black bodies by representing sexual violence, whether threatened or actualized, as the strongest evidence of the destructive force of slavery on the individual, family, and wider community. To be clear: the point of my work in this section is not to malign sexual difference or to promote homophobia, even as I discuss the same-sex abuse of slaves by white slaveowners and overseers. My examination is not guided by a moral commitment to heterosexual hegemony or to a version of African American social and political advancement that requires adherence to established cultural norms or proscriptive modes of being, sexual or otherwise. Quite the opposite: I am committed to unpacking the taken-for-granted assumptions that ground cultural norms and the social hierarchies that they uphold to discover routes to fairness—and freedom—that lie beyond these hierarchies. I proceed here with the understanding that racial and sexual ideologies are principal sources of support for asymmetric social structures that have disastrous psychic and social costs for those who live at the bottom. And I maintain that a productive site to begin to unravel these ideologies is where they converge: in the figure of the black person.

In this section, I analyze Jacobs's strategic use of same-sex sexual abuse to represent institutional slavery as morally bankrupt and perverse. Jacobs presents a sadomasochistic rendering of same-sex abuse to indicate the most profound, extreme, and damaging expression of the sexual deviance permeating slavery's various patterns. The relationship between a slave named Luke and his master qualifies as an instantiation of sadomasochistic, intra-gender abuse and reveals in general the entwinement of desire and coercion that typifies the master–slave relationship.[38] Sadomasochism here does not denote a contractual relation based on mutual enjoyment between the enslaved and the slaveholder. I use the term "sadomasochism" to pinpoint the relation between the literal sadism in the practices of the slaveholder and the literary masochism in the revelation of those practices in the text of the black author. The master's sadism is manifestly coextensive with the general practices of slavery. "Masochism" in this context does not imply any enslaved person's volition or enjoyment of the regular and regulatory sadistic protocols of slavery. Rather, it refers to the textual representation of such protocols, particularly when rendered in a sexual scenario.[39]

I should add that my analysis benefits from the recognition of slavery as a multifarious system, spawning all manner of operation and impact in particularized iterations that varied by household, region, economic position, legal mandate, and so on. I recognize also that strategies of survival, accommodation, and resistance that were adopted by enslaved people were various. The masochism to which I refer in this section is neither a sexual positionality nor an analogical social one to which I am assigning enslaved people. I am calling attention to the deployment of narrative technique used by authors of slave narratives and its attendant rhetorical and political potency in the labor of abolition. The abused black male slave, with whom the vulnerable and victimized slave-girl narrator identifies, is debased and overcome both to satisfy a despotic master and to effect authorial desires. In other words, the slave's masochistic relation to his master inheres in its textual representation; the masochistic payoff, *belonging to the narrator*, is neither her pleasure nor Luke's but exposure of the master's shameful sadism. With their focus, if not emphasis, on the underbelly of seemingly normal societal relations, slave narratives expose generally the dark and hidden side of established nineteenth-century domestic and cultural norms. Sadomasochism, as represented in *Incidents*, exposes the psychological orientation and erotic underpinnings of institutional slavery itself.

As I show in my reading of *Narrative*, Douglass argues for the eradication of slavery in patriarchal terms because it entails his—and, by extension, the possibility of all slaves'—resignification as human. Jacobs must contend with a raced and gendered self in a society that recognizes and confers economic and political power exclusively on white men, as well as with the burden of transferring slave status to beloved progeny through the reproductive capacity of her womb. Jacobs works to redeem the humanity of all slaves by embracing their matrilineal and matrifocal familial arrangements. Her strategy is to pre-figure slaves as initially and authentically "normal" and slavery and slaveown-ers as depraved, corrupt forces that debase and devastate the lives of those enslaved. She opens her narrative depicting the Brents as an intact family: a skilled carpenter, his beloved wife, and their two children, who all "lived to-gether in a comfortable home."[40] The mother, though the vector of slavery, is redeemed through her description as "a slave merely in name, but in nature . . . noble and womanly."[41] And despite the death of her mother when Linda is a small child, her maternal grandmother, Aunt Marthy, continues to provide her with the requisite maternal presence and nurturance for full subjective development, as well as the moral guidance for Linda herself to become "no-ble and womanly." The family genealogy is traced through a maternal line: "my maternal grandmother . . . was the daughter of a planter in South Car-olina, who, at his death, left her mother and his three children free, with money to go to St. Augustine, where they had relatives. It was during the Revolutionary War; and they were captured on their passage, carried back, and sold to different purchasers."[42]

Jacobs traces the family history back before the Revolutionary War, estab-lishing her own rightful placement within the national polis by putting her family at the pivotal scene of the country's formation. She establishes her own right to freedom, not only in humanistic terms, but also in legal terms, by showing that her maternal ancestors were wrongfully enslaved after their legal manumission. Moreover, through her depiction of the Revolutionary War as concurrent with her family's capture and enslavement within national borders, Jacobs ironizes the fact that the inauguration of a democratic republic in the United States coincided with the development of the most extensive, long-lasting, and brutal system of race-based slavery in the modern world. In a brief sketch of maternal history, Jacobs establishes the humanity, civility, and moral authority of the enslaved.

Jacobs depicts sadistic same-sex violence perpetuated against the enslaved by their owners to highlight the moral depravity of slavery and its ruinous effects on black individuals and families. The first insinuation of homoerotic violence occurs in Jacobs's account of Mrs. Flint's interactions with Linda. As Karen Sánchez-Eppler has demonstrated quite convincingly, given the con-ventions around what could be said to, about, and between women in relation to sexuality, Mrs. Flint's insistence that Linda describe in detail her sexual harassment by Mr. Flint must be read as itself sexually abusive, especially considering the extent to which verbal communication aids Dr. Flint's sexual coercion. Sánchez-Eppler writes, "What Mrs. Flint requires from Linda is not a protestation of Linda's sexual innocence, but the titillation of being told all. . . . For Linda, moreover, this enforced act of recounting her sexual victimization repeats the scene of sexual abuse."[43] The repetition and displacement of scenes of Dr. Flint's sexual harassment onto the relationship between Linda and Mrs. Flint implies more direct and extreme forms of sexual abuse by the mistress. It functions, moreover, to provide evidence of the failure of Southern white women to meet standards of true womanhood, a central theme of the narrative and Jacobs's primary strategy for aligning Northern white women with female slaves.

> Mrs. Flint orders Linda:
>
> "Now take this stool, sit down, look me directly in the face, and tell me all that has passed between your master and you."
>
> I did as she ordered. As I went on with my account her color changed frequently, she wept, and sometimes groaned. . . . She pitied herself a martyr, but she was incapable of feeling for the condition of shame and misery in which her unfortunate, helpless slave was placed.[44]

Proprietary customs of the nineteenth century circumscribed women's speech, forbidding discussions of the erotic lest women become associated with illicit sexuality. The mistress's insistence that Linda disclose every detail of Dr. Flint's sexual harassment is sufficient to align her with sexual impropriety. As Mrs. Flint listens to Linda's account, her skin changes color and she groans, indicating both her distress at her husband's infidelity and her sexual arousal by the tale of it. Her inability to be shamed by what she hears or to feel compassion for the victim of it demonstrates the extent to which slavery has corrupted her womanly impulses. She no longer qualifies as a true woman because she cannot *feel* and *respond* appropriately. That Linda *belongs to her*, is her "unfortunate, helpless slave," provides evidence that Mrs. Flint is complicitous with a regime that has had the effect of hindering, if not completely nullifying, her proper feminine capacities.

As Linda's position vis-à-vis Mrs. Flint makes clear, slave mistresses' dominion over slave girls provided relief from and resistance to their subjugation within patriarchal structures as well as their frustration with heterosexual imperatives. Deborah White notes, "Southern white women were powerless to strike back, were powerless to right the wrongs done them, but some did strike back, not always at Southern patriarchs, but usually at their unwitting and powerless rivals, slave girls."[45] The sexual vulnerability of slaves, particularly their slave girls, was not lost on mistresses. Their jealousy over their husbands' coerced concubinage of female slaves could be attenuated by subjecting slave girls to their own physical, psychological, and sexual torment. Mrs. Flint's persecution and pursuit of Linda continues:

> She now took me to sleep in a room conjoining her own. There I was the object of her especial care, though not to her especial comfort, for she spent many a sleepless night to watch over me. Sometimes I woke up, and found her bending over me. At other times she whispered in my ear, as though it was her husband who was speaking to me, and listened to hear what I would answer. If she startled me, on such occasions, she would glide stealthily away. . . . At last, I began to be fearful for my life. It had been often threatened and, as you can imagine, better than I can describe, what an unpleasant sensation it must be to waken in the dead of night and find a jealous woman bending over you. Terrible as this experience was, I had fears that it would give place to one more terrible.[46]

Instead of protecting Linda from Dr. Flint's sexual abuse, Mrs. Flint takes her to a concealed place near her own bedroom to re-enact it. The scene of Mrs. Flint's bending over Linda invokes a more general practice of "erotic domination."[47] Mrs. Flint's gliding stealthily away reveals her predatory aspect, and that she goes to Linda in the middle of the night connotes a sexual purpose to entering the girl's room at all. Linda worries that her mistress's activities might give way to others "more terrible"—might possibly, in other words, escalate in erotic pursuit and violence. To avoid direct association with Mrs. Flint's transgressive sexual pursuit, Jacobs presents it obliquely, a strategy I explain in detail in the first section of this chapter. She concludes the passage with an invitation to readers to speculate about Mrs. Flint's purposes for going to Linda late at night, suggesting that readers can better, and perhaps should, "imagine" what Mrs. Flint is up to, as nineteenth-century circumscriptions on public speech and Jacobs's own chastity render her unable or forbidden to "describe" it explicitly.[48]

In her reading of this passage, Spillers argues that Jacobs uses Mrs. Flint as "an analogy with the 'master' to the extent that the male dominative modes give the male the material means to fully act out what the female might only *wish*."[49] In other words, the male possesses the instrument with which to enact a phantasmagoric rape of the slave girl on behalf of her mistress. Spillers acknowledges the possibility of sexual dominance by slave mistresses but suggests that a textual conflation of Mr. and Mrs. Flint works here to insinuate more direct and extreme forms of Mr. Flint's sexual tyranny over Linda. I concur with her reading but offer the additional possibility that Jacobs alludes to a more problematic sexual arrangement altogether. The scenes between

Mrs. Flint and Linda reveal a violent masquerade in which the mistress phantasmically appropriates her husband's persona—miming his voice and body—to engage in uninvited sexual activity with Linda. This makes Mrs. Flint a sexual culprit in her own right.[50] As an instrument for the expression of the mistress's desires, the slave girl's body could be used to express sexual urges that routinely were repressed in the realm of normative heterosexual and marital relations. Moreover, Linda's textual and erotic placement between Mr. and Mrs. Flint seems a virtual ménage à trois that enacts or replicates a coercive, "real-life," polyamorous sexual arrangement on the plantation.

The story about Luke and his master demonstrates the obfuscation, if not complete undoing, of both sexual and gender normalcy under slavery. The account comes at the end of the narrative after both Luke and Linda have escaped to the North. Linda remembers Luke as a particularly degraded figure and, before she realizes that he, too, has managed to escape from slavery, laments at having left him there. She recalls, "I was somewhat acquainted with a slave named Luke, who belonged to a wealthy man in our vicinity. His master died leaving a son and daughter heirs to his large fortune. In the division of slaves, Luke was included in the son's portion. The young man became prey to the vices growing out of the 'patriarchal institution.'"[51] That Luke is given as property to the son establishes the context for homosexuality and dominance, as dominance is passed on as white men's inheritance. The vice to which this passage alludes is the young master's homosexuality, which, it is important to note, is not treated here as sexual orientation or as an identity that is natural to him. Instead, the master's homosexual inclinations are attributed to the extreme wealth of his family and the unbounded freedom of white masculine privilege. It is the patriarchal institution, with its emphasis on the master's entitlement and his unfettered control over the bodies of others, that Jacobs holds responsible for the master's homoerotic desires and behavior. For her, the master is prey to an institution that corrupts both its victims and its benefactors.

In her representations of same-sex abuse, Jacobs alludes to the protection, if not advantage, slavery provided to masters and mistresses who by culturally repressive standards were sexual outlaws or, by contemporary definitions, non-heterosexuals. She writes:

When [the young master] went north to complete his education, he carried his vices with him. He was brought home deprived of the use of his limbs, by excessive dissipation. Luke was appointed to wait upon his bed-ridden master, whose despotic habits were greatly increased by exasperation at his own helplessness. He kept a cowhide beside him, and, for the most trivial occurrence would order his attendant to bear his back, and kneel beside the couch, while he whipped him till his strength was exhausted. Sometimes he was not allowed to wear anything but his shirt in order to be in readiness to be flogged.[52]

Presumably a venereal disease or some other physical manifestation of the young master's moral degeneracy is responsible for his severe illness and bodily weakness, itself serving here as a signifier of his aberrant sexuality.[53] Because the slave body was already envisioned fundamentally as an instrument for her owner's profitmaking and pleasure seeking, the forms of seeking pleasure and making money from the bodies of slaves were exempt from either cultural sanctions or state control. As the master weakens, he continues to fulfill his sexual urges and express his frustration through sadistic beatings and sexual invasions of Luke. As in Douglass's depiction of the beating of Aunt Hester, the cowhide functions as a phallic replacement, as an instrument for inflicting punishment and sexual torture. The sex underlying the beatings is revealed in Luke's having to undress and kneel to receive his punishment, as well as his having to spend days unclothed beneath the waist. Although his back is the purported site of his whippings, Luke is allowed to wear a shirt but is made to go around with his lower parts exposed to receive his master's *additional* punishment.

Here, as in general, sadomasochism characterizes and animates the master–slave relationship. Like sadomasochism, the slave–master relationship is performative in two senses. In the theatrical sense, it requires *contrivance*: the donning of particular, unfitted, artificial, and polarized master–slave roles. Through technologies of terror and torture, slaves learned to adopt postures of passivity, and even complicity, in rituals designed to showcase the master's dominance. The slave–master relationship is also performative in the Austinian sense in that it is initiated, made intelligible, and upheld through repeated, ritual enactments of its script and spectacle.[54] If Luke resisted his treatment at all, "the town constable was sent for to execute the punishment."[55] Not only is the town constable stronger and presumably more virile, but as a representative of the state and of the law, his participation in Luke's torture sanctions it. This is so despite the fact that the sexual arrangement between Luke and his master—and now, presumably, the constable—falls outside the domain of legitimate social interactions. The constable's participation in Luke's torture also dramatizes white men's fraternity in an instance of homosocial bonding around the shared brutalization and symbolic castration of the male slave.[56] In this way, it anticipates the post-Reconstruction practice of lynching black men in large communal spectacles to shore up white masculinity after it had been assailed by black men's enfranchisement.

The account of Luke's abuse at the hands of his master reveals the cultural practices and psychic maneuvers by which domination created and carried on in slavery helped to shape white American identity in the United States. As the young master weakens, he depends on sadomasochistic ritual to establish his potency and secure his identity:

> The fact that [the young master] was entirely dependent on Luke's care, and was obliged to be tended like an infant, instead of inspiring any gratitude or compassion towards his poor slave, seemed only to increase his irritability and cruelty. As he lay there on his bed, a mere degraded wreck of manhood, he took into his head the strangest freaks of despotism; and if Luke hesitated to submit to his orders, the constable was immediately sent for. Some of these freaks were of a nature too filthy to be repeated. When I fled the house of bondage, I left poor Luke still chained to the bed of this cruel and disgusting wretch.[57]

The additional details of Luke's sexual bondage, shown by a conceivably literal chain to his master's bed, expose further the extent to which ritual sadomasochistic performance organized the master–slave relationship. This includes the sexual dimension, of course, but it also refers ultimately to the process of identity formation wherein the master comes to exist as a vital, cohesive, legitimated subject by virtue of his repeated negations and violations of the slave's body and autonomy. As the young master's condition deteriorates and he becomes completely dependent on Luke for care, he becomes even more brutal. The young master's dependence on Luke threatens to rob him of his identity as man and master because his literal survival depends on Luke's caring for him as if he were an infant, presumably feeding, bathing, and clothing him and keeping him otherwise comforted. "A mere degraded wreck of manhood," the young master asserts himself through his brutality and sexuality.

Luke is neutered, or symbolically castrated, by virtue of his subjugation as a slave, his feminized, maternal duties to his master, and his master's sexual abuse. Thus, the young master's sexual invasions of Luke do not indict the young master of sexual criminality; instead, by instantiating his complete possession and consumption of his (affectively gender-neutral) slave—according to his personal and property rights—they corroborate his status as master. As the young master's physical abilities wane, he requires more abject sexual performances by Luke so he can be satiated both physically and psychi-cally. Through the young master's rigorous disavowal of his dependence on *and desire for* his male slave—facilitated by the predominant cultural practice of denying dependence and projecting illicit desires onto black slaves—Luke's own body becomes the site and sign of his master's (homo)sexuality.

In her work on sadomasochism, Jessica Benjamin asserts that it "replicates quite faithfully the themes of the master–slave relationship. Here subjugation takes the form of transgressing against the other's body, violating his physical boundaries."[58] This, she argues, is necessary for the master to experience both the separation (or differentiation) and the recognition that are so central to subjective development. The master's self—defined always against a separate, subjugated other—is formed, legitimated, and made autonomous *and powerful* through direct (physical and sexual) domination of that other. For this process to work and to persist (in one instance and certainly generationally as in slav-ery), new levels of resistance had to be discovered in the slave for the purpose of surmounting them. Thus, as the escalating brutality of the young master's abuse indicates, the mechanisms of torture, bodily exposure, excessive toil, and requisite compliance that were standard features of slavery worked over centuries to create not only a population of slaves but also the master class.

Even though Jacobs locates her most direct and extreme portrayal of sexual abuse in a male same-sex relationship, she speaks to the general, identity-enabling character of master–slave relations regardless of gender. As Joan Dayan states eloquently, "Being a *master or mistress* became so addictive a plea-sure that the slave as ultimate possession became a necessary part of the mas-ter's or mistress's identity."[59] The subjection of black bodies in slavery and the imputation of social and sexual deviance to black people supported the de-velopment of whiteness and solidified heteronormativity as one of its main features. In other words, throughout the nineteenth century, both whiteness and heterosexuality were conceived, constituted, and stabilized through their opposition to and haunting by the specter of the black sexual deviant.

Finally, the homosexual nature of Luke's sadomasochistic bondage not only functions in *Incidents* to lessen the risk of exposure for black women (protecting the frail possibility of virtuousness on their parts). It also calls attention to the illegitimacy of master–slave relations overall. The story of Luke comes after Linda has escaped slavery in a chapter titled "The Fugitive Slave Law." It is offered as a critique of slavery, of racial prejudice throughout the entire country, and of the Fugitive Slave Law, which had the effect of na-tionalizing slavery. Luke becomes representative of all who were still in bond-age. And the diseased and decaying body of Luke's master functions as a metaphor for the institution itself. The depiction of both slave *and* master underscores Jacobs's belief that slavery, in the mid-nineteenth century, was an antiquated and perverse social system.

Literary constructions of deviant sexuality function in slave testimonies both to reveal painfully private aspects of slaves' experience and to provide a fitting metaphor for the experience and impact of institutional slavery. Sexual violence, with its elements of violation, bodily dispossession, psychic torture, and long-lived trauma, offers an apt reflection for what it felt like to be enslaved at all. Further, by exposing the institutional practices and psychic structures that enabled the debasement of the black slave and the development of the white master-subject, slave narratives reveal how concepts of personhood, citizenship, and normalcy emerged in the United States in concert with strident oppression of a population that was denied access to those very categories. Both Douglass's *Narrative* and Jacobs's *Incidents* work to expose the grand contradiction of the simultaneity of European Enlightenment and modernization and the base, barbaric social and labor systems that were imported from antiquity to support economic growth and (white) identity formation in the New World.

2

ICONOGRAPHIES OF GANG RAPE

Or, Black Enfranchisement, White Disavowal,

and the (Homo)erotics of Lynching

After chattel slavery, the most potent manifestation of the limits violently and rigorously imposed on individual and collective black American life was lynching. Pursued by white men and women with the orgiastic fury and fervor of gang rape, lynching involved the beating, maiming, mutilating, castrating, clubbing, hanging, burning of individual or small groups of (mainly) black men. Emblematic of the crisis of race hatred in America at the turn of the twentieth century, lynching exemplified the problematic and interlocking constructions of racial, gender, and sexual identity in U.S. culture, as Angela Davis, Trudier Harris, Orlando Patterson, Judith Stephens, and Walter White have all argued.[1] Lynching was touted as the spontaneous outrage of white men at the sexual violation of white women by black men. So angry were they at the putative dishonor to white womanhood that they took the law into their own hands and punished alleged black rapists in extralegal spectacles of torture, castration, and murder. Even though fewer than 40 percent of all lynchings were in response to an accusation of interracial rape, the idea of interracial rape as justification for lynching predominated. Most African Americans, however, understood lynching to be an act of racial terrorism aimed at preventing their social, economic, and political advancement. It had more to do with the effect of black cultural advancement on white manhood—and, by extension, on white community—than black men's ravishing of white womanhood. Stephens assesses, "For nearly a century, lynching was a highly visible and concrete expression of institutionalized white supremacy and symbol of the existing power relations between the black and white 'races' in the United

States."[2] While I share Stephens's estimation—and the general critical consensus—that lynching was a highly visible manifestation of white supremacy, I argue in this chapter that lynching did not reflect "existing power relations" as much as desperately *sought-after* ones. In other words, what this chapter demonstrates is that, rather than being a display of white hegemony, white racial violence in the early twentieth century was a disavowal of black humanity and a *will to whiteness*. The routinized, ritualized violence of the act and widespread white communal participation in lynching reveal a profound need on the part of whites (during Reconstruction and throughout much of the twentieth century) for some evidence that the racial order of slavery still, in fact, governed relations between black and white persons, despite the legal abolition of slavery. Lynching reflected a profound insecurity about the stability and supremacy of whiteness in the post-Reconstruction era. Southern whiteness was assailed by the perceived failure of white Southern manhood, evinced, first and foremost, by Southern white men's defeat in the Civil War and finally in the decline of the agricultural plantation system on which both their identities and wealth depended. Lynching functioned in the absence of slavery's racial organization and operational logic to fix racial categories in the post-Emancipation period and to annihilate the threat that African American men's exercise of their patriarchal and citizenship prerogatives posed to the desired (racist) social order.

This chapter analyzes imaginative accounts of lynching in Pauline Hopkins's *Contending Forces* and William Faulkner's *Light in August*. My objective in juxtaposing depictions of lynching in the novels of a prominent black American female and a white American male author is to gauge different investments in representing lynching across racial and gender lines in private and in popular culture during the decades in which lynching most terrorized the black community and vexed the nation as a whole. Both Hopkins and Faulkner depict lynching as the extreme, panicked response of white people to black men's potential parity with white men in the economic and political realms. Both writers underscore lynching as a kind of gang rape, a profound expression of communal sexual perversion—specifically, one in which the victim is gruesomely violated for the sexualized psychosocial satisfaction of a whole host of participants and spectators. There are, however, important distinctions in the authors' representations. Faulkner depicts lynching as the enactment of white men's virulent race hatred and unacknowledged desire for black men that offers a triumphant—if fragile—reconstitution of white manhood, whereas Hopkins narrativizes the failure of lynching to revive plantation hierarchies fully or to revitalize white mastery.

Although *Light in August* was published more than three decades after *Con-*

tending Forces, my discussion opens with Faulkner's novel to expose lynching as a gory homoerotic act meant to divest black men of the civic recognition, economic self-sufficiency, and patriarchal authority made possible by emancipation and enfranchisement. My discussion of *Light in August* establishes the importance of white womanhood in the context of male dominance in the social and political arena. I then read in *Contending Forces* the recovery of the absent black woman in the scene and script of spectacle lynching. Hopkins emphasizes the rape of black women as the foremost expression of white racial terrorism. To permit black men access to the conventional features and freedoms of masculinity, she de-emphasizes their victimization in lynching spectacles and highlights the sexual sadism of lynching by substituting the raped black female body for the castrated black male body. In so doing, Hopkins reveals the rape of black women and the lynching of black men to be coextensive, dual manifestations of white racial terrorism implemented to thwart black men's enfranchisement specifically and black communal advancement more generally.

Notably, both Faulkner and Hopkins use racially indeterminate figures to signify the status of post-Emancipation blackness, and both authors endow these racially indeterminate characters with particularly disruptive power. Hopkins's biracial heroes and heroines challenge widely held beliefs about the fixity of racial categories and the immutability of racial characteristics. In *Contending Forces*, biracial characters embody the aspirations of the African American community and demonstrate their qualification to enter the social and political mainstream.[3] Faulkner's racially indeterminate protagonist Joe Christmas "is both black and white," according to Thadious Davis.[4] Of course, what this means according to the one-drop rule is that Christmas is legally, if not completely culturally, black. To my mind, African Americans may be taken in general as a miscegenated group not only because of mixed racial genealogies that have resulted from rampant interracial rape during and after slavery but also because of the inevitable cultural admixture that has resulted from the presence of African Americans in America since its founding. Moreover, in the post-Reconstruction era, when black men were enfranchised—after hundreds of thousands had participated in the Civil War and helped to bring about the defeat of the South and after some had even gained the wealth and education to fare better than some of their white compatriots—racial blackness in the United States itself underwent a legal miscegenation: it became infused with some of the rights and properties of white manhood. It is this infusion of white privilege into the legal, social, and symbolic realms of blackness that participants in acts of racial violence sought to abrogate through lynching.

Violent Intimacies

Light in August was originally about white people: Lena Grove, Gail Hightower, and Byron Bunch were at the center of William Faulkner's initial conception of the novel. The murder and near-decapitation of Joanna Burden was to be the event that tied these three characters together. Joe Christmas became the central character of the novel when it became evident to Faulkner that another element, an embodied racial signifier, was necessary to get at the heart of Southern history. In Faulkner's text, the brutal murder of a white woman, followed by the quick capture and lynching of a (reputed) black man, exemplifies and encapsulates the ideological and cultural crisis of black–white relations in the post-Reconstruction era, as inflected by gender, class, and the then recent history of slavery in the South. Nell Sullivan asserts, "Christmas became so compelling that Faulkner kept adding episodes to his early life in the flashback[s]. The shift of dramatic emphasis from Lena, Byron, and Hightower to Joe Christmas reveals Faulkner's recognition of the Negrophobe myth at the heart of the (white) Southern consciousness."[5] In writing Joe Christmas, Faulkner introduced a preoccupation he would continue to work out in such novels as *Absalom, Absalom!* and *Go Down, Moses*: miscegenation and its relation to history, to slavery, and to American genealogies. For Faulkner, miscegenation, as Krister Friday remarks, serves as a "metonym for the tragic aftermath of slavery, the Civil War, and Reconstruction."[6] The fact of miscegenation—of mixed-raced bodies that could evade or straddle the color line and in their very embodiment recall the intimate and violent history of institutional slavery—provided Faulkner with a viable, living metaphor for the gruesome history, tumultuous present, and uncertain future of black–white relations in the post-Emancipation South.

Many critics have analyzed miscegenation in *Light in August* in terms of Faulkner's rendering of slavery and Southern history. I want to diverge from such standard readings to argue that miscegenation is not simply a metaphor for the messy, entangled racial history of the South; it is also the principal means by which Faulkner contemplates and represents the imperiled state of white masculinity in the post-Reconstruction era and the desire and dread underpinning white men's obsession with black manhood. Generally sexualized, degraded, and debased, the black figures in *Light in August* are placed in close proximity to white characters and spaces to demonstrate that, in the post-slavery South, black and white communities are dependent on and in some ways mutually constitutive of each other. Joe Christmas, however, is not simply someone whose racially inscrutable body reveals uncertain but possibly mixed-raced origins; he is Faulkner's definitive (albeit white) "nigger." Like many of the black characters in Light in August, Joe Christmas has little interiority and even less discernable motivation for doing what he does. Like the legible outlines of a drawing, he is a sketch figure. However, unlike the caricatured, illiterate black men or the sexualized black female and mammy figures that appear for mere seconds in the novel and abruptly leave, Joe Christmas represents Faulkner's meditation on the civic equality of black men in the post-Reconstruction era and its effect on the psyche of whites. Christmas acts out his historical moment and anticipates, if not precipitates, crises in the established economic, gender, and racial systems of that historical moment. This section principally aims to understand how Faulkner's mixed-race figure in Light in August emblematizes the crisis of the racial order in the post-Reconstruction moment. I attend specifically to Faulkner's linking of racial ambiguity and homoeroticism in the figure of Joe Christmas, arguing that he uses the historical fact of miscegenation and the perceived failure of white masculinity to critique Southern culture and history and to offer ways to revamp and reconstitute whiteness in the modern—meaning post-slavery—moment.

Although Light in August was published in 1932, nearly six decades after Reconstruction, I characterize the moment of the novel's emergence as alternately post-Reconstruction and post-Emancipation. My rationale for doing so is in part the novel's concern for the imperiled state of whiteness in the aftermath of the Civil War. More important, though, I wish to emphasize the political, cultural, and seemingly temporal stasis that gripped the South with regard to the position of African Americans during the decades between the departure of the federal troops in 1877 and the hard-won legislative gains of the Civil Rights Movement in the mid-twentieth century. As a work of fiction, Light in August shares features with other late modernist American texts. Specifically, as is the case with other early twentieth-century works of American fiction, depictions of African Americans in Light in August provide Faulkner with the means to critique fluctuations in racial, sexual, spatial, and other social arrangements in early-twentieth-century American culture and to ponder the effects of those fluctuations on white psychology. In their introduction to Prehistories of the Future, Elazar Barkan and Ronald Bush usefully describe the rac(ial)ist concept of "primitive irrationality" as "attractive to . . . [the] modern, alienated intellectual because it provided the means by which to represent the individual unconscious."[7] Marianna Torgovnick suggests that "primitives" were believed to be the "untamed selves [and] id forces—libidinal, irrational, violent, dangerous" of Europeans.[8] The commodity nature and circulation of images of blackness in the early twentieth century furnished American authors of that historical moment with a repertoire of images associated with "primitivity" through which to conjure and explore the condition of psychic fracture for the dislocated white subject under the pressure of modernity in an increasingly multiracial urbanized sphere.

At the historical moment of *Light in August*'s emergence, blackness was highly visible and widely commodified in the culture at large. As Grace Elizabeth Hale has argued, new modes of production within capitalism enabled racial stereotypes to become firmly entrenched in the popular imaginary.[9] Certainly, minstrel performances helped to preserve derogatory characterizations of African Americans as dependent slaves even as they struggled to advance socially and politically beyond that former status. Furthermore, the plantation types depicted in minstrel shows helped to create enduring beliefs about black people that lasted well into the twentieth century. As Eric Lott brilliantly elucidates, the minstrel show was "highly responsive to the emotional demands and troubled fantasies of its audiences."[10]

Blackface minstrelsy—including textual blackface—provided, moreover, a "space of fun and license" specifically to white artists.[11] In his discussion of the important influence of African American dialect and African art on American modernist aesthetics in the early twentieth century, Michael North argues that representations of blackness were used by the "moderns" to disrupt conventional aesthetic forms. He posits that "in painting and in literature, the step away from conventional verisimilitude into abstraction is accomplished by a figurative change of race."[12] Artists and writers who sought to distort, to experiment, to transform, and to invent wholly new ways to write and paint did so by importing and infusing elements of racial blackness into their artistic creations. Because blackness was itself believed to be *the very condition* of fracture, radical uncertainty, and resultant chaos both within oneself and in one's relation to the culture at large, textual blackface operated as a literary trope and practice that enabled meditations on and representations of the fragmented self in early-twentieth-century American culture. Representations of African Americans in texts of this era written by white Americans have not tended overall to reflect African American people, our inner or cultural life; these representations, instead, have marked crucial moments in the development of white American culture and consciousness.[13]

The mulatto—the putatively black but ultimately racially ambiguous figure—is one complicated and subtle manifestation of blackness. The performative quality of Joe Christmas's blackness is evident not only in his iteration of certain behavioral norms of blackness but also in his susceptibility to the violence generally reserved for black people—i.e., lynching and castration.

Christmas, furthermore, is a compelling case study of how the status of a mixed-race person can be extended to represent African American people in the post-Reconstruction era in general. Thadious Davis argues that Faulkner "provide[s] details which link Joe to the black side of Jefferson life. . . . [Christmas] enters Joanna's house like a nigger invading in the night, and he eats coarse food set for the nigger. . . . Even before he tells Joanna that he believes he is a Negro, he sees himself as the 'nigger' in her bed."[14] Race is not, nor has it ever been, completely corporeal. What determined white manhood in the nineteenth century was not simply white skin but access to the vote, to the bodies of women, to the right to defend one's country in war, to hold arms or to hold property, to acquire capital, and, especially, to the right and ability to dominate black people. What determined blackness was susceptibility to violence, a so-called inability to fend off or control primal urges, and an ultimate negation of the aforementioned rights and privileges. It is the position of black people in the aftermath of generational slavery that determines their abjectness and makes Joe Christmas a viable representation of post-Emancipation blackness in *Light in August.* My use of the word "abject" follows that of Julia Kristeva, who describes the abject as one who "disturbs identity, system, order. What does not respect, borders, positions, rules. The in-between, the ambiguous, the composite."[15] In other words, indeterminate ontology creates the position of the abject, the specter who haunts social order. Joe Christmas is abject first and foremost because his paternal lineage and, by extension, his racial origins are unknown—as traceable genealogies were unknown by the overwhelming number of emancipated African Americans. Christmas cannot be located in the strict racial economy of white over black that was inaugurated in slavery and that continued under Jim Crow segregation. He therefore remains a shadowy, haunting presence in the town of Jefferson. Described as carrying with him "his own inescapable warning, like a flower its scent or a rattlesnake its rattle," Christmas is said to look like "a phantom, a spirit, strayed from its own world, and lost."[16] Furthermore, his white body is described as "slow and lascivious in a whispering gutter filth like a drowned corpse in a thick still black pool of more than water" (107). Despite his corporeal whiteness, Christmas's identity is associated with blackness, with filth, with fluidity. He is reputed to live behind "the veil," the Du Boisian term for life within black communities or beneath the dividing line of race. The narrator describes, "None of [the townspeople] knew then where Christmas lived and what he was actually doing behind the veil, the screen, of his negro's job at the mill" (36). As has been noted almost to the point of consensus among contemporary literary critics, the difficulty *and potency* of the mixed-raced person is her epistemic uncertainty, her ability to confound and render incoherent the signifying structures of race. Krister Friday suggests, "Joe's indeterminate parentage allows him to pass as both white and black but to 'be' or have 'been' neither. Without the anchor of an origin, Joe's past and present become open, unfinished possibilities rather than certainties, making Joe's 'presence' in the novel assume a spectrality."[17] Friday's observations are useful for understanding the threat of the mixed-race person to the racial schema in general. What I want to emphasize here, however, is the condition of blackness as abject itself, as indeterminate and in-between, once it is no longer contained in slavery, or once black people have been released from the fetters of a fixed definition and status as enslaved thing. My focus then is the similarity of the threat that Christmas's white skin poses to white manhood—as it masks the so-called blackness of his "black blood" and thereby allows him white masculine privilege—and the threat that all black men posed to the racial order in the post-Reconstruction period after they had been given the vote and the legal position as head of their families.

The acquisition of citizenship rights challenged and redeemed the prior enslaved status of black manhood in the same way that Joe Christmas's white skin challenges and redeems his own purported blackness. Enfranchisement masculinized black men in that it established both their legal humanity and their U.S. citizenship; furthermore, black men's legal right to marriage and to function as fathers granted them a recognizable position within the (implicitly patriarchal) symbolic order.[18] Taken together, the status of black men in the post-Emancipation South made them akin to white men. As Robyn Wiegman describes deftly, "The [black man's] threat to masculine power arises not simply from a perceived racial difference, but from the potential for a masculine sameness."[19] Black men in the postbellum era were the same as white men, but with a difference—they were (un)desirable, uncanny, a threat. Put another way, emancipation converted African Americans from captive African slaves to U.S. citizens who spoke the same language, benefited from and believed in the principles that underwrite American democracy; like Joe Christmas's racially indeterminable self, African Americans in the postbellum era delineated difference contained within, and undermined by, similarity.

The position of African Americans after slavery posed a threat not only to the established social schema but also to the very symbolic order that gave whiteness coherence. The end of slavery disrupted the oppositional relation between black slaves and white master-citizens. Following Ferdinand de Saussure's formulation about signifying structures of languages and applying them to Faulkner's literature, Doreen Fowler writes, "Identity and meaning come about only as a result of difference, only by exclusion"; in other words, all meaning derives from and depends on difference because the meaning of a sign is ascertained only by its difference from, or the exclusion of, other signs.[20] The same holds for subjective development, wherein a subject begins to emerge at the precise moment that she ascertains her separateness, her distinction, from those on whom her existence has depended. Extended to the logic of racial formation in the United States, blackness may be understood as the chaotic, debased, and negated part of the racial dyad that defines and delimits whiteness, giving shape to its enabling boundaries.

The dialectic of race, the contingency of racial definitions, is emblematized in the figure of Joe Christmas. In a pivotal scene in the text, Christmas "stood with his hands on his hips, naked, thighdeep in the dusty weeds, while the car came over the hill and approached, the lights full upon him. He watched his body grow white out of the darkness like a Kodak print emerging from the liquid" (108). This scene exposes blackness as the frame and backdrop for the emergence of whiteness. Surrounded by the darkness of night, Joe's corporeal whiteness is contoured and given center-stage. This is imaged here despite the fact that in this very scene Joe is most concerned about his blackness, his nakedness, and its effect on the screaming white woman in the passing car. This scene reveals the epistemological uncertainty attending all racial differentiation, as race is shown to confound the visual technologies that have been put in the service of reifying it. Neither the bright light of the passing car nor the gaze of the imaginary camera exposes Christmas's reputed blackness. Instead, what racializes Christmas in this scene is his relation to the people in the car. Calling them "white bastards," he establishes his blackness relative to their whiteness (108).

Although Faulkner reveals aspects of Joe Christmas's interiority through flashback material about his childhood, his internalized racism, his sexual development, and his relationship with Joanna Burden, the main focus of Faulkner's depiction of Joe Christmas is the awe and rage he inspires in white men. Not only does Christmas exemplify the status of black men in the post-Reconstruction era; he also exposes the imperiled state of white masculinity wrought by the legal abolition of slavery. Faulkner's meditation on the state of white masculinity in the postbellum era is accomplished through his pairing of Joe Christmas and a doppelgänger in the figure of Lucas Burch, who goes by the alias Joe Brown. When Byron Bunch describes the recent arrival of two strangers to Jefferson, who now occupy the "Negro" cabin on Joanna Burden's property, he informs Lena, "Two fellows named Joe live out that way somewhere. Joe Christmas and Joe Brown" (53). The two Joes are linked first and foremost by their shared first name, Joe, and further by their outsiderness, their liquor selling, their similar economic status, and their cohabitation. It is Christmas's grandparents who attend the birth of Lena and Joe Brown's son, and Lena mistakenly thinks that Joe Christmas, not Joe Brown, has fathered her child (409). Though both men are taken for white, Christmas and Brown are described as having dark complexions. Brown's name references his color, and he is described as "tall, young. Dark complected" (55). Christmas is described as having a "dark, insufferable" face (32). What ultimately enables Lena to distinguish between the two Joes when she hears about them from Byron Bunch and to determine which has fathered her child is the white scar near Brown's mouth. Brown's white scar separates him from Christmas in that, despite his dark complexion, it designates and literalizes his racial whiteness. While Brown's dark skin might gesture toward his own potential racial ambiguity, it functions more significantly as the "black" backdrop that surrounds, and thus makes visible and emergent, his whiteness.[21] Because racial whiteness is generally unmarked and unremarked on, to become visible, determinable even, whiteness requires a marking, its own bodily inscription. In locating Joe Brown's whiteness in a scar, Faulkner makes legible and literal the racial specificity of the white body. Regardless of Joe Brown's abandonment of Lena, his refusal of patriarchal responsibility, his "negro's job at the mill," and his shacking up with Joe Christmas, Joe Brown has a more stable identity than Joe Christmas—a definitive (white) racial ontology—that determines his social desirability, justifies Lena's continued pursuit of him, and keeps him present in the novel after Joe Christmas has been lynched.

Willing Whiteness

Though handsome and spirited, Joe Brown symbolizes all that has gone awry in Southern manhood. He is unmarried; he is an alcoholic and a gambler. He resists both patriarchal and heterosexual imperatives. Instead of exemplifying the honor and chivalry of the old South, he exemplifies the decline and degeneracy of Southern manhood. David Minter explains that, in the postbellum era, Southern white men were "burdened . . . not only with indelible memories of a costly as well as humiliating defeat but also with the double burden of guilt—one born of having defended and one of having failed to defend an institution and practice that, in fact, could not be defended."[22] Brown's abdication of his familial responsibilities, his low-class status, and the frequency with which he is manipulated, dominated, and beaten by other men reveal a masculinity assailed by all manner of defeat.

Nonetheless, it is the doubling and the interracial, homoerotic desire between Joe Brown and Joe Christmas that speaks most glaringly to the failure of white Southern manhood and to the challenges posed by post-Emancipation black manhood to white identity and authority in the South. To make this point cogently, I must first illuminate the ways in which Christmas's racial indeterminacy is engendered and haunted by both same-sex desire and its policing in the town of Jefferson. In the same way that Brown and Christmas function as each other's doubles, Christmas functions in the novel as the double, the shadow, and the darker half of the white men in town. As John T. Irwin explains, "The ego's towering self-love and consequent over-estimation of its own worth lead to the guilty rejection of all instincts and desires that don't fit its idealized image of itself. The rejected instincts are cast out of the self, repressed internally only to return externally personified in the double, where they can be at once vicariously satisfied and punished."[23] As I discussed above, Joe Christmas embodies the black male threat to white masculinity even as he appears as the mirror image of white manhood. As such, he functions as an incarnation of the unspoken desires and hidden dread that some white men had for black men who were no longer their legal property.

Joe Christmas's power as a racially inscrutable figure is not simply that he resists and negotiates the identity politics that govern race and race relations in the post-Reconstruction South but also that he calls into question endogamous heterosexuality as the reigning social and sexual paradigm in early-twentieth-century American culture. Christmas's ability to effect a racial pass, or to escape definitive racial inscription, carries the distinct possibility of transgressing all sexual boundaries, first and foremost, because it allows him access to the bodies of white women. The product of a reputed black man's criminal engagement with white womanhood, Joe Christmas's sexual relationships with Bobby, other white prostitutes, and Joanna Burden violate brutally enforced restrictions on black male sexuality. The common belief in black men's predilection for desiring across racial lines was itself essential to developing theories of homosexuality, as both interracial sexuality and homosexuality were believed to be characterized by an inappropriate choice of sexual object. Heteronormative qualification at the turn of the twentieth century did not require simple heterosexuality but endogamy, as well; as customary and judicial prohibitions on interracial and same-sex coupling made clear, the proper choice of sexual object under the regime of compulsive heterosexuality was a person of the opposite sex and the same racial group.

As did black men's status generally in the postbellum period, Joe Christmas dislodges both normative racial and sexual categories, transgressing their historically enforced boundaries. As Christmas's blackness is unhinged from legible racial demarcation, and, further, as his sexual exchanges are patently non-reproductive, Joe Christmas is a figure who evades, if not defies, all manner of social and sexual regulation. In his excellent analysis of Christmas's sexuality, Jay Watson notes that "Joe's identity is so radically uncertain, making it difficult if not impossible to ascertain and fix what is sexually permissible and sexually illicit where he is concerned."[24] Christmas is an unbound and unmanageable sexual agent/signifier whose racial ambiguity *itself* obfuscates (hetero)sexual identity and precludes for him any claim to heteronormative qualification. According to Watson, Christmas's unbound racial and sexual identity both engenders and reflects a hypermasculinity that "amounts to simultaneously overdoing and underdoing of masculinity, one that spells gender trouble because its excesses . . . threaten the 'law and order' of Southern manhood itself."[25] It is important to note that Watson's definition of hypermasculinity extends beyond the predictable paradigm of a brutish and overly dominant maleness to convey instead a masculinity that is both excessive *and* (historically, internally) fractured. Although Watson's discussion of Joe Christmas does not explicitly link hypermasculinty to embodied black manhood in general, I want to emphasize precisely that connection here. Post-Emancipation black masculinity was both empowered and besieged. It furthermore had the ability to confound the racial schema and to render conventional, racially inflected, masculine hierarchies unintelligible. Watson's characterization of Christmas as "something more like conventionally defined masculinity *and* its other" speaks finally to Christmas's status both as racially indeterminable figure and as representative enfranchised black man.

The doubling of Joe Christmas and Joe Brown, with its insinuation of homoerotic desire, makes clear not only the extent to which black men's identity has been freed of some of its traditional markers but also the extent to which white masculinity has depended on these exact markers of black men's inferiority to secure its own ascendancy and legitimacy. When Brown reports to the sheriff that Christmas has murdered Joanna Burden, he is described by Bunch as speaking "'louder and louder and faster and faster, like he was trying to hide Joe Brown behind what he was telling on Christmas'" (96). In other words, the Joes' identities are so inter-imbricated that Joe Brown's narration of Joe Christmas risks his own self-erasure. Moreover, Brown's disclosure of Christmas's putative black racial ancestry "outs" Christmas not only as a black man passing for white but also, as a result of his erotic entanglements with white women and men, as a sexual deviant. Speaking of Christmas's and Brown's relation to each other, Byron Bunch postulates, "'I reckon the only thing folks ever wondered about was why Christmas ever took up with Brown. Maybe it was because like not only finds like; it can't escape from being found by its like. Even when it's just like in one thing, because even them two with the same like was different'" (87). In his description of their (uncanny) relationship, of Christmas's "taking up" with Brown, Bunch intimates that a sexual relation undergirds the two Joes' attachment.

Rooted in narcissism, a felt desire for the self with a difference, the double —by which I mean both the reflected image and the shadow—engenders and exposes homoerotic desire. Siobhan Somerville suggests that a common sexual fantasy that accompanied racial thinking in the post-Reconstruction era was that "black was to white as masculine was to feminine."[26] In other words, race supplies the difference—imagined in terms of gender—that masks and marks same-sex eroticism while exposing and emphasizing the alleged perversity of interracial desire. Somerville posits further, "In turn-of-the-[twentieth-]century culture, where Jim Crow culture erected a structure of taboos against any kind of (non-work-related) interracial relationship, racial difference visually marked [sexual] alliances. . . . In effect, the institution of racial segregation and its cultural fiction of 'black' and 'white' produced a framework in which . . . interracial romances became legible as "perverse."[27] Because interactions across racial borders were so rigorously prohibited and policed in the post-slavery South, any interracial contact outside of black labor and service to whites was believed to be criminally sexual. Two side points are relevant here. First, my invocation of sexual criminality is meant to encompass all forms of outlaw sexual practices, including interracial sex, rape, incest, and homosexuality. Second, there is no fixed distinction between black service to and sexual engagement with white people. As we know from black women's plight as domestic workers in much of the twentieth century, labor in white homes and white businesses has often included for black people the provision of sexual service to white employers.

When the sheriff hears about Brown's abandonment of Lena, he claims to have no interest in the "'wives [Brown] left in Alabama or anywhere else'" (321). The sheriff insists that his concern is only with "'the husband he seems to have had since he come to Jefferson'" (321). In designating Christmas Joe Brown's husband, the sheriff acknowledges the eroticism informing the Joes' liaison. Byron Bunch describes Brown and Christmas as "set[ting] up together [in the] old nigger cabin in the back" (79). When Christmas moves Brown into his cabin with him, he hopes to both stave off Joanna's desires for him and to make her jealous. The "nigger cabin" is the former home of slaves that ultimately will become the birthplace of Joe Brown's illegitimate child.

Throughout *Light in August*, the "nigger cabin" is the liminal, transitional space where unaccepted sexual urges—extramarital, interracial, homoerotic, violent—are explored and where character transformations are wrought.

The homoeroticism framing the Joes' liaison signifies the vulnerability of white masculinity to penetration by black men in the social, economic, and political realms. Although the intimation of a sexual relationship between Joe Christmas and Joe Brown indicates a potential for equality in an interracial alliance between white and black men, it is depicted by Faulkner as carrying with it the threat of white racial subordination. Christmas is clearly the dominant of the two Joes—Christmas is described as the "master" and Brown as his "disciple" (45). Brown imitates Christmas's mannerisms and participates in his business. One evening after beating Brown, Christmas undresses and goes outside; when he returns, he goes naked to his cot. Christmas's beating of Joe Brown coupled with his nakedness implies that the nature of Christmas's and Brown's alliance is not only homoerotic and interracial; it is also sadomasochistic, because both Joes willingly participate in a relationship of practiced physical domination and submission.

Brown is able to assert dominance over Christmas only by accusing him of having black blood, of passing for white. Before the sheriff knows about Christmas, Brown is the main suspect in the killing of Joanna Burden. Brown discloses Christmas's putative black racial origins to divert suspicion from himself—" 'That's right,' he says. . . . 'Accuse the white man and let the nigger go free. Accuse the white man and let the nigger run' " (97). To gain the social advantage over Christmas, Brown also announces his whiteness, thereby securing it and summoning the authority conferred by it. In the period after slavery, anxiety was growing within the white community about the fixity of racial categories. Rather than allow former slaves full citizenship rights, Southern whites established a system of cultural superiority and racial segregation. The rise of Jim Crow, antimiscegenation laws, and the institution of legal segregation not only mandated who could participate in government and to what extent but also divided public and private spaces along racial lines. African American bodies were literally forbidden contact with white bodies. This anxiety about interracial contact must be understood first and foremost as anxiety about an integrated body politic and the refusal of postbellum America to grant to former slaves full membership in U.S. society. The ruling in *Plessy v. Ferguson* in 1896 authorized white townspeople to determine the racial category of others and to publicize it to maintain segregation. Rumor and innuendo were essential to this project; thus, the accusation of "black blood" was sufficient evidence for one to be taken for, and convicted of being, African-descended.

Brown's disclosure to the sheriff that Christmas had once confessed to having black ancestry sets in motion the events that lead to Christmas's ultimate demise. In other words, by accusing Christmas of being black *and* of raping and murdering Joanna Burden, Brown in effect causes Christmas to be lynched. Not only does Brown's revelation of Christmas's blackness become the means by which he gains an advantage over Christmas; it also becomes the means by which he disavows his prior subordination, particularly in his erotic relation, to Christmas.

Joe Brown is not the first character in *Light in August* to allege Christmas's black racial ancestry to conceal sexual transgressions and effect his social removal. In what is often seen as the inaugural moment of his sexual development, a five-year-old Christmas hides in the closet of the dietitian who works in the orphanage in which he lives. While swallowing toothpaste and hiding amid her garments, he witnesses a sexual exchange between the dietitian and a white male intern. The sexual exchange falls beyond the requisites of proper sexuality in two regards: it is extramarital, and it is violent. The intern disregards the dietitian's repeated cries, "No! No! . . . No, Charley! Please!" and aggressively continues his sexual advances (121). Readers are not given the specific details of the sexual violation that ensues, as the scene shifts into a narrative of Christmas's sensory—oral and aural—perceptions while witnessing it. Christmas's ingestion and eventual regurgitation of the toothpaste dramatizes and mirrors the dietitian's experience of sexual assault by the intern:

> [Christmas] saw by feel alone now the ruined once cylindrical tube. By taste and not seeing he contemplated the cool invisible worm as it coiled onto his finger and smeared sharp, automatonlike and sweet, into his mouth. . . . He seemed to be turned in upon himself, watching himself sweating, watching himself smear another worm of paste into his mouth which his stomach did not want. Sure enough it refused to go down. . . . He didn't have to wait long. At once the paste which he had already swallowed lifted inside of him, trying to get back into the air where it was cool. It was no longer sweet. (121–22)

While much critical attention has been paid to the association of the toothpaste with the "pinkwomansmelling" dietitian, and therefore with femininity, I want to underscore its masculine features here. Described as a worm that coils and issues forth from a cylindrical tube, the toothpaste operates as a phallic replacement. Christmas's initiatory sexual experience then simulates nauseating fellatio as he internalizes the victimized sexual position of the dietitian. When the dietitian, ravaged and "surrounded now by wild and dishevelled hair," peers into the closet and discovers Christmas, "limp, looking with slack-jawed and glassy idiocy," she projects onto him the image of her assailant, presumably now "limp" with the satisfaction of accomplished sexual act. This is demonstrated foremost in the racial epithet she calls Christmas, in that a "nigger bastard!" hiding in her closet insinuates the black male rapist (122). Later, the traumatized dietitian fixates more on Christmas than on the intern who actually assaulted her. "She lay most of the night now tense, teeth and hands clenched, panting with fury and terror. . . . The young doctor was now even less than the child. . . . She could not have said which she hated most" (123). The dietitian displaces her outrage and terror onto Christmas. As his identity is radically unstable, both racially and sexually ambiguous, he alternately inhabits the position of violated (white) womanhood and of (now racialized) violating manhood. Foreshadowing Joe Brown's method of effecting Christmas's removal from the town of Jefferson, the dietitian relieves the shame and horror of the intern's sexual assault by alleging Christmas's black ancestry to effect his expulsion from the orphanage.

Under assault in the late nineteenth century, white masculinity asserted itself through physicality—through resemblance to and finally dominance over—black manhood. Gail Bederman explains that white manhood was constructed in the late nineteenth century as both civilized and linked to the " 'savagery' and 'primitivism' of dark-skinned races, whose *masculinity* [white men] claimed to share."[28] White men in *Light in August* are said to have more physical prowess and to be better suited to "negro jobs"—those that require maximum physical exertion—than black men (44). The revelation of Christmas's reputed blackness, which generally occurs after he has engaged in sexual activity with white women—Bobbie, the numerous prostitutes and other white women Christmas takes to bed as a young man, as well as Joanna Burden—is followed by a savage beating by the white men nearby. In the end, Joe Christmas is lynched in a communal spectacle.

In the climactic lynching scene, Joe Brown's desire for Joe Christmas, as well as its disavowal, is extended to the other white men in Jefferson.[29] Lynching's mechanized violence enacts even as it effaces a shared preoccupation with black male being and sexuality. After the ejaculatory gesture of firing a round of shots into Christmas's body, Percy Grimm stoops over and castrates him: " 'Now you'll let white women alone, even in hell,' [Grimm] said. But the man on the floor [Christmas] had not moved. He just lay there, with his eyes open and empty of everything save consciousness and with something, a shadow, about his mouth. . . . His face, body, all seemed to collapse, to fall upon itself, and from out of the slashed garments about his hips and loins the pent black blood seemed to rush like a released breath" (464–65). As Trudier Harris has usefully summarized, lynching functions as "communal rape" of black manhood.[30] By castrating him, Grimm inscribes onto Christmas's body the phallic lack characteristic of the feminine and, under the regime of slavery, of the black masculine. The shadow around Christmas's mouth is the specter of homosexuality and of race. The black blood that rushes from his body like a released breath, or new life, signifies that murder and mutilation have finally situated Christmas firmly within a proper—that is, victimized and subordinate—black racial identity.

Lynching's bloody rituals function to abate the threat of black masculine similarity and parity with white men in the post-Reconstruction era by feminizing the black male body and by simultaneously re-racializing it. As Wiegman argues, lynching enacts a gruesome, racially motivated, homoerotic encounter:

> In the image of white men embracing—with hate, fear, and a chilling form of empowered delight—the same penis they were so overdeterminedly driven to destroy, one encounters a sadistic enactment of the homoerotic at the very moment of its most extreme disavowal. . . . The lynching scenario and its obsession with the sexual dismemberment of black men to mark the limit of the homosexual/heterosexual—that point at which the oppositional relation reveals its inherent and mutual dependence—and the heterosexuality of the black male "rapist" is transformed into a violently homoerotic exchange.[31]

Grimm's final statement to Christmas bespeaks the challenge that Christmas represents to white manhood in the areas of sexual prowess and civic access, as symbolized in the figure of the white woman's body. Like McEachern's sexually charged and sadistic ritual beatings of Christmas as a child, Grimm's actions not only feminize Joe Christmas—concretizing what was believed in the early twentieth century to be a queer subjectivity—but also confirm and constrain his racial blackness. In other words, castration transfigures Christmas's hypermasculinity into the docile, emasculated, asexuality of the eunuch —or of the black male slave.[32] As lynching is a strategy for the containment of racial difference in the post-Reconstruction era, it is also the brutal enactment of homoeroticism and its panicked repudiation. The lynching of Joe Christmas functions, then, as an expression and disavowal of same-sex desire and as a violent rejection of an egalitarian, racially integrated social sphere. Finally, given the insecurity about the status of white masculinity in the face of black masculine parity and presumed greater prowess, lynching abates the threat that embodied and symbolic black manhood posed to white patriarchal dominance. Percy Grimm functions in Light in August as the white phallic authority that attempts to rejuvenate and restore white racial hegemony.

Throughout Light in August, narratives about slavery are depicted in fragmented memories of key characters—namely, Joanna Burden and Gail Hightower. Discernible in those narrated flashbacks is nostalgia for the ease and heroism of an earlier time, particularly around the figure of the white patriarch. Although neither the characters nor the novel itself display an overt longing for the reinstallment of institutional slavery, slavery does represent a neat social order in its rigid hierarchy of the races. All manner of miscegenation and diversity could be contained in slavery because the messiness of human contact—in the form of interracial sexual unions, mutually affectionate and dependent relations, violent confrontation—that inevitably erupted and to some extent undergirded the relations between blacks and whites on the plantation did not disturb the fixed, naturalized order of things that race-based slavery forcefully proscribed, policed, and preserved. It was only in its aftermath that the heinous practices and traumatic legacies of American slavery had to be confronted. The conclusion of Faulkner's novel anticipates the reconstruction of Southern white family in the aftermath of defeat in the Civil War and the enfranchisement of African American men. Depicted in the final pages of the novel are the redeemed, maternal white woman; the weathered but hardworking and upstanding white man; and the "manchild" on whom the future of the white race depends. This intact straight white family is offered as a buffer to white masculinity and a safeguard against the presence of emancipated black people in the South who demanded—and now qualified for—civic equality.

Rape and Racial Terror

Five years before Pauline Hopkins published Contending Forces, Ida B. Wells-Barnett, one of the most formidable anti-lynching crusaders, published The Red Record. The powerful pamphlet is Wells-Barnett's exposé of lynching as a practice instituted by whites to thwart the social, economic, and political advancement of African Americans in the post-Reconstruction South. Offering a counter-narrative to the predominant narrative of lynching in national circulation, Wells-Barnett historicizes the evolution of lynching as a particular form of extralegal, though state-sanctioned, racial terrorism with evidence both candid and convincing.[33] The pamphlet provides detailed accounts of individual lynchings and compiles lynching statistics by state, including criminal allegations against the victims culled from police records and responsible presses. In so doing, it effectively refutes the main justification given for lynching: black men's propensity for interracial rape.[34] In the opening chapter, "The Case Stated," Wells-Barnett reproduces verbatim the claim that she had made three years earlier in *Free Speech*: "Nobody in this section of the country believes the old threadbare lie that Negro men rape white women" for which threats of her own lynching had been made.[35] Wells-Barnett proceeds to demonstrate that during slavery and in the Reconstruction period, accusations of interracial rape were not generally leveled against black men. She recounts productively that white women on plantations from which white men were absent during the Civil War and white Northern women who lived and taught in nascent free black communities not only were safe but were *presumed* safe from sexual violation by black men. She contends, "The Negro may not have known what chivalry was, but he knew enough to preserve inviolate the womanhood of the South which was entrusted to his hands during the war. The finer sensibilities of his soul may have been crushed out by years of slavery, but his heart was full of gratitude to the white women of the North who blessed his home and inspired his soul in all these years of freedom."[36] Wells-Barnett asserts that the initial claims of black insurrection and "Negro domination" were not sufficiently incendiary to inspire or to explain masses of white people's participation in the torture and murder of black men that had become so commonplace by the late nineteenth century. As she brilliantly elucidates, the rhetoric of rape, of black men's sexual savagery and displacement of libidinal desire onto the wrong race of woman, provided the discursive cover under which racial terrorism flourished.

I open this section on Hopkins's *Contending Forces* with a discussion of *The Red Record* to illuminate the ideological positioning and discursive maneuvering of black women activists who fought for the immediate end of racial atrocities. As both Wells-Barnett and Hopkins understood, access to the full entitlements of citizenship was thwarted in the late nineteenth century by two critical developments: the legalization of Jim Crow segregation and the normalization of white racial terrorism in the form of lynching. Although a number of critics have analyzed *Contending Forces* in terms of its focus on the sexual violation of African American women, to this point no sufficient, sustained analysis of lynching in Hopkins's novel has been done. Kate McCullough, for example, asserts that Hopkins's novel "foreground[s] rape rather than African American lust as the source of miscegenation."[37] Despite the implicit appeal to lynching by virtue of the invocation of its primary justification— black men's predilection for interracial rape—McCullough does not examine depictions of lynching in the novel, although there are three, or the embedded "rape" of black manhood that lynching produces. Jennifer Putzi's reading of *Contending Forces* also centralizes black women's corporeal debasement by juxtaposing rape and beating as two distinct ways that African American women's bodies were scarred. She argues further that these "marks" of violence literalized the stigma of race and signified black women's fallen sexuality and failed maternity.[38] I depart from Putzi and McCullough and a host of other critics by arguing that, despite the novel's concentration on black women's historical victimization, collective reinvention, and rightful participation in the struggle for racial advancement, Hopkins depicts the rape of black women to construct and elaborate the lynching of black men, particularly its sexual terror. As does the rape of black women, lynching's mechanized violence obliterates the integrity of black bodies and families as a whole. Hopkins excavates the raped black woman, brutalized and abandoned at the scene of lynching, to publicize the plight of black women in acts of racial terrorism—separate from the loss of male partnership, protection, and provision that they endured as a result of the mass murder of black men.[39] As many critics have noted, Hopkins's novel is radical for centralizing black women's experiences, but I want to underscore its conservative aspect in that Hopkins subordinates black women's concerns to the largely masculinist agenda of racial uplift. In other words, by emphasizing the rape of black women as a main method of racial terror, Hopkins—unlike Faulkner in *Light in August*—avoids implicating African American men in the scene of homoerotic violence, thereby preserving black men's properly performed masculinity and qualification for the patriarchal entitlements of citizenship.

In the post-Reconstruction South, racial harm was inflicted in a number of ways, including the abrogation of voting rights and due process for black people, enforced segregation in public consumer and institutional spaces, the denial of access to viable means of economic survival or improvement, the theft and destruction of black property, and the pervasive rape of black women and girls. Fictionalizing lynching enabled Hopkins to address racism's monumental injury to black personhood and progress. As a highly visible, mainly symbolic, and unprecedentedly violent expression of racial subjection, black female activists and cultural workers organized around lynching not only to eradicate it but also to illuminate the appallingly low premium placed on African American life in general.[40] Like Wells-Barnett, Hopkins deploys lynching as a barometer for measuring both the health of various black communities around the nation and the country's general (dis)regard for its black citizens. Her novel promotes black men's fair participation in the political process as both an index and a method of collective black American racial progress. The anti-lynching advocacy that animates Hopkins's novel yields to her the most compelling point of entry into the more generalized public discourse of black advancement and resistance to racial subjugation.[41]

Returning briefly to Wells-Barnett, despite her primary focus on the victimization of black men in the lynching scenario, she brings to the fore the propensity of white men for interracial rape and the rampant rape of black women as an element of racial terror. She exhorts:

> To justify their own barbarism, [Southern white men] assume a chivalry which they do not possess. True chivalry respects all womanhood, and no one who reads the record, as it is written in the faces of the million mulattoes in the South, will for a minute conceive that the southern white man had a very chivalrous regard for the honor due the women of his own race or respect for the womanhood which circumstances places in his power. That chivalry which is "most sensitive concerning the honor of women" can hope for but little respect from the civilized world, when it confines itself entirely to the women who happen to be white. Virtue knows no color line, and the chivalry which depends on the complexion of skin and texture of hair can command no honest respect.[42]

In this passage, black and white womanhood are brought into close proximity to challenge the importance and supposed immutability of the racial binary. Virtue, a fundamental component of ideologies of white womanhood, is made a universal category to which both black and white women have claim. The "million mulattoes" who constitute an unofficial record not found in court documents but scrutable, nevertheless, in multitudes of bodies provide irrefutable evidence that the atrocity of rape has been committed widely and repeatedly against black women.[43] The supposedly chivalrous white men who justify gruesome acts of torture and murder of black men in defense of white women's honor are the same men who rape black women en masse. Wells-Barnett interrogates the legitimacy of white men's valor in protecting white women's virtue when they do not recognize and respect all women's right to freedom from sexual harm. Here she distinguishes white men from black men who "preserve inviolate the womanhood of the South," presumably regardless of race, thus insinuating that the only truly chivalrous men in the South are African American.

Feminine virtue, masculine chivalry, the safe transfer of capital to legitimate progeny, inviolable domestic space, and the maintenance of middle-class codes of conduct define the nexus of domesticity. Rather than isolating lynching as a problem precipitated by black sexual depravity and social degeneracy, black writers and imagemakers of the late nineteenth century embedded their resistance to Jim Crow and lynching within the national norm of domesticity and respectability. In so doing, they endeavored to redress racial wrongs by disproving widely held myths of African American identity that resulted in social exclusion and pervasive racial harm.⁴⁴ Black novelists incorporated features of the sentimental domestic novel in an effort to refigure African Americans as sentient, industrious, and morally and intellectually capable people whose individual impulses, collective desires, and familial organizations could be brought in line with mainstream bourgeois ideals. While I recognize Hopkins's efforts to reconfigure blackness at the site of domesticity, I want to emphasize not her adoption of sentimental modes of narration but, rather, her subversion of them. Hopkins's scenes of lynching and rape necessarily haunt and undermine her overall narrative of African American sexual and domestic normalcy.⁴⁵

In the opening section of the novel, for example, Hopkins portrays the demise of the Montfort family and the theft of their estate. That the destruction of the Montforts is brought about by white racial violence reveals the tenuousness of African Americans' claims to privacy, sexuality, progeny, and property. While I take care to avoid overstating the Montforts' racial designation as black, especially as part of the utility of racial inscrutability in Contending Forces is the disruption of racial logics, I must emphasize that, like Joe Christmas, the Montforts are phenotypically white but black in effect—both in terms of their fate and, in the case of Mrs. Montfort, in terms of her being one progenitor of the African American Smith family. For Hopkins, motivated acts of racial and sexual aggression are so entwined that she opens Contending Forces with the beating of Grace Montfort and presents it as both a rape and a lynching. In presenting the lynching of black men and the rape of black women as similar and simultaneous acts, Hopkins not only subverts the conventional marriage plot of early black fiction; she also demonstrates the extent to which white racial aggression effectively ruptures normative sexual and familial arrangements in the black racial context.

Although the first section of Contending Forces is set during slavery, it introduces the major problems of the post-Reconstruction period: antimiscegenation legislation, the discursive and legal production of entrenched racial difference, and the use of sexual and racial violence to impede African Americans' sociopolitical progress. In an often overlooked scene, Hank Davis and Bill Sampson, two lower-class white overseers, discuss the punishment of Jed Powers, a white man, who has been caught attempting to escape to Canada to marry a slave woman named Violy. Initially, Jed is sentenced to death for attempting to legalize his relationship with a black woman. Eventually, the sentence is commuted to a public whipping when the judge decides, according to Hank, that Jed "wuz young and had a chance to 'pent from the desolate ways o' his youth, of which his wurst failin wuz a-wantin to marry niggers, leastwise he'd end in hell, shure."[46] This seemingly minor incident calls our attention to the fierce policing and prohibition of cross-racial alliances (sexual or otherwise) of the post-Emancipation period, the common rhetoric that interracial romance was a crime against humanity, nature, and God, as well as the fact of white men's desire for black women.

Historically, of course, the most common expression of white men's desire for black women has been rape, which operates also as a weapon of racial terror.[47] Hopkins recontextualizes lynching as black female obliteration by figuring its standard violence—sexual assault, ghastly disfigurement, and deadly outcome—as gang rape. In a scene that foreshadows the rape of Sappho Clark and the lynching of her father, the Montfort plantation is descended on by local whites. Both Mr. and Mrs. Montfort are rumored to have African ancestry. This insinuation is enough to justify the white townsmen's disregard for their phenotypic whiteness and to divest them of their freedom and property rights. In addition, Mr. Montfort plans to emancipate his slaves gradually, a gesture that would seem to support abolition and, by extension, black liberation. Led by Anson Pollack, the white townsmen murder Mr. Montfort, steal and divide his property, kidnap his children, and beat severely Grace Montfort. Hazel Carby convincingly describes Mrs. Montfort's beating by Hank and Bill as gang rape: "In a graphic and tortured two-page scene, Hopkins represented the brutal rape of Grace in the displaced form of a whipping by two vigilantes. Her clothes were ripped from her body, and she was whipped alternately 'by the two strong, savage men.' Hopkins's metaphoric replacement of the 'snaky leather thong' for the phallus was a crude but effective device, and 'the blood [which] stood in a pool about her feet' was the final evidence that the 'outrage' that had been committed was rape."[48] Grace Montfort is not only gang raped, as Carby brilliantly decodes; she is also tortured and murdered. Here, Hortense Spillers's characterization of black women's historical subjection by traditionally masculine disciplinary procedures, specifically torture and mutilation, is aptly illustrative. Spillers notes that black women have not only been the "target[s] of rape—an interiorized violation of the body and mind—but also the topic of specifically externalized acts of torture and prostration that we imagine as the peculiar province of male brutality and torture inflicted by other males."[49] Throughout the ordeal, Hopkins vividly describes Grace Montfort's

HE CUT THE ROPES THAT BOUND HER, AND SHE SANK UPON THE GROUND AGAIN. (See page 69.)

"He cut the ropes that bound her, and she sank upon the ground again."
General Research Division, The New York Public Library, Astor, Lenox, and Tilden Foundations.

shrieks, fainting fits, and copious blood flow as the two men take turns brutalizing her. Later, as a result of her corporeal debasement, Grace Montfort dies. Turning to the illustration that opens the novel, I wish to point out that Hopkins deploys the iconography of lynching to depict Grace's beating and rape.

The illustration shows the tortured body of a woman seemingly lifeless on the ground. The stake to which she was tied is erect behind her. While one man eyes the noose, the other looks at her with cruel satisfaction. The whip in one man's hand descends from his crotch area, like an elongated penis, while the whip in the other man's hand takes the shape of a noose. In the written account and its visual illustration, Hopkins brings the rape–lynching dyad into such proximity that the acts morph into each other on the landscape of Grace Montfort's mutilated body.

Gendered implications exist for both black men and women involved in black women's corporeal and sexual subjection, particularly by white male gang violence. In her thorough and astute study of sexualized Ku Klux Klan violence in the postbellum South, Lisa Cardyn analyzes the ritualization of (gang) rape, genital mutilation, and sexual torture of black women by marauding white men in the post-Reconstruction South. She argues that in addition to satisfying sadistic sexual urges in theatric displays of black female defilement, white men frequently raped and sexually tortured black women to reinvigorate plantation norms in the decades following the Civil War and Reconstruction. In effect, white male sexual violence denied black women bodily autonomy and denied black men uncontested paternity and other privileges of hegemonic masculinity. Cardyn suggests, further, that sexual humiliation was an important feature of whites' racial violence. She reports that "numerous reports [exist] of freedwomen outraged in this manner [by rape, genital mutilation, sexual torture] often in the presence of family members powerless to intervene on their behalf."[50] Prior to being lynched, black men were frequently made to endure the spectacle of beloved female family members' sexual subjugation. This witnessing entailed a de-phallicization of black masculinity. The inability to defend female kin from sexual violence, in other words, had an emasculating effect on black men, who could not protect black women from the very crimes for which they themselves were routinely lynched.

To highlight black male valor, Hopkins reverses crucially the order of events by having Charles Montfort murdered *before* his wife's violation. Grace Montfort "uttered a wild cry of agony as . . . Hank Davis [tore] her garments from her shoulders" (68). She called to her husband to save her, but "there was none to answer the heartrending appeal. He who would have shed his heart's best blood for her, lay cold in death" (68). In killing off Charles Montfort before the gang rape of his wife, Hopkins both maintains his masculine heroism and eliminates the possibility of his unwitting participation in a homoerotic encounter. Cardyn observes, "Gang rape is a crime often fraught with homoerotic overtones. . . . One need not adopt a strictly psychoanalytic approach to recognize that part of the allure of raping in groups is precisely the fact that others are available to witness and participate in the act and applaud their collective accomplishment. Moreover, there is a way in which watching violent sex is itself a sexual act."[51] In the post-Reconstruction South, the gang rape of African American women by midnight marauders rose to prominence as a main component of racial terror inflicted through sexual torture. Black men who were forced to witness the sexual torture of their mothers, sisters, daughters, wives, and so on were triangulated into a homoerotic exchange with white men through mechanisms of spectatorship and shame. By having black men effectively excised from the gang-rape scenario by virtue of their own prior murder (here and later in the novel), Hopkins allows black men conventional markers of manhood while interrogating the masculine qualification of those white men who were driven by sexual predation to engage in sadistic sexual performances with black women and black men alike.

Recovering Her, Refiguring Him

In Contending Forces, the domestic sphere instantiates the social, political, and economic relations of society at large. Much of the novel proper centers on the activities of the Smiths, descendants of the doomed Montfort family, under the direction of Ma Smith, who operates a successful boardinghouse after the death of her husband. A prosperous and principled single mother, Ma Smith raises two children, Dora and Will, as representative, gendered embodiments of the socioeconomic aspirations and cultural ideals of the black bourgeoisie. Set in 1896, the year in which Jim Crow segregation was legalized, the novel depicts the oppressive force of racism on the domestic tranquility of this New England family. Hopkins reveals how de facto residential segregation, poor education, and economic deprivation plague even African American communities in the north. The narrator laments:

> The masses of Negro race find for employment only the most laborious work at the scantiest remuneration. A man, though a skilled mechanic, has the door of the shop closed in his face among the descendents of the liberty loving Puritans. The foreign element who come to the shores of

America soon learn that there is a class which is called inferior and will not work in this or in that business if "niggers" are hired; and the master or owner, being neither able nor willing to secure enough of the despised class to fill the places of white laborers, acquiesces in the general demand, and the poor Negro finds himself banned in almost every kind of employment. (83)

As the narrator makes clear, the defining characteristic of whiteness is its putative difference from resident blackness. The national consolidation of whiteness in the postbellum period guaranteed distinct social, economic, and psychic advantages to all who could claim whiteness, regardless of national origin, class, or education.[52] In the same ways that they solidified white identity across class boundaries in the South, racial terrorism and structural racism solidified white identity despite cultural differences in the North.

The normalization of racial atrocities in the South entailed a devastation of African American life in the North, as well.[53] Jacqueline Goldsby's incisive argument that lynching was neither "regional [nor] aberrant" but part of a wider nexus of American modernity is useful to my thinking here.[54] Cognizant that lynching and sexual terrorism simply epitomized and reinforced racial hierarchies in the nation at large, black activists mobilized against lynching not as a peculiar regional practice but as a national norm. In Contending Forces, the American Colored League is an organization convened in part to eradicate lynching and other manifestations of white supremacy. Members of the league debate the relative merits of militant versus unarmed resistance. At one meeting, Luke Sawyer comes forward and discloses the details of the lynching of his father and adoptive father and the sexual torture of their female kin. Luke's father had held property and run a store. The success of his store placed a neighboring white storeowner's business at risk and enraged the townspeople. Finding him unresponsive to their coercive efforts to evict him from the town, a white mob surrounded Luke Sawyer's house and set it aflame. Luke recounts, "My father had arms. He raised the window of his sleeping-room and fired into the mob of cowardly hounds. Thoroughly enraged, they broke open the doors back and front, seized my father and hung him to the nearest tree, whipped my mother and sister, and otherwise abused them so that they died the next day. . . . I saw all this, and frenzied with horror, half-dead with fright, crept into the woods to die" (257). Luke's father's willful defiance of the white mob attests to his bravery. His choice to arm and defend his family from white invasion underscores his rightful position as head of that family. It is only after Luke's father is hanged—that is, irrevocably incapacitated—that the white mob is free to murder Luke's mother and siblings. That his mother and sister are brutally raped is encoded in the general language of injury; the woman and girl are beaten and "otherwise abused." The death of both mother and daughter following the sexual violence of the white mob signals both their violation and their virtue. Finally, as a child at the time of these atrocities, Luke is unable to defend or avenge his parents and siblings. His primary function, then, is that of a witness who uses the incontrovertible evidence of firsthand experience to vitalize anti-lynching resistance. His damning testimony against lynch mobs is what inspires the American Colored League to decisive action.

Hopkins centralizes male competition and sexual predation as the twinned motivations of lynching. Her fictive renderings of lynching make clear two critical points: (1) that sexual sadism is a driving force in the development of the rituals of lynching; and (2) that sexuality in general has been instrumental in waging racial warfare to manufacture white superiority. Mr. Beaubean, Luke's adoptive father, is lynched, and his daughter is kidnapped and repeatedly raped. Like Luke's father, Mr. Beaubean is an educated and upstanding landowner. Neither a rapist nor a criminal of any sort, he is lynched because he threatens to bring legal action against his white brother for kidnapping his daughter Mabelle—later Sappho Clark—and forcing her into concubinage and prostitution. Voicing the popular sentiment that black women are "a direct creation by God to be the pleasant companions of men of my race," the white brother offers Mr. Beaubean one thousand dollars as remuneration for his sexual usc of Mabelle, a gesture that not only fails to redress the injury to Mr. Beaubean's daughter but that also turns Mabelle's father into her pimp (259). Outraged, Mr. Beaubean shuns his brother's offer and vows to avenge his daughter by judicial means. That night, he is murdered.

In absenting black men from their families, in violating the virtue of black women, and in supplanting black men's contribution to the reproductive process, white terrorism hampered the evolution of healthy black familial patterns in the postbellum period. This point is illustrated in Sappho Clark's having a child after she is repeatedly raped by her white uncle, and it is expressed most directly through the character of Will Smith, who espouses vehemently, "Lynching was instituted to crush the manhood of the enfranchised black. Rape is the crime which appeals most strongly to the heart of the home life" (271). Challenging the prevailing narrative of lynching as retaliation for the violation of white female bodies and white families, Hopkins makes clear that the only endangered women and families in the post-Reconstruction South were African American. Figuring personal privacy, economic prosperity, political ascendancy, and familial sanctity as a contest for access to black female sexuality and reproduction between brothers of different racial designations allows Hopkins to expose the sexual subjugation of black women as fundamental constituents of black and white American identity and cultural formation. Moreover, that the ruin of the Beaubean family is brought about by a white family member bespeaks the shared genealogy, mutual constitution, and combined cultural development of white and black America, a point that by itself reasonably supports Hopkins's call for egalitarian social relations and the equitable distribution of political and economic resources between the races.

Finally, lynching frequently involved the castration of black men, a symbolic gesture that temporarily grants white men possession of the black phallus and its mythic power. Trudier Harris describes lynching rituals that involved not only castration but also gender mutilation in which white men divided the severed penis into souvenirs to be shared among themselves. She writes, "For white males . . . there is a symbolic transfer of sexual power at the point of executions. The black man is stripped of his prowess, but the very act of stripping brings symbolic power to the white man."[55] In severing the penis from the black man's body and taking it into their literal possession, white men who participated in lynching rituals appropriated the symbolic and sexual power they themselves had ascribed to black masculinity. In addition to the vote, emancipation protected the male prerogative of black men to serve as heads of their families and as legal husbands and fathers and thus granted them a recognizable place within the symbolic order. Considering Jacques Lacan's insistence that woman is the phallus, I suggest further that the rape of black women functioned also as a phantasmagoric castration of black men that allows white men to appropriate the black phallus to access, presumably, greater sexual prowess and to exercise greater social authority.

In Mabelle Beaubean's survival of her ordeal and rebirth as Sappho Clark resonate the resilience and forward progress of African American life. Unlike Grace Montfort and Luke Sawyer's mother and sister, Sappho is not destroyed by sexual assault. Instead, as Richard Yarborough poignantly describes it, she "pass[es] through the cleansing fire of pain and exploitation and emerg[es] the purer for it."[56] Sappho becomes an upstanding member of the black community, claims the child born of her assault, and marries Will Smith, the novel's hero. Here, Hopkins's skillful manipulation of the sentimental tropes of domestic fiction is clear. As the feminist literary critics Jane Tompkins and Nina Baym have demonstrated, the domestic novel is itself a subversive literary form.[57] Although it generally reinforces capitalist values by celebrating middle-class comfort and wealth, it also encourages examination and reform of problematic social institutions and practices. In general, the protagonist of sentimental domestic fiction has fallen through the cracks of defective social systems, and although she is blameless, she suffers. Through a long and meticulous process of acculturation and through strict adherence to established codes of middle-class decorum and morality, the protagonist usually survives her initial difficulties to experience personal advancement, usually through installment in a marriage and secure domestic space. Baym characterizes the heroine of the sentimental novel as one who achieves by novel's end "a strong conviction of her own worth as a result of which she does ask much of herself. She can meet her own demands and, inevitably, the change in herself has changed the world's attitude toward her so that much that was formerly denied her now comes to her unsought."[58] What is particularly powerful about sentimental fiction is that the protagonist who starts out as a social outcast emerges by the end of her tale as the decisive moral authority of her text. In other words, like Sappho as the redeemed and lofty heroine of *Contending Forces*, the protagonist of the domestic novel embodies the critique of her society and provides the model for its improvement.[59]

By making white racial aggression and sexual violence the twinned concerns of her novel and by debunking the myths that were used to justify lynching, specifically the rape of white women by black men, Hopkins narrativizes the activist position held by Wells-Barnett and other anti-lynching crusaders at the turn of the twentieth century. Instead of turning to the ballot or to the pulpit to stage her protest, she turned to fiction, to the realm of expressive culture. In the preface to *Contending Forces*, Hopkins articulates the merit of black fiction. She states, "It is the simple tale unassumingly told, which cements the bond of brotherhood among all classes and all complexions. Fiction is of great value to any people as a preserver of manners and cultures—religious, political and social. It is a record of growth" (13). Hopkins recognizes the importance of a black literary tradition to the advancement of black people. For one, such literature depicts African American life from the vantage point of African Americans. It demonstrates the capacity of African Americans for reason and for imagination and thus serves as one cultural contribution that African Americans offer the world. Moreover, as Hopkins notes, fiction supports the construction of ideology and allows her to inculcate moral codes in keeping with programs of black racial uplift. After declaring the importance of fiction, Hopkins notes its documentary function, suggesting that "the incidents portrayed in the early chapters of this book actually occurred" (14). In the final analysis, fiction allows Hopkins to record blacks' experience, to condemn U.S. racial hatred and inequity, and to agitate for black liberation by incorporating political work in the artistic enterprise. Her novel, like *Light in August*, ends with a wish for the reconstructed family in which men inherit the entitlements of patriarchy, women enjoy men's provision and protection, and children of dangerous and illicit sexual liaisons are incorporated into legitimate families. Of course, the reconstituted family with which *Contending Forces* concludes is African American, mere generations from the regime of racial slavery, anticipating the redress of historic and collective violation and poised anxiously at the gate of the new century.

3

DESIRE AND TREASON IN MID-TWENTIETH-

CENTURY POLITICAL PROTEST FICTION

I define nationalism as the activation of a narrative of identity and interests. Whether or not it is concrete in the form (or even the possibility) of a state, this narrative is one that members of a social, political, cultural, ethnic or "racial" group tell themselves, and that is predicated on some understanding—however mythologized or mystified—of a shared past, an assessment of present circumstances, and a description of or prescription for a shared future. Nationalism articulates a desire—always unfulfillable—for complete representation of the past and a fantasy for a better future.
—Wahneema Lubiano, "Standing In for the State"

Neither culture nor its destruction is erotic; it is the seam between them, the fault, the flaw which becomes so.
—Roland Barthes, *The Pleasure of the Text*

As my investigation of lynching and its fictive representation in the previous chapter illuminates, African Americans inhabit the fault lines of U.S. culture. Neither fully assimilated nor completely excised, black Americans exist at the crossroads, occupying a liminal position in the U.S. cultural imaginary—in politics, in popular culture, in socioeconomic organization. Straddling the barrier, the border, that both unites and stratifies the country in all relevant arenas, African American culture activates within its various communities and in the wider culture all manner of desire. In the prior chapter, I examined lynching as an enthralling and sexualized encounter meant to reactivate the legal, customary, and political structures of racial slavery. At the heart of the lynching ritual is a ruse of pleasure. The price of refusal, of African American resistance to the (re)installation of de facto enslavement—the systematic optimization of black mental and material capacity for the general benefit of white people—is a hideous and terrifying synecdoche: individual black bodies are mangled and murdered to subdue, and to substitute for, an entire population.

At the turn of the twentieth century, African American writers grappled with lynching's incredible symbolic potency, but out of political necessity they often eradicated African American desire from their considerations. As I have argued in the preceding chapters, African American cultural producers, spokespeople, and members of the rising middle class have endorsed and enacted the politics of respectability throughout much of the history of African American political struggle. The politics of respectability has been one attempted route to mainstream acceptance, but it has also functioned as a means of communal civic protection. Thus, even in fictive treatments of lynching, black American writers took care to disassociate the brutal illegalities of the lynching act from the legal, civil, and proprietary romantic liaisons of black citizens. Thus, manifestations of all but the most socially acceptable desires were left out of public presentations of African American life, particularly in post-Reconstruction literature.

The present chapter moves forward a few decades to investigate explicit (and often illicit) representations of desire in mid-century black American writing. I contend that in no period of African American literary production has the depiction of desire been so prominent as in the protest fiction of this period.[1] Often in the explicit register of political desire, yet with a discernible subtext of personal aspiration and romantic feeling, the literature produced by African Americans during the movement for civil rights and for black power provided the cultural corollary—the literary expression, that is—of African Americans' wish to be free finally and, nearly as important, to be themselves. Much black American fiction produced during this era grapples with the dual dimensions of racial desire: the desire to have recognized the possibility, the plausibility even, of black individuation and the desire for African Americans as a collective to achieve full inclusion in mainstream national life.[2]

Importantly, in mid-twentieth-century African American literature, the duality of racial desire is most often explored via depictions of illicit cross-racial desire. The overt thematic preoccupations of mid-century protest novels often center on interpersonal relations between white and black characters. Representations of cross-racial sexual desire provide a space for black writers to investigate—and to interrogate—broader possibilities for meaningful civic cooperation and political equality between the races. These novels operate subtly according to the supposition that the level of personal and political freedom that African Americans have achieved or may exercise since emancipation may be indexed by the nation's collective response to the question: *would you let your son or daughter marry one?*

Cross-racial love engages with the civil rights agenda in two meaningful ways. First, it grants African Americans the power of choice in sexual matters across the racial boundary. For black women, this equates to freedom from sexual assault by white men and the right of legislative redress in cases of interracial rape. It grants black women, moreover, the option to participate voluntarily in interracial sexual liaisons and domestic partnerships. For black men the power of sexual choice entails an expansion of sexual entitlement. Black masculinity is thereby buffered by right of access to sexual partners with various racial affiliations, attributing to it one of the distinct and historic phallic privileges of white masculinity.[3] Second, interracial romance engages with the civil rights agenda by granting to black and white citizens the legal right to marry. The removal of any legalized or customary barrier to romantic unions between black and white Americans allows a greater exercise of enfranchisement. Specifically, intermarriage enables cross-racial couples to secure their union within a social and legal contract that acknowledges their sexual bond, consolidates and potentially augments their wealth, and makes their offspring socially recognizable heirs and citizens. Finally, beyond its tangible benefits intermarriage is a powerful metaphor for successful political, economic, and civic integration. The most popular and the most vocal proponent of civil rights, Martin Luther King Jr., for example, frequently presented social and political integration as beneficial to all Americans, regardless of race. In *Letter from the Birmingham Jail* he writes, "We are caught in an inescapable network of mutuality, tied in a single garment of destiny. Whatever affects one directly, affects all indirectly."[4] King's rhetoric of mutuality, of shared destiny, invokes the figurative national house.[5] His rhetoric implies, furthermore, that nationhood may be characterized—and thus should be experienced—as membership in a united family.

It is worth noting that literary depictions of interracial love and longing in midcentury black writing are haunted by both enacted and imagined violences against black men and women, as if to suggest that the swiftest and most predictable result of interracial contact in the United States is the continued subjection of African Americans. In this way, midcentury novels engage intertextually with black American writing of the prior era, which saw the predominance of fictive lynching, in order to measure racial progress since the post-Reconstruction period and since the Great Migration of African Americans into northern cities. Registering both the audacity of individual desire and the force of history to circumscribe racial subjects and their social relations, novels such as Ann Petry's The Narrows (1953), Ralph Ellison's Invisible Man (1952), Chester Himes's If He Hollers Let Him Go (1945), and James Baldwin's Another Country (1962) issue a productive caution about (seemingly benign) white liberalism and the efficacy of interracial struggles for equality. Moreover, these novels examine the problem of racial standardization and the individual toll it takes on black subjects to embody and uphold "the race."[6] In other words, in addition to querying the promises and the pitfalls of integration, these novels take an interrogative approach to ideologies of monolithic blackness and prescriptive, uniform racial struggle.

To be clear, I do not wish to advance the argument that representations of interracial love and sex in mid-twentieth-century black American novels should be read narrowly *as* political allegories of the nation's failure to develop a just and egalitarian political and social landscape after slavery. In fact, a very important function of these representations is their contemplation of an ethos of love. bell hooks argues, for example, that the lack of sustained commitment to love as an underlying premise in the struggle for racial advancement renders the project of racial uplift inadequate. She writes:

> Without love, our efforts to liberate ourselves and our world community from oppression and exploitation are doomed. As long as we refuse to address fully the place of love in our struggles for liberation we will not be able to create a culture of conversion where there is a mass turning away from an ethic of domination.
>
> Without an ethic of love shaping the direction of our political vision and our radical aspirations, we are often seduced, in one way or another, into continued allegiance to systems of domination—imperialism, sexism, racism, classism.[7]

Midcentury African American writers who depict cross-racial longing often take seriously the transformative power of interpersonal connectivity to foster ethical citizenship. These writers investigate the possibility of transforming the felt desire of sexual intrigue into a broader political vision and enactment of social and racial equality. In many ways, this chapter, focused mainly on James Baldwin, explores precisely this point: to what extent does meaningful contact and interpersonal *knowing* between members of different races inspire ethical cooperation and political equality? In addition, to what extent does the meaningful inhabiting of a nationalist posture require African Americans to assert black personhood, in part, by accepting the diverse identificatory and desiring practices *within* the racial collective?

An equally important function then of representing unsanctioned interracial desire in mid-twentieth-century African American novels is the opportunity it grants black American writers to contemplate black subjectivity *outside* the traditional requirements of racial identification and to grapple with personal longings that exceed the parameters of social protest. As Guy Mark Foster smartly observes, in the African American cultural context the practice of desiring beyond one's racial group is "cultural taboo," as it is "deemed a form of betrayal of other blacks, if not self-hatred against oneself for being black."[8] The same taboo, of course, frequently applies to intra-gender desiring, a point that I will explore in detail in my analysis of Baldwin's writing. While maintaining my focus on the political ramifications for mid-twentieth-century struggles for racial equality, the current chapter unfolds to achieve three main goals. First, opening with Petry's *The Narrows*, I show how representing interracial romance engenders a broader analysis of the formative influence of histories of racial oppression and antagonism on racial subjects, despite their experience (and even expression) of unsanctioned desire beyond their racial locale. Second, moving to analysis of *Another Country*, the main focus of this chapter, I study Baldwin's juxtaposition of racial standardization and sexual variance, arguing that the novel may be read as Baldwin's attempt to locate himself as a queer black writer in the civil rights movement and to instantiate its goals. Finally, I read Baldwin's last novel, *Just Above My Head*, as a literary meditation on the history of racial struggle in the United States and the viability of Black Power as a lived philosophy. Incorporating its main themes of self-love and self-determination, *Just Above My Head* transforms Black Power from nationalist politics to the philosophy and practice of African American communal love. As such, the novel puts forth a vision of racial equality that does not make integration its ultimate endpoint, but neither does this vision require racial uniformity or separatism. I argue ultimately that, in both *Another Country* and *Just Above My Head*, Baldwin presents the black esthete and the homosexual as figures of cultural renovation, as paradigmatic embodiments of personal freedom and political reform in both the civil rights and black power eras.

Straddling the Border

In *The Narrows*, Ann Petry portrays the doomed interracial love affair between a wealthy white heiress and a black man educated at Dartmouth to query the national commitment to racial reconciliation in the wake of the civil rights movement. Set in the residentially segregated New England town of Monmouth, the novel chronicles the relationship between Link Williams and Camilla Treadway Sheffield from first meeting through passionate romance to disastrous separation, concluding with Link's lynching after Camilla falsely accuses him of rape. Despite its preoccupation with the force of sexual desire to liberate individuals from the binds of social convention and law, the novel emphasizes the tenacity of racial distinction in the United States. Foregrounding the enduring problem of racial caste, Petry illustrates the power of history to interpellate racial subjects and to circumscribe their social relations, regardless of their individual efforts and longings.

In *The Narrows*, history—in particular, the history of slavery and Jim Crow—is an inescapable bind, becoming the biggest impediment to progress, racial and social. This is not to suggest that history negates collective social advancement or individual enactments of desire. Historical subjects are human and therefore necessarily agential. It is important, however, to acknowledge Petry's revelation of how deeply rooted racial oppression remains in the middle of the twentieth century. The historical implementation of hierarchical, race-based sociopolitical machinery continued to manifest in the mid-twentieth-century present, and it continued to produce racial subjects, shape the expression and thwart the fulfillment of their desires, and sabotage their destinies.

Notably, the novel does not merely present a historical account of U.S. race relations to show their operative force in the present; rather, it employs history as the main component of its analytic apparatus. By concluding with the lynching of its main character for trespassing the racial-sexual boundary, both the world and the world of *The Narrows* are made intelligible *and operable* through historical reference and through repeated re-enactments of the past. Michael Barry offers a persuasive reading of the significance of history in the novel. He posits, "The same ineluctable stories play themselves out again and again in the short history that we are privy to. The repetition obviously has great ramifications for the social protest content of the novel. For the social horrors resulting from twentieth century racism and corruption and cruelty appear to be eternal dilemmas."[9] To establish the centrality of U.S. racial history to her narrative, Petry names her protagonist Link Williams, after the president, politician, and slave emancipator Abraham Lincoln. Link is a historian whose proudest memory from high school is successfully reading an entire archive of the history of U.S. slavery. After graduating from Dartmouth Phi Beta Kappa, Link returns home to research and write a new racial history of the United States.

Despite his familiarity with U.S. history, Link rejects commonplace assumptions about race and thereby resists its regulatory codes. For example, the central plot opens when Link rescues a terrified woman from an attacker on the docks in his impoverished, segregated part of town. Although the woman is fair, blond-haired, and blue-eyed, Link does not immediately recognize her—Camilla Treadwill Sheffield—as white. Given the repeated generational and sexual violations of black women by white men, racial difference does not necessarily entail bodily demarcation. He compares Camilla's physical traits to those of African American women he knows, seeking more discernible, definitive markers of her racial identity. Physical examination, he understands, is insufficient: her skin is "as white as" Mrs. Ananias Hill's; her eyes are as blue as Mamaluke Hill's mother's; her hair as "shimmer[y]" as his own adopted mother Abbie's.[10] Camilla's legible, phenotypic whiteness alone does not determine her racial status. The novel thus critiques the one-drop rule as a viable determinant of racial categories, even as it proceeds to condemn the exclusionary real-estate and economic disinvestment practices that effectively segregate and stratify communities by race in northern cities.

The potential for racial inscrutability, or racial misrecognition, undermines race as a reliable taxonomic tool—although, to be sure, such racial inscrutability does make legible a history of sexualized racial conquest marked in the flesh of slavery's descendants. Petry challenges the notion that racial difference is solely a matter of bodies and thereby interrogates the logic of biological determinism. More importantly, she foregrounds the history of material and political inequality in the making of race. As the novel makes clear, race is formed and lived through asymmetric social structures. Its intelligibility depends on the differential entries to and exercises of power that race allows. My reference to power here does not support the notion that it belongs exclusively to whites, although to be sure whiteness does confer on white people the privilege of maintaining socioeconomic structures and cultural machinery that guarantees their own benefit. I wish to recognize, though, that the power operates insidiously and implicates all subjects. Thus, every social being has some access to power. By emphasizing the different racial positionalities inhabited by Link and Camilla, I seek to expose the ways in which whiteness functions to consolidate social privilege and finite economic resources. In a sense, as I demonstrated in the previous two chapters, whiteness operates not as a discrete racial identity per se but as the ideology and apparatus of privilege in the United States.

On the night that Camilla meets Link, she is in the segregated black part of town, the Narrows. When Bug Eyes, Link's Southern friend, sees her, he immediately recognizes her whiteness. Bug Eyes's prompt and disdainful recognition resonates with the regional Southern history: sharecropping; Jim Crow segregation; the ordinary, everyday assaults on black dignity; and frequent extralegal enactments of white power. In the South, Bug Eyes's failure to see Camilla's whiteness might have led to an accusation of insolence or a worse behavioral trespass that could have cost him his life or property. Link soon concedes, "Bug Eyes . . . was right. The lady is white. That surprised condescension in the voice is an unmistakable characteristic of the Caucasian, a special characteristic of the female Caucasian" (72). Camilla's performance of superiority, despite the potential for gender subordination and under the condition of her own rescue by Link, exposes her whiteness. In other words, as Link soon perceives, it is not the phenotypic traces that determine a person's race but her relationship to power.[11]

The road on which Camilla and Link drive after her rescue symbolizes their momentary dislocation from history as they experience the dawning of physical attraction. The road grants a modicum of freedom as the bourgeoning lovers submit to the dangerous undertaking of physical proximity and, further, of their desire. In the car, Link's rescue of Camilla from a would-be assailant is soon forgotten as they recede into their respective social locations. He drives her Cadillac both to calm her and to become better acquainted with her. He soon realizes that, despite their peculiar meeting, his confusion about her race, and his heroism that saves her, the history of racial oppression and antagonism continues to shape their encounter; they are somehow, in other words, oppositional subjects. Camilla begins to issue demands as if Link were either her chauffeur or her black brute rapist or a frightful amalgamation of the two:

> She said, sharpness in her voice, arrogance in her voice, something he couldn't quite give a name to, not as uncontrolled rage, but controlled rage, rage because the chauffeur was late, the chauffeur talked back, was impudent, impertinent, had to be put in his place, "I want to go back. Stop and turn the car around." . . .
>
> [Link contemplates.] She thinks I'm going to rape her. I'm due to rape her, or try to, because I'm colored and it's written in the cards that colored men live for the sole purpose of raping white women, especially young beautiful white women who are on the loose. (79)

Attracted, enthralled, Link rejects Camilla's assumptions. He continues driving, talking to her sweetly, tempting her. In so doing, Link refuses to allow racial difference or its concomitant structuring of sociopolitical and economic arenas to negate this instance of felt desire. While social interactions were not criminalized in the pre–civil rights North as they were in the South, they were nonetheless regulated by community vigilance and histories of custom. The strong customary prohibition against Link's and Camilla's close proximity as they drive in her car is mitigated by her resignification of this early interaction as one between an affluent white woman and her black chauffeur. In pursuing Camilla, Link pursues an illicit attraction that is self-generated and that offers the possibility of self-fulfillment. It is a desire that exceeds the boundaries of socially accepted, cross-racial proximity and sociality but that is irresistible because it emanates from the depths of *individual* feeling.

As Link and Camilla drive around in the middle of the night, they literally have nowhere to go. Not even a black establishment would serve at this hour a man and a woman whose "colors don't match" (74). Abandoning the prohibited and heavily policed codes of black male and white female liaisons, Link and Camilla surrender to the intrigue of the other and the opportunity of this new romantic horizon. The road Link refuses to abandon becomes a literal site of liminality, the porous boundary between the black and white parts of town. In this moment before dawn when only one car travels it, the road is ahistorical and atemporal. The road promises emancipatory progress as the newly formed interracial couple move farther and farther away from their respective racial communities and thus from racial restriction.

Link's pursuit of cross-racial desire offers temporary respite from regulatory norms of bourgeois blackness. Throughout much of Link's childhood, his adoptive mother, Abbie, instills in him the importance of being a "credit to The Race" (141). As do many members of the African American middle class, she extols the virtues of bourgeois decorum, educational attainment, sexual propriety, and stringent moral upkeep. Link recalls, "She said colored people (sometimes she just said The Race) had to be cleaner, smarter, thriftier, more ambitious than white people, so that white people would like colored people. The way she explained it made him feel as though he were carrying The Race around with him all the time. It kept him confused and a little frightened, too. At that moment The Race sat astride his shoulders, a weight so great that his back bent under it" (138). Abbie attempts to inculcate moral codes and class ambitions that are in keeping with programs of black racial uplift. Candice Jenkins offers an incisive explanation of the disciplining character of middle-class black American culture. She coins the term "salvific wish" to describe the black bourgeois effort to "protect or save black women, and black communities more generally, from narratives of sexual and familial pathology, through an embrace of conventional bourgeois propriety in the arenas of sexuality and domesticity."[12] Abbie subscribes to the pervasive black middle-class practice of (re)figuring blackness as normative and assimilable to enable African American entry into the national mainstream and group access to the full benefits of unqualified citizenship.[13] She commands Link to be respectable, thoughtful, well-mannered, neat, moral, *repressed*. Although they emanate from a parental wish for Link's prosperity and from the inclination to protect him from the hazards of white supremacy, Abbie's instructions are anxiety-ridden and so inspire dread and rebellion in the child. As he undertakes his relationship with Camilla, Link transgresses the racial requirement of endogamous coupling, which presumably builds solid, thriving, prosperous black American families. His transgression is pronounced all the more when Abbie discovers the couple in Link's bed and tosses them promptly and aggressively out of her house.

The hope of Link's and Camilla's union and its symbolic promise of a racially reconciled and genuinely egalitarian nation are shown in the early stages of their relationship. On their first date, Camilla recounts her high-school experiences as an isolated, overweight teenager who suffered much derision at the hands of her peers. Camilla's experiences resonate with Link as he remembers the social exclusion he encountered as the rare black student at an integrated elementary school. Ridiculed by his white teacher, taunted by classmates, and cast as the minstrel character Sambo in a school play, Link recalls debilitating racial shame: he "was ashamed of the color of his skin" (135). Camilla and Link find common ground in their formative experiences of social outcasting, which helped to establish their individual dispositions. The alliance of their adolescent experiences functions for them—and for the reader—as a means by which the distance created by race-based structural imbalances and repressive conduct codes is bridged. The second time the burgeoning couple meets, Camilla lies to Link, telling him that her last name is Williams. Coincidentally, it would seem that the two share a last name. Considering the power inhering in the patronym in the Western cultural context as the name that is contractually conferred on the wife during marriage and which descends through the male line, the unexpected sameness of Camilla's and Link's last names suggests the possibility of their inhabiting permanently the role of intimate partners and progenitors. When Link later asks Camilla to marry him and she agrees, this possibility, as a wish and as an intention, is confirmed. As I explain in the opening of this chapter, intermarriage signals a meaningful advancement in the African American movement for civil rights. Petry highlights the social and legal ramifications of intermarriage, making clear that its illegality is an abrogation of citizenship. Weak Knees, a cook who has nurtured and mentored Link since childhood, cautions him about pursuing an interracial romance. He states, "If a man got to have a piece of white tail then he ought to live in some other country, a country where they don't give a damn about such things" (304). Through Weak Knees's declaration, Petry raises the issue of cross-racial romance and its culmination in legalized marriage to the status of national concern—or, rather, a concern at the heart of national belonging and the rights of citizenship. Considering the coincidence of a shared last name even before marriage, the interpersonal connection between Link and Camilla seems so internally solid that it precedes, and exceeds, the bounds of legal sanction or marital contract.

That is, of course, until Link learns that Camilla's last name is not Williams. Here Petry demonstrates the tenacity of U.S. slavery to frame racial interactions of subsequent periods and to impede racial progress in general. As soon as Link discovers Camilla's true identity, the couple is reinscribed into a historical schema that denies them personalized, sexualized access to each other and that negates the very possibility of their abiding love. The wealthy heir of an arms manufacturer, Mr. Treadway, and the current wife of Mr. Sheffield, Camilla Williams is in fact Camilla Treadway Sheffield. Because of her status as the current wife of a wealthy white man, the possibility of her legal and enduring romantic partnership with Link is exposed as both farcical and socially irredeemable. Realizing this, Link (re)interprets Camilla's romantic desire for him as exploitative sexual possession by a white mistress:

> Part of his mind parroted, I bid two hundred; look at his teeth; make it three hundred; the gentleman says five hundred; look at his muscle, look at his back; the lady says one thousand dollars. Sold to the lady for one thousand dollars. Plantation buck. Stud.
>
> He had been in love with her, wooed her, won her, thought that there was between them that once of a lifetime kind of love. . . . All of it inside of him when he kissed her on the tip of her nose, and asked her to marry him.
>
> Bought and sold, he thought. Bought at an auction, sold again at the death of the owner, part of an estate to be disposed of at the death of the owner, along with his horses and cows. Presents. She was always giving him presents. . . . Kept man. Stud. (280)

For Link, there is no other culturally available or politically applicable context for him to imagine Camilla's voluntary participation in their cross-racial romance. Because of the illegality of interracial coupling and because of the rigorous and violent prohibition of black men's sexual access to white women that was secured by penal law and extralegal enactments of racial terror in the period after abolition, Link does not experience cross-racial love as an aspect of personal freedom or a legitimate right of citizenship. The relationship, furthermore, does not entail a broadening of his sexual prerogatives or object choices. This, again, would put him on par with white men and thus make the relationship a *symbol* of his successful advancement to the cultural and political mainstream. Once the personal and political promises of the romance are nullified, Link conceives of his sexual relationship with Camilla in the only historical terms bequeathed to him: his sexual use as the stud of a white mistress under the condition of his enslavement.

There is a noteworthy slippage in gender-specific pronouns in Link's imaginative construction of his sale to Camilla at a slave auction: sold to *the lady*, part of the estate of the owner, along with *his* horses and cows. I would like to suggest that this slippage bespeaks the neutrality of gender in enactments of white power. Or, to put it another way, although gender difference clearly shapes social manifestations of white power, whiteness itself operates in spite of gender, particularly in terms of the organization and solidity of wealth and social privilege. In fact, in Camilla's case, after her affluent father dies and leaves her the heir to his great fortune, her wealth increases through marriage. The material disparities maintained by whiteness across gender, particularly in a town economically stratified and residentially segregated by race, is encapsulated in Link's sardonic accusal, "Or did your husband, the captain, pick me out to make you happy?" (314).

The great de-equalizer in Camilla's and Link's relationship, regardless of the momentary unity and parity they experience as lovers who bear a single marker of marginalized identity subordination (his race, her gender), is the seemingly unassailable power of racial whiteness to maintain its tangible and exclusive privilege.[14] As Link's evocation of the slave auction makes clear, it is the propertied aspect of whiteness—by which I mean not simply its historical right of self-possession but also its historical protected right to purchase and to claim *as property* black persons—that accounts for the insidious and seemingly insurmountable differences between the category of the black and the category of the white in the United States. A consideration of the Lockean concept of the self is helpful here, as it defines the human as the sole proprietor of her person, property, will, and capacity. Locke's concept provided the discursive and juridical framework for the development of a democratic republic in the United States, as well as the very notion of individual freedom it was designed to protect. Enslavement, perpetual structural inequity, and the continued sociopolitical marginalization of African Americans have effectively transformed individual freedom from a set of guaranteed rights and legal protections pertaining to the enfranchisement of discrete individuals to a set of group entitlements that accrue specifically to whiteness, or to those with uncontested white racial identification.[15] The subjection of black people throughout the nation's history and ongoing, racially inflected socioeconomic asymmetry maintain the solidity of racial whiteness and make the accumulation of wealth one of its main hallmarks.

The economic basis of racism is a main thematic concern in the novel, as the Treadway Sheffield estate is frequently depicted in contradistinction to the decrepit landscape of the Narrows, where the black people live.[16] Reflecting on their relationship, Link contemplates, "Maybe she was in love with me. Maybe I know too much about the various hells white folks have been cooking up for colored folks, ever since the Dutch man of the warre landed in Jamestown in 1619 and sold twenty Negras to the inhabitants, just as though they were cows or horses or goats" (329). Even as he admits the possibility of a genuine and heartfelt encounter, Link is aware of the formative binds of history on individuals and nations. Despite their passionate love, disparities in wealth, in quality of life, and in opportunities for social and material improvement make legible and immutable Camilla's and Link's racial difference.

The Narrows concludes by reiterating its sober perspective of midcentury race relations. After Camilla accuses Link of rape, her family's reputation suffers. What, after all, was she doing out on the docks in the Narrows so late at night? Camilla's husband and mother seek retribution by kidnapping and murdering Link. The scripts and stereotypes are familiar enough: when a black man is accused of sexually assaulting a white woman, he is lynched, simply. As Evelyn Brooks Higginbotham reminds us, lynching "maintain[s] racial etiquette and the socio-economic status quo."[17] Re-creating the contentious and violent racial landscape of the South in her novel, Petry queries the nation's readiness for African American participation in the specified realms of social, economic, and civic life. Written one year before the historic ruling in Brown v. Board of Education (1954), the novel anticipates ameliorative legislation on the part of the state but warns black Americans of the hazards of too quickly forgetting the longstanding, socially entrenched, psychic and material harm caused by racism. The insinuation here is that the state's judicial appeasement of African Americans may not sufficiently remedy centuries of economic exploitation, social subjection, and political exclusion.

Although by no means a proponent of racial essentialism, Petry constructs in The Narrows a novel that upholds the tenacity of racial difference as it pertains to the socioeconomic and political hierarchization of U.S. national life. Different from Baldwin, whom I read in the next section, Petry offers a startling refutation of progress by emphasizing the formative and seemingly unbreakable bind of the nation's originary and persistent rac(ial)ist organization. Returning repeatedly to the site of origin—that is, to the site of slavery—*The Narrows* refuses to succumb to cultural amnesia by resisting the appeal of cross-racial rapture, whether in erotics or politics.

Black Masculinity and the Ruse of Redemption

The mid-twentieth century was the critical juncture at which African Americans renewed the struggle for racial equality with a determination and militancy unmatched since the mid-nineteenth-century struggle for the abolition of institutional slavery. Central to the rhetoric and practices of black liberationist struggle were theories of the rights and responsibilities of African American manhood. Whether articulated by the foremost spokesperson for civil rights, Martin Luther King Jr., or embodied in the culture's most visible representatives of black nationalism, Malcolm X and the Black Panthers, the ideologies of civil rights and black power were fraught with anxieties about proper masculine qualification, public bearing, and social presentation. Theories about sexuality and (proper) masculinity historically have informed the development of political programs in the black, and in the larger American, community, and these theories have shaped and been shaped by black political figures from Frederick Douglass to Eldridge Cleaver.[18] Derogatorily referred to as "Martin Luther Queen," James Baldwin was disparaged for failing to qualify as a proper black man even as he was a spokesperson for black social advancement during the civil rights era.

By 1962, the year the novel *Another Country* emerged publicly, Baldwin had already become an active participant and foremost spokesperson in the mid-century struggle of African Americans for full civil rights. Writing the novel in the late 1950s and the early 1960s, he was preoccupied with the racial dilemma in the United States and the events that led to the civil rights movement, including the lynching of Emmett Till, the Montgomery bus boycotts, and the landmark legislation *Brown v. Board of Education* that mandated desegregation in education. Baldwin unwittingly became a spokesperson for the racial dilemma in the United States. Inhabiting the persona of a witness, he continually unmasked white Americans' fantastical beliefs about black people and how these beliefs enabled the construction and preservation of whiteness. As Will Walker postulates, "James Baldwin's uncompromising negative critique of American political culture extends beyond nationalist critiques in terms of the complexity of its psychological depth and discussion of how both black and white identities have been formed in the Americanization process."[19] Baldwin wrote prolifically about Americans' general amnesia and apathy with regard to the history of racial slavery, as well as its covert continuance in other forms of racial dominance. And he wrote obsessively about the effects of longstanding denigration and exclusion on the psychology and in the material lives of black people.

The publication, as well as the content, of *Another Country* dramatizes Baldwin's effort to locate or excavate a place for himself, a black queer artist, in the movement for black social, economic, and civic equality.[20] Attending primarily to Baldwin's linkage of black masculinity and sexual variance, this section reads *Another Country* as Baldwin's civil rights novel. Here, more than elsewhere, Baldwin interrogates the political efficacy and philosophical cogency of integration, as well as the practice of nonviolent agitation as the main method by which to procure civil rights. Questioning the place and productiveness of white liberalism in the struggle for racial equality, the novel lays bare the brutal history of black and white race relations and their destructive and often fatal consequences for African Americans. Although the setting is New York and Paris, the novel is preoccupied with the American South and with lynching and other forms of racial terrorism that secured white Southern domination in the first half of the twentieth century.

Another Country exposes the mutual constitution of racial definitions and sexual ideologies by illustrating how both the black person and the sexual outlaw function in U.S society as social outsiders, as figures who are constructed as the Other, the scandalous, the unrepresentable. Rufus, the black musician, and Eric, the white gay actor, are central characters in the novel who have intimate relationships with men and women, black and white. Reading Rufus and Eric as doppelgängers, this section contends that Baldwin depicts (and links) the black esthete and the homosexual as figures of cultural reformation, as those who most embody and influence the journey toward personal freedom and widespread social and political transformation in the civil rights era.

I proceed in this section by first reiterating the connection between nonheteronormativity and racial blackness. I attend specifically to the ways in which ideologies of sexuality affect the subject formation of black men, linking, finally, black men's identity to civil rights rhetoric and goals. All of this prepares the way for my discussion of *Another Country*. In reading the novel, I discuss Rufus and Eric in the most detail because they emblematize Baldwin's investment in the philosophical and political aims of civil rights. Even though these characters figure in the plot less than other characters in the novel, they are most significant because they are the main love objects of the other characters and, more important, because it is through them that the other characters are able to perceive themselves and be transformed.

The operative logic underwriting my discussion is the recognition that the sexual practices and domestic arrangements of disenfranchised groups—specifically, the impoverished and the African-descended—are often cited to justify social inequities and to deflect attention away from asymmetric social structuring and the unfair distribution of rights and resources in U.S. society. As I have reiterated in each chapter, the ideological and institutional regimes that disqualify African Americans from participation in the body politic have exploited heteronormativity as the primary index of inclusion and exclusion, of marginalization and belonging. In her thoughtful essay "Living at the Crossroads," Rhonda Williams posits: "Western racist discourses routinely construct "blackness" as a problematic sign and ontological position. In so doing, the architects of cultural and (social) scientific racism historically have represented black communities, black families, and black bodies as the bearers of stigma, disease, danger, violence, social pathology, and hypersexuality. . . . The conventional social scientific wisdom is clear: the 'problem' is that so much black sexuality and kinship formation transgresses the boundaries of married (and therefore healthy) heterosexuality."[21] Because heteronormativity ultimately organizes the family and centralizes masculinity in the service of patriarchal, civic, and political power, the family has long been regarded as the microcosm of the nation. The family is the unit that both rationalizes and regulates identity to designate the citizen-subject a rightful member of the body politic. Nationalism depends on tropes of the patriarchal, patrifocal family.

To further explain the foundational theoretical linkages binding political inclusion, heterosexuality, and racial difference, I turn to the work of Roderick Ferguson. In *Aberrations in Black: Toward a Queer Color of Critique*, he rigorously maps the mutually supporting systems of patriarchy, racism, sexuality, and material prosperity. Using the work of Max Weber to examine rationality as the organizing principle of capitalism and state practice, he argues that sexuality is "fundamentally an irrational force" whose regulation is secured through heteronormativity.[22] Registering the productive caution to avoid equating homosexuality with all non-normative sexual practice, Ferguson notes nonetheless that "common law marriages, out-of-wedlock births, lodgers, single-headed families, [and] nonmonogamous sexual relationships" all fail to meet the heteronormative ideal, and these unorthodox sexual practices and familial arrangements have long been associated with African Americans. Noting, furthermore, that historically homosexuality and heterosexuality have enjoyed relatively unencumbered proximity to each other in African American communities, Ferguson reiterates that non-heteronormativity, like irrationality, has long been regarded a black racial characteristic.

The perceived historical failure of black men to fulfill the legal obligations of paternity and to achieve the financial security that grounds heteronormative households has long been seen as the main culprit in African American disenfranchisement and dispossession and widespread social malaise. The normalizing and disciplining of sexuality entails its restriction to state-sanctioned, monogamous marriage. Not only do these marriages define and constrain women's identities, but they also authorize men as the primary participants in legal, economic, and political matters. Ferguson explains, "African American familial forms and gender relations were regarded as perversions of the American family ideal. . . . Questions concerning material exclusion—as they pertain to African Americans—were displaced onto African American sexual and familial practices, conceptualizing African American racial difference as a violation of the heteronormative demands that underlie liberal values. Presuming African American violation of those demands became the justification for subordinating African Americans."[23] The uneven distribution of wealth, the denial of equitable political and property rights, and grossly disproportionate access to quality education as a means of improving economic status all effectively curtail black people's power in both the domestic and political arenas. Structural racism is truly, then, the main impediment to black people's social, economic, and political progress.

For African Americans, attaining economic prosperity, entering the cultural mainstream, and accessing the entitlements of citizenship historically have meant conforming to hegemonic heterosexual and patriarchal ideals.[24] Since Reconstruction, black familial arrangements have been under the surveillance and supervision of state agencies and the social sciences alike. The Freedmen's Bureau, established to oversee the transition of former slaves into civil society, encouraged black people to register their marriages legally and to provide for their families. Despite the coercive manner by which government agencies attempted to inculcate white American bourgeois cultural values in black communities, African Americans took great pride in the legal right to marry and to claim their children as their legal descendants. For many, these rights attested to their new condition as free men and women. Linking marriage to enfranchisement, Claudia Tate postulates, "To vote and to marry . . . were the two civil responsibilities that nineteenth-century black people elected to perform; they were the twin indexes for measuring how black people collectively valued their civil liberties."[25] Long denied the right to legal marriage and to legal parentage, newly freed African Americans considered legal marriage as both a civil liberty and a civic duty. Speaking of the years immediately following abolition, Ann duCille posits, "Marriage rights were a long-denied basic human right—signs of liberation and entitlement to both democracy and desire."[26] For African Americans, conformity to heteronormativity signaled access and recognition in the political sphere and thus racial advancement in the social sphere.[27] Despite the century and a half that have passed since the formal abolition of slavery, and despite contemporary views of heterosexual hegemony as repressive and exclusionist, many black people still regard the nuclear black family as both the index of and the stepping stone to racial progress. For this reason, Williams argues, "Family tropes are vital today, and function in part to circulate specific notions of racial authenticity."[28]

Despite their distrust and avowed rejection of Anglo-European cultural standards, proponents of black nationalism in the mid-twentieth century endorsed fiercely mono-racial political struggle and endogamous heterosexual couplings and families. In addition to the opposition civil rights proponents and activists faced from racist white Americans, they faced opposition to the goal of full integration from African Americans who were struggling with more covert but nonetheless potent forms of racial discrimination in northern cities. Beginning in the late 1950s and 1960s and continuing throughout the 1970s, black nationalist thought found a base in urban centers all over the United States. At first through the founding of the religious and cultural movement the Nation of Islam and later, most notably, in the radical political and social movement for black power, black nationalists challenged the aims of the civil rights movement to integrate black and white America. Perceiving that integration entailed wholesale psychic and social assimilation into the white cultural mainstream, and thus meant conceding to notions of white cultural superiority, black nationalists opted instead for ideologies of political and economic independence and militaristic resistance to white racial terrorism.[29] Deploying the rhetoric of revolution, black nationalists sought to seize state power as it pervaded the lives of black people and to develop in its place logics and (communal) infrastructures that were racially affirming and preserving. Black nationalism thereby valorized black racial identity in cultural expression and advocated self-determination in economic attainment.

As a general rule, black nationalists propagated endogamy and heterosexuality not only as "natural" erotic and domestic practices but also as necessary ones for black people to survive racial oppression.[30] Responding to the historical and contemporary threat of black extinction, black nationalists believed that the creation of black families and reproduction of black children would both prevent genocide and restore patriarchal legitimacy to black manhood. Here, the precise meaning of Phillip Brian Harper's perceptive critique becomes clear. He asserts, "Social autonomy is precisely what constitutes conventional manhood, no matter what the racial context. Given the racio-political context operative in the United States since the moment of its founding, in which the denial of social autonomy had been a defining characteristic of African American experience, it is not surprising that such reclamation of that experience as was represented in the Black Power movement should be conceived in terms of accession to a masculine identity."[31] As Harper cogently elucidates, the concepts that have always underwritten unimpeded cultural and political access or, more simply, full citizenship in the United States are the same concepts that delineate the masculine subject. It is not surprising, then, that the struggle for black social advancement historically has been a simultaneous struggle to reconfigure black masculinity.

James Baldwin understood that black manhood was severely diminished and besieged in the American context, even as he recognized that black men preoccupied the popular imagination, operating as the culture's fantastical, fetishized phallus. For him, though, capitulating to mainstream concepts of masculinity would not resignify black men's humanity or guarantee civic equality for black Americans. Although Baldwin did attend to women's issues and offered complex representations of black and white womanhood in many of his novels, his overall preoccupation, I would argue, was defining and expanding constructions of masculinity so that black men, gay men, and men who were artists could claim manhood as the initial step to defining themselves and to gaining social recognition and civic entitlements. Despite Baldwin's skepticism about whether legislation would produce racial equality or whether passive civil disobedience was a likely method for curbing white racial violence, Baldwin advocated the principles of interracial cooperation and moral uprightness that characterized civil rights philosophies. He promoted the experience and expression of individual desires that were prohibited in both white and black cultural traditions—most notably, interracial romance and homoerotic love. Baldwin believed that the acceptance of forbidden desires would help to remedy racism—the most extensive, virulent, and destructive manifestation of the denial of desire.

Structurally, *Another Country* pairs Rufus and Eric as twinned heroes. Opening with the death of the black bisexual musician, the novel concludes with the promising romantic union of the white gay actor and his lover, Yves, recently arrived from Paris. "Book One" narrates Rufus's experiences: his love affair with the white Southern woman, Leona, and the final months of his life before despair, isolation, and a ruinous racist climate drive him to commit suicide. "Book Two" narrates Eric's experiences: his discovery of homosexuality, his sojourn in Paris, and his ultimate return to New York. "Book Three" opens with the lovemaking of Eric and Vivaldo, a scene that conjures Rufus through an erotic enactment of mourning (his loss) and that ultimately lays him to rest. Textually, Rufus and Eric are linked by virtue of their artistry, their queer desiring, and their momentary romance. After Rufus's death, an event that haunts the novel's other main characters—Vivaldo, Ida, Cass, and Richard—Eric returns, an agent of character and cultural transformation, to help them make sense of and make peace with it. Rufus and Eric, furthermore, are dual incarnations of Baldwin. Rufus epitomizes the endangerment and the estrangement suffered by the racial outsider in U.S. society, and Eric epitomizes the alienation experienced by the sexual outsider. Both lived in Baldwin.[32] That Baldwin pairs black and white queer male figures as the centermost forces in his novel's psychic core and as architects and harbingers of social reform bespeaks and performs his own civil rights advocacy.

Although *Another Country* takes place primarily in New York and Paris, it is preoccupied with the legal and extralegal practices of racial terrorism that underwrote legal segregation in the South. Rufus's primary erotic relationships are with two white Southerners, Leona and Eric. The practice of lynching black men who surpassed their predetermined denigrated political and class location and who thereby violated stringent race codes was a Southern tradition. As I showed in my discussion of Ida B. Wells's activism in the previous chapter, the claim that lynching was a response to the rape of white women is racist lore. Both the fallacy of black men's raping white women and the threat of lynching are explored early in the novel. Rufus's and Leona's first sex takes place on a balcony in Harlem overlooking the George Washington Bridge, from which Rufus will later plunge to his death. The scene of their lovemaking invokes the violence and danger of the South, with resonant insinuations of interracial rape and the concomitant threat of lynching:

> He pulled her to him as roughly as he could. He had expected her to resist and she did. . . . He knocked the glass out of her hand and it fell dully to the balcony floor, rolling away from them. . . .
>
> "Oh God," she murmured, and began to cry. At the same time she ceased struggling. Her hands came up and touched his face as though she were blind. Then she put her arms around his neck and clung to him, still shaking.[33]

What begins as a forcible sexual act becomes a consensual exchange, as Leona joins Rufus:

> Her fingers opened his shirt to the navel, her tongue burned his neck and his chest; and his hands pushed up her skirt and caressed the inside of her thighs. Then after a long, high time, while he shook beneath every accelerating tremor of her body, he forced her beneath him and he entered her. . . .
>
> And she carried him, as the sea will carry a boat, with a slow, rocking and rising motion, barely suggestive of the violence of the deep. They murmured on this journey; he softly, insistently cursed. . . . Tears hung in the corner of her eyes and the hair at her brow was wet. Her breath came with moaning and short cries, with words he couldn't understand, and in spite of himself he began moving faster and thrusting deeper. He wanted her to remember him the longest day she lived. And, shortly, nothing could have stopped him, not the white God himself, nor the lynch mob arriving on wings. . . . A moan and a curse tore him while he beat her with all the strength he had and felt the venom shoot out of him, enough for a hundred black-white babies. . . .
>
> Her eyes were wet still, deep and dark, her trembling lips curved slightly in a shy, triumphant smile. . . . "It was so wonderful," she said, and kissed him. (21–22)

The grammar of rape and violent death conditions Rufus's and Leona's sex. Their exchange is nonetheless both violent and tender. I invoke the dual connotations of tender here: as that which is gentle and as that which is sore or bruised from a prior wound. Rufus's and Leona's tenderness belongs to them, born of their instantaneous, genuine desire for each other and born of their own individual hurt histories. Their violence, however, demonstrates their position as historical subjects, acting out their nation's racial drama.

Rufus manhandles and curses Leona because she is a white woman. As a white woman, she has been placed on a pedestal as the epitome of femininity, virtue, and desirability and as such has had the power to negate both black femininity and black masculinity. Speaking specifically of black masculinity, my main concern here, white women's sexual attraction and availability to a black man has carried the distinct threat of his annihilation, his castration, his masculine undoing. This is the basis of Rufus's rage, and yet it is more internally imagined than outwardly enacted. Although he intends sexual assault, Rufus's violent erotic gesture is undone by Leona's complicity, her own volition and desire for his sex. As he is having his way with her, she is having her way with him. She smiles triumphantly, even as he has cursed and attempted to injure her. Rufus's fantasy of virility, which would fulfill black nationalist dictates to reproduce, is untenable here, as well. His reproductive capacity, which would be shown by Leona's impregnation with "a hundred black-white babies," is undone by her later disclosure of infertility.

Despite their love for each other, Rufus's and Leona's relationship is besieged by racism: the dominant culture's and what they have imbibed and internalized of it. Through the depiction of the novel's many white characters Baldwin illustrates that racist attitudes often covertly subtend benign liberalism. In the case of Leona, she discounts hostile stares from white neighbors, disregards her loss of employment for having a black boyfriend, and endures their friends' condescension and Rufus's rage. All the while, she naively insists to Rufus, "Ain't nothing wrong in being colored" (50). There can be no doubt about the fundamental truth of which Leona speaks; however, her declaration to Rufus overlooks the obliterating psychological and material impact of being raced on him. Leona's assurance seems trite, and merely echoing white liberal sentimentalism, it verges on ignorance. In the figure of Leona, as in the depictions of the various white characters in the novel, Baldwin reveals the pitfalls of white political innocence. Enraged, frustrated, and feeling utterly unknown and alone, Rufus brutalizes Leona. Black nationalism is invoked in the image of "her tears [falling] on his dark fist," signifying Rufus's own adherence to established codes of black masculinity that nonetheless disparage his love of Leona and that render him insufficient in terms of both his racial and gender identity (23). Rufus's relationship with a white woman, his "peddling his ass" when he is starving, and his homoerotic romance with Eric all indicate his failure to fulfill heteronormative standards and, by extension, black nationalist mandates.

Rufus's romantic entanglement with Eric bears striking similarity to his relationship with Leona. Eric and Leona are white Southerners, and Rufus's relationships with both characters signify his departure from cultural injunctions on heterosexuality and on racial purity and authenticity. After Leona has been driven insane by Rufus's abuse, and by her husband's before him, Rufus descends into unbearable, unutterable despair. Starved, guilt-ridden, and isolated, he hurls himself off of the George Washington Bridge. The central event of the novel, Rufus's death haunts the other characters. It moreover initiates their meditations on their own lives, on the racial dilemma in the United States, and on their complicity in Rufus's death. His suicide also gives each central character the courage to reclaim and express his or her own repressed desires. Ida, Rufus's sister, labors to understand her brother's personality and peril by infiltrating his former life and becoming lovers with his best friend, Vivaldo. Vivaldo endeavors to get past his secret jealousy of and estrangement from Rufus, and for Rufus's blackness generally, by loving Ida and by making love with Eric. Attempting to escape a loveless and constricting marriage and domestic life, Cass enjoys a brief but passionate love affair with Eric. And Eric remains preoccupied by Rufus, to the point of being nearly possessed by him. Rufus's memory is central in Eric's psyche not only because Eric continues to love him, but also because Rufus is utterly and inexorably gone from the world.

Recalling their romance, Eric wonders whether he earned Rufus's hatred because of his own unconscious racism. He ponders:

> Was it the body of Rufus to which he clung, or the bodies of dark men, seen briefly somewhere, in a garden or clearing, long ago, sweat running down their chocolate chests and shoulders, their voices ringing out, the white of their jock-straps beautiful against their skin—and the water splashing, sparkling, singing down!—one with his arm raised, laying an ax to the base of a tree. Certainly he had never succeeded in making Rufus believe he loved him. Perhaps Rufus looked into his eyes and seen all those dark men Eric saw, and hated him for it. (194)

A native of Alabama, Eric was accustomed to the presence of black field hands, and he longed for them. Magnetized by their "chocolate chests" and "jock-straps," along with the stereotypically manly labor they performed, he does not contemplate their individual selves or the impossible conditions of their lives. Eric objectifies black men. He earns Rufus's disdain, as did Leona, because his tantalization by the mythical black penis undermines his capacity to recognize in black men both their especial individuality and their complicated humanity. Because of the racializing effects of sexual alterity, Eric's homoeroticism is linked to a black racial identity. He initially casts homoerotic desire as an obscene descent into darkness, as if to suggest that his sexual proximity to a black body has contaminated him, and his participation in illicit sexual practice costs him the civility and propriety of bourgeois whiteness (197). His first sexual experience is with a black boy, LeRoy, whose race has already banished him from the sphere of hetero-normalcy and who therefore serves as a safe and obvious choice for Eric's aberrant sexual experiments. Eric remembers, "That day. That day. Had he known where that day would lead him would he have writhed as he did, in such anguished joy, beneath the weight of his first lover? He was frightened and in pain and the boy who held him so relentlessly was suddenly a stranger, and yet this stranger worked in Eric an eternal, a healing transformation" (206).

The racializing effect of Eric's homosexuality is exemplified in a warning that he gets from LeRoy: "You better get out of this town. Declare, they going to lynch you before they get round to me" (206). Recognizing the danger that their budding intimacy poses for both of them—namely, because they bespeak Eric's liberal racial attitudes, LeRoy's interracial friendship, and both of their homosexuality—LeRoy encourages Eric to leave. Of course, it is Eric's whiteness and economic advantage that grants him the mobility to escape the South. LeRoy, who does not enjoy white racial privilege, cannot plan such an escape as he lacks access to the economic means of geographic mobility. Further, because he does not work for Eric's family, LeRoy's friendship with Eric is considered a form of social infringement in that it violates the strict codes of racial segregation. Eric's sexual awakening, finally, places LeRoy's literal life in grave danger, not his own. This volatile racial situation then is what Eric fails to recognize and what Rufus can never forget.

Eric's first days in New York City after he leaves Paris echo Rufus's final days in the city before committing suicide, signaling that Eric's arrival will suture social divisions that caused and were caused by Rufus's untimely and irreversible departure. New York seems for Eric to have "no sense of the exigencies of human life; it was so familiar and so public that it became, at last, the most despairingly private of cities. One was continually being jostled, yet longed for the sense of others, for a human touch" (230). On Rufus's last night alive, he walks around New York, isolated, "one of the fallen—for the weight of the city was murderous—one of those who had been crushed on the day, which was everyday, these towers fell. Entirely alone, and dying of it, he was part of an unprecedented multitude" (4). Both Rufus and Eric find New York City abrasive, enormous, daunting, and overcrowded yet lacking the spirit of human compassion and the inspiration for human contact. Expecting to be joined soon by Yves, his Parisian lover who evokes for Eric "somehow, somewhere . . . Rufus," Eric will survive the city whose fierce racist climate destroyed Rufus in part because he is white, but more importantly, because his identity and his desires are not bound by social categories. He loves and is confidently loved.

Despite their different racial locations, Rufus and Eric are strikingly similar. Their racial difference nevertheless determines radically different outcomes for their lives. Both men are artists. As an actor, Eric's craft pushes him beyond a singular, fixed identity and opens him to the full range of human experiences. It allows him, further, to reach and to transfigure others. Rufus is a jazz musician, a drummer; his craft is conditioned by his racial identity and binds him further to it. Jazz is characterized in *Another Country* as the "beat," the oral/aural manifestations of historical black suffering and persistent, hopeful black aspiration. Rufus's father explains to him, "A nigger . . . lives his whole life, lives and dies according to the beat. Shit, he humps to that beat and the baby he throws up in there, well, he jumps to it and comes out nine months later like a goddamn tambourine. The beat: the hands, feet, tambourines, drums, pianos, laughter, curses, razor blades" (6). Racial epithet aside, Rufus's father explains that, as an expressive form that exists in synecdochal relation to black experience, the beat characterizes, contains, signifies, and sustains black life. In other words, jazz and other black musical forms translate black experience into rich cultural expression. The tropes of family and reproduction pervade this passage, suggesting that black musical forms are organic and intrinsic to black experience. In reciprocal fashion, black music and black existence give birth and continual rise to the other. For example, when Vivaldo struggles to make sense of Rufus's cruelty toward Leona, he thinks of Rufus's drumming: "He had never associated Rufus with violence, for his walk was always deliberate and slow, his tone mocking and gentle: but now he remembers how Rufus played the drums" (66). Although jazz has the power to express the longings and long-time sufferings of black life, it does so obliquely. As a highly sophisticated, non-linguistic, and non-visual aesthetic form, it does not signify experience transparently or readily communicate internality.[34] The message in the music requires a listener attuned to the emotive subtext, and a translation. Rufus's musicianship confirms his status as artist, a maker of beauty, and member of the black community. And while drumming provides a medium for his soul's expression, it nonetheless maintains the mystery of his internal struggle.

Eric's acting, on the other hand, enables him to occupy and to understand a number of subject positions simultaneously. It also promotes direct—that is, substantial and translatable—communication with his audience. Watching Eric's film debut, Vivaldo has the sense that he has "caught a glimpse of who Eric really was. . . . It was the face of a man, of a tormented man. . . . It was a quality to which great numbers of people would respond without knowing to what it was they were responding. There was great force in the face, and great gentleness. . . . It was a face which suggested, resonantly, in the depths, the truths about our natures" (329–30). For Eric, acting provides a method and medium for the transcendence of rigid, socially scripted roles. Acting empowers him to convey to others his own emotion, experience, and felt sense of human complexity. As an actor, Eric's identity is fluid, and this is what compels his safe explorations of love outside bounded, sanctioned territories. In other words, it is in part Eric's artistry, his particular mode of cultural production, that enables him to succeed where Rufus has failed. His skill as an actor, his ability to produce different personae and intermingle multiple subject positions at once, enables Eric, finally, to bare Rufus's introjected insides to the other characters in the novel who must now move beyond guilt and melancholia over Rufus's suicide.

Throughout the novel, Vivaldo, Rufus's best friend, wonders whether he could have saved Rufus's life and why, in fact, he did not. Eventually, he accepts that his homophobia and his racism, both disavowals of his desire for Rufus, prevented him from embracing Rufus when an embrace alone may have prevented his fatal jump. Vivaldo's lovemaking with Eric begins with a dream of Rufus's suicide and their eventual lovemaking: "Rufus came hurtling from the air, impaling himself on the far spiked fence which bounded the meadow. . . . Vivaldo watched Rufus' blood run down, bright red over the black spikes, into the green meadow. . . . Then, to his delight and confusion, Rufus lay down beside him and opened his arms. And the moment he surrendered to this sweet overwhelming embrace, his dream, like glass, shattered, he heard the wind at the windows . . . and found that it was Eric to whom he clung" (332–33). Waking up in Eric's arms, Vivaldo submits to homoerotic love, and this initiates his healing from the loss of Rufus. Thinking of Rufus, he wonders what same-sex lovemaking had been for him: "Rufus had certainly thrashed and throbbed, feeling himself mount higher, as Vivaldo thrashed and throbbed and mounted now" (386). Eric's body serves Vivaldo as a curative agent and as a conduit for resurrecting and finally releasing Rufus. Described in terms of falling, plunging, thrusting, and being overtaken, Eric's and Vivaldo's lovemaking re-enacts Rufus's death by falling and drowning. Their lovemaking serves as a cleansing and rebirth for both men, who afterward "lay together, close, hidden and protected by the sound of rain" (386). The gentle rain here is distinguished from the violence of the raging river that claimed Rufus's life. In their lucid, persuasive article "Beneath the Black Aesthethic," Andrew Shin and Barbara Judson suggest that James Baldwin celebrates "the male body not as a juggernaut of power but as a sensorium of comfort—the body as harbor and refuge, recapitulating the infant's relation to the mother, enjoying an amorphous, passive sexuality, a luxuriant dependency, played out, however, between men."[35] In terms that denote maternal nurturance, Eric's and Vivaldo's lovemaking restores each of them and prepares them to move confidently and safely into their romantic partnerships: Vivaldo with Ida, and Eric with Yves.

Another Country ends with Yves's arrival in New York. The novel, which has journeyed so laboriously through pained interpersonal relationships within genders and across races, ends romantically with a simple wish for nurturing spaces for the queer artist/activist in the United States. Repudiating standards of masculinity and racial imperatives that exert repressive social control, Baldwin concludes his novel with the wise maxim that love, equality, and brotherhood are the most reliable indices of a just society. Thus, the other country to which the title of this novel alludes is not an imaginary place or a nation that exists in an alternative or distant geographical region. It is the country that Baldwin most desired to see realized in the United States—one in which equal protection and equal access would be guaranteed to all without regard for their sexuality, gender, or race.

Coming Home

I opened my discussion of *Another Country* with the proposition that the novel instantiates Baldwin's effort to locate a place for the black queer artist in the movement for black social, civic, and economic equality of the 1950s and 1960s. Attending primarily to Baldwin's linkage of black masculinity, sexual variance, and racial standardization, I have treated *Another Country* as Baldwin's civil rights novel. Even though the novel indicts overt white racism and its subtle manifestation in white liberalism, it nonetheless touts Baldwin's conviction that civil rights could be achieved only by the collective desire and cooperative struggle of both black and white Americans. Both African and Anglo Americans would have to own their nation's bloody history and together solve the persistent problem of racial caste.

This chapter reaches its conclusion via an analysis of a key textual moment in Baldwin's final novel, *Just Above My Head*. The scene, as I will demonstrate, illustrates Baldwin's reconsideration and recontextualization of black nationalism as a viable philosophy and political strategy in the bid for American pluralism. I argue, in other words, that Baldwin taps the tremendous power and pathos of African American life as both diagnostic and didactic tool for the benefit of the nation as a whole. To be clear, *Just Above My Head* is about black people. It traverses the tumultuous middle decades of the twentieth century, depicting the horrors and the hopes of African American experience, moving from North to South to Europe to Africa and back to the United States to render visible the efforts of a historically degraded and excluded people to *belong* to and in the country of their birth. In *Just Above My Head*, Baldwin reconfigures the meaning and the practice of black solidarity to espouse an ethical, inclusive, humane regard for self, family, and compatriots. This section unpacks and extends the astute contention by Eddie Glaude Jr. that "Baldwin's invocation of the beauty of black life and struggle constitutes a profoundly democratic act aimed at rescuing democratic ideals from the ghastly implications of the idolatry of color."[36]

The scene to which I refer rehearses the ritual of black familial gathering: a gorgeous, lazy afternoon; the joyful consumption of so many sumptuous dishes; the protective shelter of parents and extended relatives; the enjoyment of children and their instruction in the ways of being and the ways of living. The gathering scene frames the novel's entire narrative progression, as if Baldwin wished to proffer an existential claim about origins and endings. At nearly six hundred pages, the novel is sprawling and exhausting, but its main lesson may be gleaned, it seems to me, by scrupulous and careful study of the opening depiction of an African American family's afternoon meeting in the presence of food and music to recollect the past, to instruct the young, and to memorialize the dead.

Hall Montana, the narrator of *Just Above My Head*, dances with his daughter Odessa. His wife, Ruth, dances with their son Tony. Julia Miller, Hall's former love, plays the music and keeps watch. The family awaits the arrival of Jimmy, Julia's brother and Arthur Montana's lover. Arthur Montana is the dead protagonist of this novel, a musician like Rufus in *Another Country*, queer like Rufus, gone like Rufus. It is noteworthy that Arthur dies violently, prematurely at thirty-nine, the same age as Malcolm X and Martin Luther King when they were assassinated in 1965 and 1968, respectively.[37] The novel's engagement in acts of mourning and memorializing the strong, the beautiful, the promising, the black dead assumes a collective function as it comes to refer ultimately to the black liberation struggles of a bygone era.

In the aftermath of Arthur's life and his passing, the family must make sense of his existence to gain a deeper understanding of their own. Although his queer desiring practices take Arthur outside of uplift-oriented articulations of black identity, the novel does not spend long periods on excursions that exceed the territory and the politics of African American culture. Specifically, the love of Arthur's life is a black gay man, like himself, a musician like himself, a lover and a brother. The novel is narrated from Hall's first-person perspective. Lynn Orilla Scott argues convincingly that Arthur's untimely demise "connotes a terrible internal violence (psychological as well as physical) that kills Arthur and seriously wounds Hall's psyche. Arthur's death in a pool of blood takes on metaphorical dimension . . . reflecting a crisis in black life. Hall's narrative becomes an effort to stop the blood loss, to repair the wound, and to make vivid the ties of kinship. By reconstructing Arthur's life in memory and story Hall hopes to end his own nightmares and sense of alienation."[38] Hall's narration weaves together fragments of his own and Arthur's life, and he imaginatively reconstructs the events in Arthur's life that he himself did not witness. The narrative commingling of Arthur's and Hall's life stories textualizes Baldwin's vision of intra-racial unity *and* inclusivity. In other words, the novel's narrative structure enacts Baldwin's commitment, on one hand, to racial preservation in the form of African American socioeconomic and political equality and, on the other hand, to the expanded potentialities of black being and belonging.[39] Baldwin's dual commitments are encapsulated in the scene of black familial gathering at the moment in which Tony asks his father, Hall, the question that has plagued him since his uncle Arthur's death:

> "What was my uncle—Arthur—like?"
> "Well—why do you ask? *You* knew him."
> "Come on. I was a baby. What did *I* know?"
> "Well—what are you asking?"
> "A lot of the kids at school—they talk about him." . . .
> "What do they say?"
> "They say he was a faggot."
> [After a pause, Hall tells his son] "Okay. Your uncle was my brother, right? And I loved him. Okay? He was a very—lonely—man. He had a very strange—life. I think that—he was a very great singer."
> Tony's eyes do not leave my face. I talk into his eyes. . . . "You want the truth, I'm trying to tell you the truth—anyway, let me tell you baby, I'm proud of my brother, your uncle, and I'll be proud of him until the day I die. You should be, too. Whatever the fuck your uncle was, and he was a whole lot of things, but he was nobody's faggot."[40]

After a brief pause, Tony looks away from his father. Hall asks him:

> "What did *you* think of your uncle?
> [Tony] looks down; unwillingly, he smiles.
> "I thought he was a crazy, beautiful cat." He looks at me. "I loved him—that's why—" Tears drip from his nose; he throws his head back. "I just wanted you to tell me," he says. (29)

Tony's conversation with his father illuminates the many layers of (social, behavioral, sexual) regulation that Arthur, as a black gay man, had to confront and surpass to achieve communal acceptance—or, in Baldwin's words, "a place at the welcome table." Tony opens the conversation by referencing his uncle's reputation as a "faggot" (presumably within the black community) and the social derision that attaches to such an outlaw sexual identity. In this important moment of gendered, generational instruction, Hall proclaims—and thus demonstrates—pride in Arthur. He does so despite his misconceptions, or simply misgivings, about his brother's sexuality, as demonstrated by his initial silence and awkward stutters. Hall's further declaration that his brother was "nobody's faggot" destabilizes the link between sexual identity and gender performativity that is especially entrenched in African American communities.[41] Hall's assertion finally assures Tony that Arthur was no more compromised than other African American men who are similarly besieged by the ravages of American racism. The recovery of Arthur's proper manhood in a racialized, *familial* context enlightens Tony, and it underwrites Baldwin's reconsideration and reconfiguration of black nationalist ideals.

Tony's avowals of love and acceptance of his uncle recall, although they reverse, the open letter that begins *The Fire Next Time*. In "My Dungeon Shook: Letter to My Nephew on the Hundredth Anniversary of the Emancipation," Baldwin lovingly instructs his nephew and namesake James to survive racism by determinedly, defiantly, and indefatigably refuting white hegemonic norms, as they rely on the subjugation and social marginalization of black Americans. Based on its cultural construction and its historic socioeconomic mistreatment, the category of the black is a virtually uninhabitable, inoperable positionality. Baldwin knows this. With unsparing candor, he writes:

> This innocent country set you down in a ghetto in which, in fact, it intended that you should perish. . . . You were born where you were born and faced the future that you faced because you were black and *for no other reason*. The limits of your ambitions were, thus, expected to be set forever. You were born into a society which spelled out with brutal clarity, and in as many ways as possible, that you are a worthless human being. You were not expected to aspire to excellence: you were expected to make peace with mediocrity. Wherever you have turned, James, in your short time on this earth, you have been told where you could go and what you could do (and how you could do it) and where you could live and whom you could marry. . . . The details and symbols of your life have been deliberately constructed to make you believe what white people say about you.[42]

Addressing his nephew, Baldwin diagnoses the U.S. racial schema, particularly as it underwrites political stratification and the uneven distribution of material resources in the country. Baldwin warns his nephew and his readers about the damage racism does to individual black lives. Notably, in his articulation of so strident an oppositional stance to white hegemony, Baldwin aligns himself with black nationalism. Will Walker convincingly makes the case that not only in his later writings but also as early as the publication of *The Fire Next Time*, Baldwin expresses black nationalist leanings. In his perceptive assessment, *The Fire Next Time* "articulated a common black nationalist theme of rejection of American ideals based on the belief that white supremacy was the limit of American democracy."[43] Walker's point is well taken here. The perceived decline in Baldwin's writing and literary significance has long been attributed to his waning advocacy of integration as a social goal and his (supposedly) new problematic alliance with black nationalism.[44] As I demonstrate in my reading of *Another Country*, despite his faith in human and national progress and, more importantly, in the power of shared experience and interpersonal connectivity to foster civic cooperation, Baldwin interrogated white liberal prescriptions for racial equality and rejected outright any insinuation of intrinsic black racial failure.

Baldwin's open letter to his nephew illustrates this point emphatically. In the letter, as in *Just Above My Head*, Baldwin establishes the familial context as the most profound and efficacious site for *national* revelation and instruction. In continuous search of opportunities for black self-making, Baldwin assures his nephew (and, by extension, all black Americans) of his innate personal value, despite predominant devaluations of black people. He commands his nephew (and, again, all African Americans) to live according to his own design and determination and to resist constantly the discursive, social, and institutional curtailments that historically exploited *and* excluded African Americans. Baldwin instructs his nephew and his reader, "Please try to remember that what they believe, as well as what they do and cause you to endure, does not testify to your inferiority but to their inhumanity and fear. Please try to be clear, dear James, through the storm which rages about your youthful head today, about the reality which lies behind the words *acceptance* and *integration*. There is no reason for you to try to become like white people and there is no basis whatsoever for their impertinent assumption that *they* must accept *you*."[45] Amid his impassioned plea, Baldwin registers plainly his skepticism about the place of integration in the struggle for racial equality. He also makes an important distinction between the full enfranchisement of African Americans—with all of the personal freedoms, civic protections, and economic opportunity it promises—and whites' approval. The former, Baldwin clarifies, is a goal; the latter is not.

In summation, *Just Above My Head* shares the productive impetus of *Another Country*: both novels are motivated by Baldwin's desire to create a national landscape in which he, the black queer artist, exists and furthermore embodies innovative conceptions and enactments of personal and political freedom.

Baldwin understood that the dark male figure functions in the American cultural imaginary as the founding "queer" subject, as the Other, the unrecognizable and unrepresentable, and the socially cast out. Mining the progressive potential of this cultural positioning, Baldwin portrays the black aesthete and the homosexual, or simply the black queer artist, as both exemplar and measure of social reform. In chapter 1, I analyzed Harriet Jacobs's mid-nineteenth-century depiction of interracial homoeroticism as the most severe expression of racial denigration. She portrays Luke's sexual enslavement by his white master as an illustration of his complete abjection, his utter dehumanization. A century later, James Baldwin depicts interracial, homoerotic sexuality as the most profound and promising demonstration of African Americans' entry into the realm of the social, of their final admittance into the U.S civic and political body. For him, the general acceptance of unacknowledged and unaccepted desire signals America's coming of age and a final preparedness to admit its historically marginalized members into the national interior. Rather than demonstrating the utter loss of humanity as it does in Jacobs's *Incidents*, interracial homoeroticism is portrayed in *Another Country* as the promise of its reclamation. *Just Above My Head* locates homosexuality within the specific African American cultural context to emphasize diversity within the racial collective and to measure African Americans' capacity for intra-racial love and self-acceptance. Despite its challenge to racial protocol, same-gender love functions in Baldwin's conception as one potential thread in the complex philosophical and political apparatus of black nationalism, not in explicit contradistinction to it.

4

RECOVERING THE LITTLE BLACK GIRL

Incest and Black American Textuality

The race or group mother is the point of access to a group history and bodily identity, but she is also the cultural vehicle for fixing, ranking, and subduing groups and bodies.
—Laura Anne Doyle, *Bordering on the Body*

In a society ordered by hierarchies of power based on race, class, and gender, no one is more powerless, hence more vulnerable, than a poor black girl.
—Cheryl Wall, "Introduction," *Changing Our Own Words*

Within the first few pages of *The Women*, a book that is part memoir, part elegy, and part cultural criticism, Hilton Als reproduces, for the sake of further exposition on "Negress identity," the caption of a *New York Times* article. The article tells of the rape of a three-year-old girl, the swift arrest of her uncle for the rape, and the reaction of the toddler's mother, who refuses to discuss the case publicly as she "just want[s] to go back to [her] apartment to rest."[1] Although the article appears without photographic documentation or any explicit mention of the racial identity of the abused child, her uncle, or her exhausted mother, Als notes a constellation of coded references that lead him to believe that this is a black family. The mother has had six children, three of whom are in foster care. The mother and her brother have different last names, suggesting that at some point she married. The absence of paternal outrage at the child's sexual victimization, however, suggests that those earlier attempts at familial legitimacy have by now failed. Als sums up the mother as an "inbred Negress who made her way to New York and bad men and children swollen with need and the welfare system."[2] He thus alludes to the critical import of social, economic, and political factors in narrating incest. Shocked that such a crime was committed by "kin," the child's mother refuses to disavow her relation to the child's rapist, unwilling as it were "to give her brother up, regardless of the facts."[3] The mother's disbelief that her "kin" has so injured her child seems to Als further evidence of the family's racial blackness. "Kin" serves in this instance as a nebulous sketch word for people connected through blood relations but not necessarily constrained and sanctioned as "family" according to the requirements of culture—that is, material self-sufficiency, patriarchal hierarchization, patronymic authorization, and so on. Als concludes, "I attached black faces to this narrative of 'kin' gone awry, pants down around the ankles, a mother's need for 'rest' after an atrocity committed against someone else."[4]

Als is clever, cutting, and compassionate in his description of black familial ruin so vast and devastatingly wrought that a grown man seeks and finds sexual relief in the fragile flesh of his three-year-old niece. The account ultimately, though, is less concerned with the child, who is lost to the reader, if not to the world, and more concerned with the black mother, the primary subject of Als's text. For Als, the mother's mute bewilderment at her brother's sexual assault of her toddler exemplifies what he calls "Negress identity" and one of its main hallmarks: the failure of (self-)articulation in the face of terrible, tireless experience. Als writes, "Angry or silent, colored and female, her starched cap of servitude firmly in place, she carries a tray loaded with forgiveness, bitterness, rancor, anger, defensiveness, and slatternliness. She has rejected language."[5] Subtly reprimanding and ridiculing the black mother for her refusal of rage but co-optation of the traumatic effects of "an atrocity committed against someone else"—namely, the inability to speak—Als's brief synopsis of child rape presents the black mother as the quintessential "Negress." We are never given the woman's name; she exists solely in terms of relationality: she is the victim's mother, the rapist's sister. According to Als, it is the black mother's perpetual being in and being for others, coupled with her lack of self-knowledge and failure of self-articulation, that make her such a powerful symbol of black identity and the sacrificial lamb of most of its cultural expression. After all, in the U.S. cultural and political context, the most recognizable and enduring symbols of social and sexual degeneracy and of historical black victimization are the single black mother and, of course, the little black girl.

To understand these predominant figurations of black female identity and to begin mapping the contours of my study in this chapter, I wish to underscore the mother's co-optation of her daughter's injury in Als's account, her momentary *being in* her daughter, to make a larger claim that undergirds much of my analysis here—namely, that the predominant perceptions of black women and the historical uses of their labor have brought black motherhood and black girlhood into such unbearable and convoluted proximity that their differences eventually bottom out. Or, to put it more concretely, the single black mother and the little black girl exist along the same continuum of black female representation, morphing into and out of each other, revealing one aspect of black women's lives while occluding others. Racial enslavement created a legacy in which black motherhood and black girlhood appear to be one and the same, for institutional slavery abnegated legal motherhood, denied all female-bodied black people the self-authorizing rights obtaining in sex and reproduction, and imposed generalized African American (social, material) dependency through totalized racial regulation. The ideologies of black motherhood and girlhood that arose during slavery to excuse rampant rape and the forced removal of black children from their mothers—mainly black women's sexual irresponsibility and maternal inadequacy—find their contemporary correlates in stereotypes of the unwed teenage mother and the welfare queen.[6]

It is not entirely surprising, then, that incest, generally perceived as the girl child's sexual surrogacy and at times premature maternity, is represented in Als's treatise on black womanhood. In the late twentieth century, literary depictions of incest in texts that center on black women abound. A cursory review of late-twentieth-century texts written by African Americans that depict in particular father–daughter incest illuminates the emergence of a literary trope. Maya Angelou's *I Know Why the Caged Bird Sings* (1969), Alice Walker's "The Child Who Favored Daughter" (1973), Gayl Jones's *Corregidora* (1975), Toni Morrison's *The Bluest Eye* (1979), James Baldwin's *Just Above My Head* (1979), Alice Walker's *The Color Purple* (1982), Carolivia Herron's *Thereafter Johnnie* (1991), and Sapphire's *Push* (1996) are some of the best-known and highly lauded texts. Notably, all of these novels were published after the historic passage of the Civil Rights Act in 1964. Recognizing incest as a prominent motif in contemporary black women's literature, this chapter treats incest not simply as traumatic, individual sexual injury but as a *figurative* sexual arrangement that epitomizes black familial ruin in the post-civil rights period. My main contention in this chapter is that, as in Als's depiction, representations of incest in contemporary black American literature bespeak racism's profound and incessant injuries to black children and black women, epitomizing the disintegration of the black family under the pressures of civil rights retrenchment, reinvigorated black patriarchy, dwindling communal supports, negligible economic resources, and urban decay.

This chapter proceeds by examining incest as the central trope through which black female identity and black familial dilemmas are figured in African American women's writing in the period after black Americans were purportedly granted equal rights before the law. Elizabeth Barnes posits, "Narrativizing incest reveals the ways in which discourses of sex, gender, class, race, desire, intimacy, family, domination, love, and violence inform, and have informed, understandings of personal, political, and cultural experience."[7] Analyzing key textual moments in Morrison's *The Bluest Eye*, Jones's *Corregidora*, Octavia Butler's *Imago*, the final book of her Xenogenesis series, and Sapphire's *Push*, I argue that representing incest allows black American women writers to highlight the effects of civil rights retrenchment and the waning popularity of a largely masculinist black nationalist agenda on black families in the late twentieth century. By noting the hierarchy of familial relations obtaining in father–daughter incest, as well as the failure of civil rights legislation and refigured patriarchy under black nationalism to produce necessary improvements in many African Americans' lives, my analysis interrogates both phallocentric racial struggle and the nuclear, heteronormative model of family as necessary requirements for collective racial progress. In so doing, I illuminate the methods by which representing incest allows black women authors to critique, first, the institution of the family as imagined and invigorated by black nationalism's masculinist rhetoric and requirements, which bear a mimetic relation to hegemonic U.S. masculinity, and second, federal and local government policies that neglect structural transformation and instead vilify poor black families for their failure to conform to nuclear heteronormativity.

My analysis opens by tracing the evolution of the incest narrative from the earlier rape narrative so common in slavery and its literary representation. In so doing, I show how contemporary African American women writers expose the continued relevance of slavery to black familial formation and interrogate black men's exercise of patriarchal prerogatives in the contemporary moment. My reading of Sapphire's *Push* highlights incest as the cumulative effect of the violences of state racism and its various economic, social, and political consequences in the lives of black women and girls. By locating agency and desire in the raped girl child and by replacing ruined families with alternative kinship arrangements, Sapphire transfigures incest from parent–child rape and pedophilia into a more general indictment of state policies that fail to protect the interests, bodies, or destinies of black female children. This chapter concludes with Octavia Butler's unique deployment of incest within the genre of science fiction. Her final novel in the Xenogenesis series, *Imago*, depicts incest not as evidence of extreme black psychical, familial, and communal deformation resulting from racial oppression; instead, sibling incest is figured as a faulty but innovative circuit of desire that carries the possibility of a fierce familial cohesion and effort toward racial preservation. Taking a cue from the authors under consideration, this chapter reads incest not as absolute negation, unimaginable and non-navigable longings and crossings, but as a site from which to begin to unravel and repair harrowing black familial dilemmas and to critique society for its egregious neglect of black women and children.

In Awful Slavery

In the preceding chapter, I read James Baldwin's mid-twentieth-century novels in light of the aspirations and the eventual disappointments of civil rights movement outcomes. I analyzed *Just Above My Head* for its celebration of black familial love and communal survival in the face of continued racism. One aspect of *Just Above My Head* that was not treated exhaustively in the previous chapter but that makes its mark in this one is the depiction of incest in the black family. The central drama in the Miller household is the repeated rape of the child evangelist daughter by her father. As shown by my opening discussion of *The Women*, both black male and female writers deploy literary incest to shed light on contemporary black familial problematics, particularly as they result from racism's sundry effects. Ralph Ellison's portrayal of the Trueblood family in *Invisible Man* is one of the earliest and most thoroughly theorized depictions of incest in the African American literary canon.[8]

It is Baldwin's account of incest in *Just Above My Head*, however, that has much in common with the many depictions we find in black women's writing in the second half of the twentieth century. These are, namely, the daughter's repeated violations by a father figure; the father figure's attempt to conceal or overcome masculine inefficacy through authoritarian behavior in the household (traditionally the feminine/mother's domain); and the mother's absence, if not her explicit (or simply silent) collusion with the sexual abuse of her child. Christine Froula provides an apt description of the family dynamics shaping and shaped by father–daughter incest:

> The family situations of incest victims: a dominating, authoritarian father; an absent, ill, or complicitous mother; and a daughter who, prohibited by

her father from speaking about the abuse, is unable to sort out her contradictory feelings of love for her father and terror of him, of desire to end the abuse and fear that if she speaks she will destroy the family structure that is her own security. . . . This silencing ensures that the cultural daughter remains a daughter, her power suppressed and muted; while her father, his power protected, makes culture and history in his own image.[9]

While Baldwin is not the main focus of this chapter, I appreciate his origination of incest as a motif in fiction centered on black families as it was bequeathed to his literary daughters—Toni Morrison and Gayl Jones foremost among them.

In this section, I read *Corregidora* to track the evolution of the incest narrative in African American women's texts. In its social commentary and political operation, the incest narrative in black-women-authored fiction of the late twentieth century is a reformulation of the rape narrative of the century before in black women's personalized narratives of slavery. Darlene Clark Hine notes, "Virtually every known nineteenth-century female slave narrative contains a reference to, at some juncture, the ever present threat and reality of rape."[10] This is not surprising, as sex and reproduction constituted a main component of enslaved women's labor. Rape, forced concubinage, and mediated reproduction were part and parcel of enslaved women's lives. Saidiya Hartman reminds us that legally the sexual exploitation of black women by the master class (and I include white women here) was a "legitimate use of property."[11] The sexual abuse of enslaved people was an occurrence so commonplace that it acquired the status of "unspoken but normative condition."[12] As it was a standard feature in the daily catastrophe of slavery, rape became a central trope in black women's accounts of their enslavement, even when presented obliquely or as seduction.[13] Like rape, the incest motif is rooted in slavery. As in twentieth-century African American fiction, incest in the nineteenth-century slave context epitomizes familial disarray. It bespeaks the most hideous possible outcome for families whose members were not only forcibly dispersed but also forcibly mated according to the dictates of the market and the designs of individual slaveowners.[14] The anxiety of participating inadvertently in incestuous relations energized the enslaved person's desire to legitimize and legalize filial bonds and to gain access to and maintain family records. Nonetheless, even without physical enactment between black kinfolk, incest can be understood as an organizing principle of plantation life in that it exposes the exploitative and intimate relations between slaveowners and their human property. In other words, as a trope, as a sexual arrangement that also operates in a representational apparatus, incest reveals the extent to which slavery was, first and foremost, a domestic institution—economically supported and judicially enforced but home-based nevertheless.

Because plantations were both proto-factories and home spaces, interactions between members of the master class and enslaved African Americans were necessarily conditioned by—and, to a certain extent, experienced as—the spatial, behavioral, and consanguineous bonds of family. Hortense Spillers describes, "Under the conditions of captivity, the offspring of the female does not 'belong' to the mother, nor is s/he 'related' to the 'owner,' though the owner 'possesses' it, and in the African-American instance, often fathered it, *and, as often*, without whatever benefit of patrimony."[15] Spillers, following Claude Meillassoux, articulates the captive slave's general state of kinlessness, or permanent formal, legal, and social orphanhood, wherein biological and affective ties of family are rendered null and void in favor of the master's official (physical and financial) ownership of the slave. She writes, "In those cases where [slave masters] were begetters of children, the puzzle of fatherhood is fully elaborated. As 'owners' of 'human property,' they impede the operations of kinship."[16] Spillers observes that, even without the benefit of legal or social recognition, slaves were often begotten by their owners, creating the situation of consanguinity in the absence of acknowledged paternity. Spillers reminds us further that the rights of paternity, patrimony, and patrilineality are enacted specifically in the arena of property and inheritance; they are particularly "the vertical transfer of a bloodline, of a patronymic, of titles and entitlements, of real estate and the prerogatives of 'cold cash,' from fathers to sons and in the supposedly free exchange of affectional ties between a male and a female of his choice."[17] While enslaved subjects were not the legal heirs to or the likely beneficiaries of their owner's wealth, they were nonetheless moveable parts of it: purchased, branded, mated, reproduced, sold. We might then view the enslaved as (frequently biological) children who were exchanged, like daughters, to advance the monetary interests of powerful, propertied fathers. Denied legal claims to self-ownership—that is, to legal autonomy conferred by citizenship and the rights of property possession and family—enslaved subjects remained the perpetual dependents of their owners. And masters were, in a twisted and self-serving plantation schema, "fathers" to a population for whom legal paternity was not as much nullified as it was vacated.

Considering, then, the "parental" relation obtaining between masters and their captive humans, slavery, as Janice Doane and Devon Hodges assert, "was a paternalistic institution in which white men economically and sexually exploited people they defined as their dependents."[18] Understood this way, the coerced sexual enactments between slaveowners and the enslaved—with the usual elements of betrayal, seduction, ambivalence, and brutality—resemble incest. I turn now to Gayl Jones's novel *Corregidora* for extended exemplification. Framed as a wish for productive expression in song, Ursa, the protagonist of *Corregidora*, mourns her great-grandmother's (and, by extension, her own) incestuous slave past: "I wanted a song that would touch me, touch my life and theirs . . . A new world song. A song branded with the new world. I thought of the girl who had to sleep with her master and mistress. Her father, the master. Her daughter's father. The father of her daughter's daughter. How many generations?. . . . How many generations had to bow to his genital fantasies?"[19] Ursa's song is not merely for Great Gram, her great-grandmother, but also for Linda Brent, the protagonist of *Incidents in the Life of a Slave Girl*, the representative girl child/mother in slavery, and for all of the female enslaved. Ursa, the blues singer, the white Corregidora's granddaughter and great-granddaughter, wants a song that can serve as both testimony and progeny. Ursa has been mandated by her mothers to "make generations"—that is, to bear children to serve as animate, corporealized evidence of the sexual authorities of the slave plantation: "The important thing is making generations. They can burn the papers but they can't burn conscious, Ursa. And that's what makes the evidence. And that's what makes the verdict" (22). After a brutal injury by her husband results in a hysterectomy, Ursa loses her capacity for childbearing, and she learns to fulfill the maternal, ancestral mandate to "make generations" with song, a different kind of record in the flesh.

In this passage, Ursa seeks the right words, the right melody to mourn and memorialize Great Gram, the kidnapped African girl child who was forced into slavery and prostitution by her figurative father upon arrival to the New World. Great Gram was her master Corregidora's favorite concubine, his most exquisite prostitute, his "gold piece" placed in the sexual service of both her master and mistress. Great Gram tells Ursa, "He wouldn't sleep with [his wife], so she made me sleep with her, so for five years I was sleeping with her and with him. That was when I was thirteen to eighteen" (13). As a dependent in their household, removed as a small child from the legitimate care of her African parents by the unrelenting, consumptive force of slave trade, a child, Great Gram was not only physically enslaved but also sexually enslaved by her "foster" parents. Jones implies Corregidora's double relation to Great Gram in the loaded, fragmented sentence, "Her father, the master." The linkage of the terms and the practices of fatherhood and slaveowning conjoins the authority of the father with the tyranny of the master. Such an alignment rebukes the predacious slaveowner while paving the way for Jones's more generalized critique of the father in the (Western) paradigmatic nuclear family and its reinvention under black nationalism. The Corregidora family's incestuous (re)production continues into another generation as Great Gram becomes the grandmother of Corregidora's children after he begins also raping their daughter.

Incest as familial legacy, as slave (post)memory, is a main theme of Jones's novel. I invoke "postmemory" in the sense Marianne Hirsh uses it to describe the process by which second-generation Holocaust survivors internalize their parents' Holocaust memories. Hirsh postulates that children of survivors of collective cultural trauma, such as genocide or slavery, remember those traumas

> as the stories and the images with which they grew up, but that are so powerful, so monumental, as to constitute memories in their own right. . . . Postmemory is a powerful form of memory precisely because its connection to its object or source is mediated not through recollection but through projection, investment, and creation. That is not to say that survivor memory itself is unmediated, but it is more directly connected to the past. Postmemory characterizes the experiences of those who grow up dominated by narratives that preceded their birth, whose own belated stories are displaced by those of the previous generation, shaped by traumatic events that they can neither understand nor re-create.[20]

Hirsh's definition of postmemory applies both to Ursa and to Mama. Mama has retained Great Gram and Grandmama's memories of Corregidora's plantation and imbibed their lessons so extensively that her own life experiences are overshadowed. Neither Mama's identity nor her desires find meaningful expression. Ursa eventually realizes that, since she is not Corregidora's direct incestuous progeny, she is not necessarily one of *his women* (103). Her struggle, then, is to reconcile the slave past with its aftermath in the present, to discover or to invent a trajectory, a trace, from then to now, that can pierce slavery's vast terror, only to leave it behind. Ashraf Rushdy deftly characterizes Ursa's journey and Jones's authorial effort in *Corregidora*. He posits, "Jones traces the specific and complex ways that an ancestral slave narrative works on the terrain of family as the family produces and reproduces the modern desiring subject. Jones focuses on the subject of desire as constituted historically in order to show how both the spectacular and the hidden experiences of slavery, especially the historical subjection of desire, operate in the formation of contemporary African American subjectivity."[21] Ursa's subjective formation occurs within the fraught enclosures of slavery's wounds and in tales of maternal trauma. She is formed in shrieks and shadows, in the repeated incantations of

Corregidora's sexual insanity: "The words repeated again and again could be a substitute for memory, were somehow more than the memory. As if it were only the words that kept the anger" (11). The sexual wounding her mothers have endured assumes the status of cultural condition as Ursa learns the meaning of racial subjection in the explicit, and nearly exclusive, register of sexual violation. Ursa's search for self exemplifies the search for black American women's subjectivity in the post-civil rights era. Ursa undertakes the collective journey: to re-humanize the formerly commodified self, to locate one's value beyond mere worth in dollars, and to pursue personal desire—even those desires that, when exercised and expressed by black women, have been historically, tragically mistaken for complicity.

Conceptually, incest signals the subjugation and the creation of desire. As such, incest serves as a symbol of Ursa's familial legacy, as well as her journey beyond it. Once the incest taboo is transgressed, all hell breaks loose. Once enacted, in other words, incest can neither be eliminated nor contained. The perpetuity of incest's violation underlies Great Gram's memory of Corregidora and his proliferating abuses, "Ole man, he just kept rolling" (42). There is simply no going back to the time before pedophilia, before incest, and there is no predating it.[22] Ursa's recollection of Great Gram exemplifies incest's inevitable proliferation. Ursa remembers Great Gram's staged recountings of enslavement. "Great Gram sat in her rocker. I was in her lap. She told the same story over and over again. She had her hands around my waist, and I had my back to her. . . . Once when she was talking, she started rubbing my thighs with her hands, and I could feel the sweat on my legs. Then she caught herself, and stopped, and held my waist again" (11). Great Gram's firm grip on Ursa's five-year-old body limits the child's movements and undermines momentarily her sense of corporeal autonomy. Great Gram's intense caress of Ursa's thighs literalizes to some extent her articulations of sexual terror. In this instance, talk becomes tactile, and it penetrates Ursa's young consciousness. Combining tactility and narration intensifies Ursa's instruction, demonstrated by the production of bodily fluid, sweat, before Great Gram submits to her own self-willed restraint. Because Ursa comes to her great-grandmother's staged and routinized accounts of Corregidora's sexual depravity with no pre-knowledge of sex, Great Gram's recollections have the effect of sexualizing the child.

Elizabeth Breau's observation is useful for making sense of this scene: "The sexual exploitation practiced by white slave owners distorted the sexuality of both master and slave and blurred the familial boundaries that ensure observance of the incest taboo."[23] Whether or not Great Gram intentionally mishandles or molests her great-granddaughter is less relevant here than incest's notable power to signify continued, reshaped violation in the transition from plantation existence to contemporary black family life. Ursa is subjected to and traumatized by incest through ritualized sexual triangulation with the incestuous Corregidora, her great-grandmother's touch and talk operating as the primary modes of inclusion and transmission.

The sexual invasion of a girl by a mature woman is depicted explicitly later in the novel. The scene functions most evidently as an introduction and a swift repudiation of lesbianism as a potential erotics of repair. Jones acknowledges the possibility that intra-gender love between (African American) women can provide respite and solace from the authority and abuses of (refigured black) patriarchy. However, she ultimately disavows the curative elements of lesbian love and in so doing presents more forcefully a violating sexuality only hinted at in the interactions between the Corregidora women of different generations. In a state of semi-consciousness, Ursa remembers tidbits of conversation she had with her husband Mutt, his physical assault, and her consequent infertility. "Even my clenched fists couldn't stop the fall. That old man still howls inside me. You asked me how did I get to be so beautiful. It wasn't him. No, not Corregidora. And my spirit, you said, like knives dancing. My veins are centuries meeting" (46). Ursa's meditation on her fall, and on the possessive love and domestic violence that caused it, is punctuated by her reflections on Corregidora. She grapples with his location in her history, in her genealogy. She is not—African Americans in general are not—the descendent simply of slaves but of slave masters, as well. Concubine daughter, Ursa was formed out of sexuality's pursuit under the most extreme and totalizing case of social subjection. In linking Mutt's physical brutality to Corregidora's sexual depravity, "centuries meeting" in her own lived experience, Ursa's remembrance conjoins the slave master and the patriarch, whether husband or father.[24] Jones thereby exposes power's undue concentration in the male figurehead in all intra-familial matters, including those that involve the extended, enslaved family of the plantation household and those of the contemporary African American family.

Returning to the women in this scene, Ursa awakens fully to a hushed conversation between her friend Cat and Jeffy, the young girl who only moments before had climbed into her bed and fondled her breasts in a befuddled attempt at lesbian seduction. Ursa recounts:

> I struggled out of sleep. My eyes felt as tight as fists, but they opened.
> Then I heard Cat talking.
> "If you bother her again I'll give you a fist to fuck."

"I ain't going to bother her again."

"I said if you do you got my fist to fuck."

There was silence.

"I could've told you she wouldn't."

"What? You ask her?"

There was a loud slap, and then low crying. (46–47)

This moment between Cat and Jeffy may be read as a concretized instantiation of the erotic dimension of Ursa's relationship with her grandmother. The exchange does not make clear whether Jeffy's lesbian desire is produced by her own self-originated inclination, or whether Cat's seduction has contributed to the creation of the desire. It seems apparent that, either way, the older woman is the one who inducted Jeffy into the eros of woman love and the one with whom Jeffy shares her primary libidinal attachment. Cat is possessive of Jeffy and of her desire, warning her not to pursue Ursa and, by implication, other sexual partners. Cat's sexual possessiveness recalls Great Gram's commodification of Ursa's body—or, more specifically, her desire to harness its reproductive capability to record history. Great Gram wants the misery of slavery documented in Ursa's flesh. She slaps Ursa when Ursa questions her narrative of the past, as Cat slaps Jeffy in an effort to contain Jeffy's woman-loving proclivities. Cat's physical aggression is, of course, markedly different; she wishes to conceal her own lesbianism and implication in child sex. To maintain her secrecy, as well as her exclusive access to Jeffy, she threatens a patently aggressive and painful sexual encounter: a fist to fuck.

Rather than fixate on Cat's sexual threat, I will complete my reading of *Corregidora* by observing the signification of the fist itself. The fist that appears in this scene is not unlike Rufus's fist, onto which Leona's tears silently and powerlessly fell in Baldwin's *Another Country*. By the time Cat threatens to use her fist, Ursa has already invoked the fist twice—once in the literal sense, and the other as a simile. Her clenched fists could not stop her fall, her eyes as tight as fists. It is important to note that in the African American cultural context, the fist is first and foremost the emblem of black power, its gestural proclamation. Rushdy postulates:

> Critiquing what she calls the "new strictures of exclusion" and the "new hegemony" established by the Black Power intellectuals and Black Aesthetic theorists, Jones complicates the racial formation operative in Black Power by exposing its historical roots, by dwelling on the ways that contemporary concepts of authenticity in black communities are connected to historical master discourses on plantations. [. . .] Troubled by the ways

black cultural nationalists eschewed cultural forms (blues), downplayed the importance of formative historical periods (slavery), and argued for rigid regimentation of racial identity (black is, black ain't), Jones used her palimpsest narrative to explore how the complex of desire, sexuality, and racial identity, like the intersubjectivity created in family narratives, offers both enabling and constricting options.[25]

The fist is re-signified in these passages to capture black women's subversive sexuality and oppression. In other words, it exposes black women's unwitting support of black nationalism's patriarchal imperatives, even as it decries African American women's subordinate social status and sexual subjection. The fist signifies the failure of black nationalist philosophy to address and correct *every* crisis in African American families and communities. Its relative impotence in gendered, intra-racial matters is made evident by the failure of the fist to prevent Ursa's injury, which, notably, is caused by intra-racial, gendered violence. Finally, black nationalism's regulatory restriction is signaled by the metaphoric fist that disallows Ursa's lucid vision, and its unwitting subordination of black women is implied by Cat's fisted sexual aggression.

As does Great Gram's insistence that Ursa's sole reason for living is "making generations," the fist operates in this scene as a symbol of the ways in which, when adhering to essentialist, masculinist programs of racial uplift, African American men *and* women inadvertently validate the ethos—and participate in the practice—of dominance. Jones's novel critiques both state and black nationalist imperatives that centralize black masculinity in African American cultural renovation and political resistance.[26] She denounces attitudes in the reformed and empowered black community that limit African American women's zone of activity to childrearing and home building in support of black patriarchy. *Corregidora*, finally, challenges notions of the contemporary black American family as simply slavery's dysfunctional trace, as sociological studies of the midcentury often presented it.[27] Jones cautions black women from the wholesale adoption of the hetero-patriarchal dictates of the normative nuclear household and urges instead a refashioning of black familial love and a new understanding of black women's (re)productivity.

Misshapen Maneuvers

Although my study considers to some extent the social, economic, and political circumstances that, perhaps, give rise to incestuous occurrences in black American families, I must reiterate that an in-depth sociological or legal exposition on the matter is beyond the immediate goals of this chapter, and my training. My concern here is with what incest—generally perceived and represented as the most intimate, and hence disturbing, kind of sexual violation—signifies in African American women's writings of the contemporary era. Sabine Sielke postulates, "Narratives of sexual violence ponder not an alien and uncontrollable part of human nature but the power dynamics of a particular culture."[28] To reiterate, my examination of incest is pursued to illustrate black women authors' stunning commentary on African American life in the post-civil rights period and, further, to reveal the power of literary incest to upset conventional narrative possibility. My thinking here follows that of Elizabeth Barnes, who posits, "The literary study of incest sharpens our awareness of trauma as a social and cultural, as well as personal, experience."[29]

As incest specifies a particular kind of traumatic experience, it forecloses the possibility of its own straightforward, linear narrative reproduction. Incest is an activity so loaded with implausible and imprecise meaning, so symbolic in its repudiation of order, that it trumps its own telling. Narratives of incest are necessarily conditioned by some level of unintelligibility and therefore require all manner of artful, misshapen maneuvers to end up on the page. These artful aesthetics—including disruptive chronologies; the representation of fragmented (and demented) subjectivities; multivocal and multilayered narration; and the interplay among the tragic, the obscene, and the parodic—give rise to formal innovations in the African American women's novel of recent decades. As this section demonstrates, since incest precludes the victim's successful entry into linguistic and social order and undoes the possibility of linearity and evolutionary progress in both life and narrative, telling incest gives black female writers the opportunity to generate social critique in the midst of an immense exercise of creative license.

Toni Morrison's first novel, The Bluest Eye, is an excellent early exemplar. Although many critical analyses of incest in The Bluest Eye take Cholly Breedlove as their focus, I choose to examine Mrs. Breedlove's participation in her daughter's disaster to make a larger case about incest, narrative, and African American women's writing in the post-civil rights period. As I argue in my reading of Corregidora, sexual predation on the slave plantation prefigures sexual transgressions and other forms of violence within black families in the mid- to late-twentieth-century historical context. The implicit presupposition here is that the specter of white masculinity de-phallicizes African American manhood, divesting it of the social and symbolic sovereignty generally accruing to the patriarch. This logic goes: the black patriarch's loss of phallic authority in the familial domain causes systemic dysfunction, shown foremost by black poverty and eruptions of violence in the household, particularly the sexual abuse of daughters. In the case of *The Bluest Eye*, Cholly, the rapist father, endures as a youngster an experience that is akin to rape. As he and his girlfriend, Darlene, are engaging in exciting, clandestine first sex in the woods, they are discovered by two white men. Their sex interrupted, Cholly and Darlene attempt to conceal themselves and their sex acts. The white men order Cholly to continue copulating with Darlene as they use flashlights to illuminate the nearly naked bodies of the two black teenagers, hold guns to clarify and enforce their terror, and giggle throughout the ordeal.

> "Get on wid it, nigger," said the flashlight one.
> "Sir?" said Cholly, trying to find a buttonhole.
> "I said, get on wid it. An' make it good, nigger, make it good." . . .
> With a violence born of total helplessness, he pulled her dress up, lowered his trousers and underwear. . . . He could no more than make-believe. The flashlight made a moon on his behind.[30]

By assuming the role of voyeurs and directing Cholly's sexual performance, the white men hijack Cholly's position in his sexual exchange with Darlene. As armed, uninvited intruders who control the sexual action, they become rapists by proxy. The flashlight on Cholly's buttocks signals his scopic penetration; it operates, like the guns at the men's sides, as the phallic instrument by which the rape is effected. Despite his simulation of forceful sex with Darlene, Cholly is rendered impotent by the comparative masculine power of the white men, whose status is secured by the codified and legalized system of white-over-black ascendancy in the Jim Crow South and by the death technology of a gun.

Many critics read this scene as the crucial precursor to Cholly's rape of his daughter. The logic of their reading draws on popular psychological discourse that views sexual abuse through the lens of history: victims become victimizers. Their analyses also, as I state above, regard the history and overblown operation of white masculinity, specifically in terms of racialized sexual conquest, as prohibitive of full black patriarchal expression. Minrose Gwin's essay "Hereisthehouse" has been particularly influential in this line of reasoning. Gwin argues that as Cholly rapes Pecola, "The materiality of the kitchen merges in space/time with the southern woods of Cholly's remembered youth, where, in the midst of his first sexual experience, he himself as a young African American male was sexually victimized by white men."[31] Echoing Spillers's claims that racial harm entails the obfuscation of intra-familial gender roles so that "father" and "daughter" lose their ontological fixity, Gwin concludes that Cholly's "act of sexual violence toward his daughter is therefore haunted by his positioning and victimization as 'daughter.'"[32] As "daughters" in the metaphorical national family, feminized and subordinated to white "fathers" in the apparatuses of politics, law, and class, black men (mis)align with the actual positionality of girl children in their homes.

While acknowledging the genuine utility of this observation, I would like to hazard, or simply to add, something a bit different. Cholly's incestuous act of violence reunites Pauline and Pecola in a new act of birthing and, in so doing, supports the novel's anachronistic, multilayered, dialogic, and dialectical narrative structure. I am relying on Lacan's contention here: since the absence of the maternal body makes necessary the substitutions inherent in language's acquisition—and, I would add, use—the reinstallation of the maternal body after father–daughter incest shapes Pecola's capacity for speech, her sociality, and, most interesting to me here, the formal aspects of Morrison's novel itself. Morrison entangles Pauline Breedlove in Pecola's rape, framing its before and after with images of the maternal body. In fact, referring to the impact of Cholly's figurative rape, she writes explicitly, "It was Pauline, or rather marrying her, that did what the flashlight did not do" (160). When Cholly rapes his daughter, he is re-enacting not his own symbolic rape by a band of white marauders but, rather, the tenderness he once felt for his wife. In the kitchen that day, "The sequence of emotions was revulsion, guilt, pity, then love." Cholly is driven by a distorted desire that is both romantic and paternal. It was "not the usual lust to part tight legs, but a tenderness, a protectiveness," Morrison writes (162). Pecola faints under the pressure of her father's loving brutality. "Cholly stood up and could see only her grayish panties, so sad and so limp and sad around her ankles" (162). Pecola's loss of consciousness instantiates (and anticipates) her total psychic disintegration. After her rape she recedes into a state of in-animation, a limp and lifeless genitalized object signified only by her underwear. Personified, her panties become Pecola's mark; their grayness reveals her poverty and degradation; their limpness shows the catastrophe of her father's sexual assault on her self-composition. When Pecola awakens, she remembers neither Cholly nor the rape. Instead, she "connect[s] the pain between her legs with the face of her mother looming over her" (162). Inarguably, incest is the founding prohibition in any psychoanalytic account of identity formation and sexual economy within the constrained space of nuclear families. As lover to her father, the girl child clearly has no place in the nuclear household and is necessarily driven out—or driven insane. Pecola, ravaged, demented, rambling bewilderment after father–daughter sex, is banished to the time before fathers—beyond social recuperability, that is—and restored to a symbiotic relation with her mother, the first face she sees.

Pecola's rape is an inverted re-enactment of her birth. Her victimization recalls her mother's invasive, sexualized handling by doctors at a medical facility when she was giving birth to Pecola. Pauline remembers: "He gloved his hand and put some kind of jelly on it and rammed it up between my legs. When he left off, some more doctors come. One old one and some young ones. The old one was learning the young ones about babies. Showing them how to do. When he got to me, he said now these here women you don't have any trouble with. They deliver right away and with no pain. Just like horses. The young ones smiled a little. They looked at my stomach and between my legs. They never said nothing to me" (125–26). The doctors' disregard of Pauline's humanity as a woman in labor is self-evident. They do not look at her or speak to her directly. They do not administer adequate pain medication, and they compare this black woman's delivery of her child to that of a horse. The language that Pauline/Morrison uses to describe the doctor's examination—"rammed it up between my legs"—implies aggressive sexual invasion. Making a series of gendered, racialized associations, Pauline projects her shame and poor treatment during childbirth, the pain between her legs, with the face of her newborn daughter: "The baby come. Big old healthy thing. . . . But I knowed she was ugly. Head full of pretty hair but Lord was she ugly" (127). Michael Awkward describes Pauline's response to her daughter as "the projection of the shadow, and its resultant scapegoating."[33] Susan Willis suggests that Pauline experiences both cultural alienation and internal self-division, writing that she "lives a form of schizophrenia."[34] Willis's and Awkward's postulations emphasize the similarity of Pauline's and Pecola's interior (emotional and psychic) landscapes. Both have imbibed white standards of beauty as they pervade and drive mainstream cinema, household items, toys, and other elements of commodity culture. I want to go as far as suggesting that, given their shared racial psychosis, Pecola seeks, and in moments achieves, communion with her mother in her mind-split, self-generated dialogue at the novel's end.

Morrison explores the perils and potential traumas of black female embodiment, the main theme of The Bluest Eye, by re-associating the child and maternal body and by discovering alternative modes of articulation and communication within the realm of the imaginary, or what Awkward calls Pecola's "schizophrenic, double-voiced" self-talk. The transgression of the incest taboo prohibits narrative assembly and disclosure in that it prevents the child's access to and expert management of language through oedipalization.

As the victim of incest, Pecola cannot manage its narrative reconstruction, as incest enforces her retreat into prelinguistic, pre-Oedipal time.[35] The suppression of unruly desire and submission to the Law of the Father require a movement away from embodied connectivity to the mother, a leave taking of the realm of the imaginary. Successful resolution of the Oedipus complex through the regulatory repudiation of incest is rewarded with access to linguistic capability and, further, with admission into social order.

The Oedipal drama preconditions narrative structure and coherence. In her influential *Visual and Other Pleasures*, Laura Mulvey postulates, "The Oedipus complex shares some of the features of the tripartite narrative of ritual structure. If the dyadic relationship between mother and child corresponds to the initial stative phase, then disrupted by the Oedipal moment, its journey populated by desires, anxieties and contradictions, then the third phase would correspond to the resolution and closure around the Law of the Father and his symbolic order."[36] Narrative consists typically of three parts: beginning, middle, and end. The middle space of the narrative is the space allocated for pleasure, disruption, unpredictability. But the subversive potential of the middle section is contained and foreclosed by the overall construction of the narrative, which depends in general on conformity to linguistic norms and, by extension, to social organization and regulation. Given its curtailment of the resolution of the Oedipal complex, incest drives child victims to the time before sociality. I provide this extended discussion of oedipalization in relation to narrative to suggest that, by returning her protagonist to the time before fathers—before coherent communication and narrativization, that is—Morrison eschews narrative convention and its gendered (read: masculinized) implications for narrative authority. She constructs instead a multilayered and multivocal narrative to tell a story of racial shame and communal self-hatred, homing in on the suffering of one little, embodied black girl.

Unlike other critics who claim that Morrison abandons her deranged protagonist to the space of psychic negation, the nowhere of subjectivity and sociality, I want to emphasize Pecola's bifurcated consciousness.[37] Morrison places Pecola within dialogic communion with an other, a figure with the same psychic landscape as she and her mother, who speaks to and for her. Referring to the blue eyes the deranged Pecola believes she has finally acquired, Pecola and her other confer:

They really are pretty, you know.

I know. He did a really good job. Everybody's jealous. Every time I look at somebody, they look off.

Is that why nobody has told you how pretty they are?

Sure it is. Can you imagine? Something like this happening to a person, and nobody but nobody saying anything about it? They all try to pretend they don't see them. Isn't that funny? . . . I said, isn't that funny?

Yes.

You're the only one who tells me how pretty they are.

Yes.

You are a real friend. . . . (195–96)

Though not explicitly her mother, Pecola's other evinces maternal qualities in her adoration, nurturance, and guidance of Pecola. Together, Pecola and her other attempt to make sense of the social isolation Pecola experiences following her loss of sanity. They surmise that it is due to jealousy because Pecola has attained startling blue eyes when, in fact, it is due to shame. The members of Pecola's community recognize that parental abuse *and* their collective mistreatment of her have caused her mental and emotional ruin. They are, moreover, aware that an internalized disdain of blackness in its most legible phenotypic expression is what initially caused their mistreatment and outcasting of Pecola. In positing the possibility that jealousy inspires their refusal to look at her, Pecola names the communal self-hatred that has resulted in her own demise. Pecola's other joins with her in this diagnosis of racial shame, even as she joins her in the experience of it.

In that incest catalyzes both Pecola's mind split and the final disintegration of her black American family, incest functions in *The Bluest Eye* as the primary lens through which Morrison examines the legacy of racial domination and its mind-bending toll. Beyond its utility in the aesthetic shaping of Morrison's novel, the incest motif in *The Bluest Eye* showcases the most painful aspects of black women's experience by capitalizing on the violated body's signification in the absence of effective, linear speech. The girl child's sexual wounding *itself* names the traumatic violations engendered by the mutually supporting systems of capital, racism, and patriarchy, thereby augmenting black women's (self)articulations and repairing, to some extent, the mute condition of Als's "Negress."

Welfare Reform and Alternative Ethics

Shifting my focus from an examination of the aesthetic and, by extension, psychoanalytic implications of literary incest, in this section I analyze how African American women's incest narratives acquire explicit socioeconomic and political resonance. In her novel *Push*, Sapphire deploys the incest motif to propel a narrative of social, economic, and heterosexist critique. Set in the late 1980s at the height of so-called welfare reform, the novel examines numerous state agencies whose purported mission is to serve society's most vulnerable and disenfranchised members but that instead entangle them in self-perpetuating cycles of poverty that include inadequate education, exploitative labor, sexual and reproductive policing, and judicial surveillance. *Push* clearly depicts the problematics of familial dysfunction, ranging from child physical and sexual abuse to malnutrition and inadequate health care and the overuse of media technology to replace personalized intra-familial engagement, but the novel's dramatic core occurs in sites of public service—public schools, welfare offices, shelters, hospitals, and the like. Exposing the failure of these government agencies, and the people employed in them, to respond effectively to the needs of one horrifically abused black girl, Sapphire paints an almost unbearable picture of African American life abandoned and rotting at the center of urban decay. In its treatment of race as the principal determinant of social and material outcomes in the United States and in its bleak depiction of African American lives besieged by U.S. racism, Sapphire's novel operates within the longstanding tradition of African American literary protest.

Push reads as much as a cautionary tale as it does protest fiction. The trouble befalling its protagonist, Precious Jones, is heart-wrenching if a bit far-reaching. An almost absurd composite character, Precious aggregates within her brief fictive life nearly every imaginable hazard that could befall a young black American woman. She is undereducated, destitute, HIV-infected, underhoused, repeatedly raped by both of her parents, twice impregnated (before attaining the age of legal adulthood) by her father, expelled from school, and finally coerced prematurely into menial labor under misguided welfare-reform statutes. In its recognition of the failure of government to guarantee the inclusive exercise of citizenship or equitable allocation of material resources on behalf of black Americans, the novel interrogates the efficacy and legacy of civil rights legislation to bring meaningful change to African Americans' lives. The novel chronicles Precious's journey toward healing and wholeness through her acquisition of literacy with the help of a supportive network of other marginalized women of color.

Precious's recovery begins when she takes a pre-GED literacy course, along with other impoverished, illiterate women of color who have suffered familial neglect, sexual violence, and labor exploitation, at a community-based adult learning center called Each One Teach One. Based on a student-driven, interpersonal model of instruction, Precious's literacy class is taught by the dreadlocked lesbian poet Ms. Rain, whose name signals for the novel (and for many of its female characters) cleansing, rebirth, revitalization, and continued nurturance. By centralizing a community-based alternative school and a nontraditional teacher in Precious's recovery, the novel promotes the development of humane, fail-safe communal infrastructures that can intervene in individual and familial crises in under-served communities rather than continued reliance on state agencies and apparatuses.

To appreciate fully Sapphire's social commentary, it is necessary to consider the 1980s and 1990s a critical period that inaugurated not only misguided and detrimental welfare reforms but also a generalized expansion and racialization of urban poverty. To adequately historicize the novel and fully contextualize its concerns, I take here a brief detour from my analysis to sketch the history of public assistance and its shifting relationship to racial asymmetries. My point in doing so is to illuminate the confluence of welfare reform and the repeal of civil rights statutes. As I elaborate in the opening of this chapter, the retrenchment of civil rights contributes to the particular circumstance of black familial malaise in the current era and thus becomes an underlying theme in black women's contemporary narratives of incest.

By the mid-1980s—that is, within two short decades—white backlash in both northern and southern states had significantly thwarted the full implementation of civil rights for African Americans and caused an almost complete dismantling of affirmative action. A cornerstone of civil rights legislation, affirmative action had been instrumental to rethinking and retooling American democracy and economic equality. It was designed to monitor inequality, to reduce poverty, and to redress the centuries-long exploitation and social degradation of African Americans. Helene Slessarev observes, "For many whites, the passage of two major civil right bills concluded their commitment to racial justice. Further attempts to expand access to better housing, education, and employment were fiercely resisted in the North. The reaction was swift and forceful. . . . By 1966, a flurry of conservative candidates, including Ronald Reagan, won elective office . . . arguing that government should do less, not more, and that strong civil rights enforcement threatened white liberty"[38] The appointment of conservative Supreme Court justices during the era of Ronald Reagan and George Bush led to the rescission of key affirmative action laws that had been designed to protect African Americans from discrimination in housing, education, labor, and health care. Robin D. G. Kelley notes the important role of the state in determining individual and group economic and social outcome. He contends, "Many of the problems that minority workers and students face, and many of the benefits that white workers and students receive, are not merely the product of thrift and hard work in a free-market economy but outcomes determined largely by government policy."[39] Without legislative protections to guarantee suitable education and vocational training, inclusive hiring and promotion, and equitable compensation in labor, African Americans were left to the discretionary impulses of racial bias and capital.

Further intensifying racial poverty, the rising tide of global economic restructuring entailed a minimization of local employment opportunities for black Americans. With the international outsourcing of labor, positions that had long been occupied by African Americans and businesses that had helped to preserve the vitality of urban spaces simply vanished. Furthermore, a national economy increasingly dependent on the incarceration of black men, combined with an educational system that fails to prepare impoverished black students adequately to compete in existing job markets, helped to keep multitudes of African Americans in utter destitution in the final decade of the twentieth century.[40] In this period, more than any earlier period, urban black families came to rely on public-assistance programs for basic material survival.

It is important to reiterate that prior to the civil rights movement, African Americans had been excluded in the main from the benefits of public-assistance programs. The considerable constriction of welfare assistance that began during the Reagan era and peaked with President Bill Clinton's signing into law the Personal Responsibility and Work Opportunity Reconciliation Act of 1996 must be understood, then, as coextensive with the curtailment of other key political, economic, and civic gains of the civil rights movement. Dorothy Roberts, advancing Linda Gordon's work, provides a useful genealogy of the evolution of welfare from "mother's pensions," dispensed locally at the state level, to federally mandated and funded public assistance for masses of the poor. A maternalist paradigm fueled the logic, rhetoric, and early machinery of welfare legislation. Designed initially to give relief to impoverished white mothers who were either widowed or deserted by irresponsible husbands, welfare assistance enabled women to forgo low-level employment to stay home and rear children. As such, it advocated women's central role in the home as homemakers and caregivers. However, impoverished black women, who historically had provided low-wage menial or domestic labor, were largely disqualified from welfare benefits. Extending the meaning and the effect of disenfranchisement codified under legal and de facto segregation, "The first welfare legislation was intended for white mothers only. Administrators either failed to establish welfare programs in locations with large Black populations or distributed benefits according to standards that disqualified black mothers."[41] A triumph of civil rights legislation was the inclusion of poor African American women and children as beneficiaries of public support, including welfare. The extension of this basic right of enfranchisement for a brief period in national history, however, did not guarantee the full integration of African Americans into the U.S. polity; nor did it last very long.

The eventual bifurcation of public assistance into Social Security (relief for ill or aging taxpayers) and welfare (provision for the destitute) helped to preserve cultural logics that have further isolated black Americans from the majority of U.S. citizens. In the visual register of popular media and in the discursive register of political reform, black families currently are identified exclusively with welfare, portrayed not only as its predominant recipients but also, in the main, as illegitimate, exploitative ones. Coalescing into dominant tropes of the unwed teenage mother and the welfare queen, the misrepresentation of blacks' use of welfare reinvigorates age-old stereotypes of African Americans' social degeneracy, economic irresponsibility, perverse propensity, and cultural dependency—especially as African American women and children are perpetually distinguished from the dignified or deserving poor.[42] The stigmatization of black Americans' participation in welfare is reflected back to Precious, the protagonist of Push, via the media technology of television. As she watches a horror flick on television, she believes that she sees her family, depicted as vampires. "I know who I am," she surmises. "I know who they say I am—vampire sucking the system's blood."[43]

By naming her protagonist Precious, Sapphire inscribes the little black girl's value as a person and as a citizen. As Doane and Hodges postulate, "Sapphire develops the humanity of Precious so that the reader fully . . . understands that child members of the urban black poor fully deserve resources and opportunities to grow."[44] Because the nation has not consented in general to the entitlement of black women and children to economic support, equitable education, and suitable housing and health care, black families, like Precious's, are stigmatized in national culture as thieves, as illegitimate recipients of the privileges of citizenship, and as the largest drain on the material resources of the nation. For the past three decades, welfare reform has exposed and exemplified the national refusal (at the popular and juridical levels) to allow African Americans ordinary rights of national membership or to extend to them ordinary resources of the state. No longer supported by a maternalist ethic that advocates homemaking and childrearing, welfare—now in blackface—surveils, polices, and punishes black families for the economic despair that has resulted from globalized economic restructuring, post-industrializa-tion, and the retrenchment of affirmative action and, moreover, for their flawed adherence to the dictates of bourgeois heteronormativity.[45]

Welfare has become a punitive state apparatus that monitors and regulates the sexual and reproductive activities of black people. Its reform hinges on removing black women from home spaces and placing them in positions of menial labor rather than on effectively purging structural inequities that main-tain racial poverty. The overhaul of welfare under the Clinton administration effectively limited stipendiary support to growing families; restricted allow-able timeframes for families to receive public assistance; disqualified con-victed drug felons from receiving welfare altogether; and required women with children older than one to enter the labor force, whether as skilled or unskilled laborers or as unpaid Work Experience Program (WEP) workers.[46] As the federal government ceded its role in the centralized administration of public assistance, it granted states the power to fund and implement pro-grams that would reduce the nation's welfare rolls at the local level. Without federal oversight, the programmatic exploitation and marginalization of Afri-can American women proliferated as various states implemented policies to force impoverished black mothers off welfare and into severely underpaid janitorial and domestic labor.[47]

The intensification of poverty in black communities precipitated by civil rights retrenchment, as exemplified by the history of welfare reform I have sketched, assumes centrality in African American women's narrative of incest, which focus generally on the obliteration of black families in the current period. A strident condemnation of welfare reform pervades Push. In a strik-ing scene, for example, Precious considers her social worker's recommenda-tion that she quit school, terminate her welfare usage, and secure employment as a home attendant. The assumption underlying this recommendation is that there is some social inadequacy or criminal propensity that disqualifies Pre-cious from public support. As a teenage single mother, she is (presumably) guilty for her iteration of the so-called sexual deviations of blackness. As a welfare recipient, she is guilty (apparently) of detracting from the hard-won sustenance of the ordinary taxpayer. The removal of welfare support from Precious and her child would function, then, as redress for her supposed crimes, as would her continued impoverishment. Precious contemplates:

> If I'm working twelve hours a day, sleeping in people's houses like what
> Rhonda usta do, who will take care of Abdul? The ol white people had her
> there all day and all night, "on call," they call it. But you only get pay for 8

hours (is the other 16 hours slavry?) so that's 8 x $3.35 = $26.80 dollars a day, but then you is not really getting that much cause you working more than eight hours a day. You is working 24 hours a day and $26.80 divided by 24 is $1.12. Rhonda say ol bitch would ring a bell when she want Rhonda in the night. Home attendints usually work six days a week. I would only see Abdul on Sundays? When would I go to school? Why I gotta change white woman's diaper and then take money from that and go pay a baby sitter to change my baby's diaper? (121)

Precious interrogates the efficacy of welfare-to-work policies that foreclose educational possibilities for unskilled women and that displace mothers as primary caregivers. Precious is mindful of the similarity between a home attendant and a domestic worker. As a conscientious parent, she prefers serving as her small child's primary caretaker and perceives that a paid babysitter would not likely offer the same quality of care. After calculating the wages for a full-time home attendant, she assesses that the forced termination of her participation in welfare to procure her labor as an underpaid domestic worker would signify a virtual refigured enslavement. In other words, Precious smartly intuits that welfare reform initiatives such as WEP and workfare—which require African American women to perform arduous and largely uncompensated labor and which do not result in any notable improvement in material or economic positioning—dangerously approximate the conditions of U.S. slavery and, in so doing, present a sanitized reinstallation of it.

Sapphire's overall criticism of state agencies and public-service apparatuses is twofold. On one hand, state agencies fail to serve the country's most vulnerable populations because of inherent, historical, and systemic biases against black people, women, the poor, and the undereducated, among others. On the other hand, these agencies fail because their policies and protocols preclude human(e) intervention and therefore disallow effective, affective responses to people in crisis. Some cases in point: after she delivers her baby at age twelve, Precious is informed that the child has Down syndrome, the genetic defect resulting from its incestuous heredity. Although she is too young to even comprehend the extremity of her child's disability, Precious sobs:

I crying for ugly baby, then I forget about ugly baby, I crying for me who no one never hold before. Daddy put his pee-pee smelling thing in my mouth, my pussy, but never hold me. I see me, first grade, pink dress dirty sperm stuffs on it. No one comb my hair. Second grade, third grade, fourth grade seem like one dark night. Carl is the night and I disappear in it. And the daytimes don't make no sense. Don't make no sense talking, bouncing balls, filling in between dotted lines. Shape? Color? Who care whether purple shit a square or a circle, whether it purple or blue? What difference it make whether gingerbread house on top or bottom of the page? I disappears from the day. (18)

Despite her illiteracy and the purported mental ineptitude that preserves it after years of public education, Sapphire equips Precious with a sharp intellect and an equally strong moral compass. What starts as grief for a disabled child becomes a lament of personal history and familial impairment that is transformed ultimately into an indictment of urban public school education. Precious does not receive adequate care at home. Her mother does not do her hair, bathe her, or wash her clothes. Her father exploits the full capacity of her sexual use without regard for her age and without even the ruses of affection that at times accompany incest. This domestic life constitutes Precious's nighttime existence. During the day, at school, Precious is re-victimized by extreme institutional neglect. Her teachers ignore her, continue their lessons, promote her despite all evidence of devastating abuse by her parents and despite her inability to focus, to remember, to speak. Precious recognizes and mourns her social undesirability even as she is aware of her corporeal utility. This is the conundrum of her existence as an embodied black woman. She is profoundly usable, profitable, enjoyable even (primarily to her father) but somehow still without value: no one holds her.

The hospital where Precious's two children are born is an equally deficient public-service site. Even though she delivers her father's child as a preteen, she is sent back home where her jealous mother nearly kills her and her father continues to rape her. When Precious returns to the hospital after the birth of her second child four years later, seeking protection from her parents and suitable housing for herself and her newborn, she is informed coldly by the nurse on duty, "Lots of people get out hospital wlf no place to go. . . . You not so special" (77). She is then sent in a van with other homeless people to the decrepit armory, where she and her newborn sleep on a plastic-covered mattress surrounded by criminals, prostitutes, mentally ill clients, and drug abusers. Ms. Rain's response to Precious's plight is starkly different from that of the nurses and the social workers who are also familiar with her narrative:

I can tell by Ms. Rain face I'm not gonna be homeless no more. She mumbling cursing about *what* damn safety net, most basic needs, a newborn child, A NEW BORN CHILD! She going OFF now. Rhonda come in behind her. No class, all Each One Teach One is on the phone! They calling everybody from Mama to the mayor's office to TV stations! Before this day is up,

Ms. Rain say, you gonna be living somewhere, as god is my witness. As GOD is my witness! (79)

As a part-time instructor at an adult learning center, Ms. Rain is neither formally required nor especially equipped to procure safe, suitable housing for Precious. Ms. Rain is motivated to do so by what might be considered a compassionate but appropriate reaction to Precious's predicament; she follows the unspoken, quotidian rules that govern humane sociality and ethical citizenship. Ms. Rain prioritizes Precious's basic need for housing over the ordinary events of the day. She cancels class, invites her students to assist their colleague, and uses all routes and resources available to her to help Precious find a home.

In the midst of her impassioned denunciations, and presumably when speaking to various agency administrators and state officials, Ms. Rain appropriates the rhetoric of public service and of welfare reform. She decries the "safety nets" that have been established supposedly to prevent members of the urban underclass from slipping further into destitution and social malaise but that nonetheless fail the most vulnerable citizens. Ms. Rain's membership in and placement at the intersection of various underrepresented and underserved communities—she is, again, a black lesbian poet—allow her to communicate from the incontrovertible position of *experiential* authority. Exploiting fully her employment in a community-based institution to assist Precious, Ms. Rain models the behavior befitting those in public service. She feels and does what Precious's previous teachers, guidance counselors, social workers, doctors, and nurses *should have* done. Moreover, Ms. Rain demonstrates the determination, creativity, and self-empowerment that members of underserved communities must exercise to salvage themselves, their families, and community members from the manifold crises that assault everyday urban black life.[48]

Push promotes an ethos of self-love and communal self-reliance that resonates strongly with black nationalism. However, Sapphire destabilizes the excessive phallic authority awarded to black men under black nationalist philosophies that propagate standardized models of racial solidarity and heterosexuality. Black nationalism is represented most strongly in the figure of Louis Farrakhan, whose speeches teach Precious about African American enslavement and give her a language within which to conceptualize the interrelation among structural racism, poverty, and black familial impairment. Precious recognizes her incestuous relationship with her father as violent and violating only after hearing Farrakhan's discussion of rape on the slave plantation:

"Farrakhan say during slavery times the white man . . . take any black woman he want and if he feel like it he jus' gone and do the do on top of her even if her man there. This spozed to hurt the black man even more than it hurt the woman getting rape—for the black man to have to see this raping" (68). Even as he is presented as an admirable proponent of racial uplift, Farrakhan's marginalization of African American women's experience and his unqualified endorsement of resurgent black patriarchy are clearly problematic.

In its textual construction, Farrakhan's vision of racial redemption and political progress is flawed because it disallows diversity and multiplicity within the black racial context. He is presented as an apologist for black men's sexual predation, which, he implies, African American men learned at the hands of offending white slave masters. His energetic support of hetero-patriarchal couplings entirely excludes alternative sexualities. Throughout the novel, Ms. Rain embodies a challenge to the masculinist and heterosexist underpinnings of black nationalism. In a poignant scene in which Precious declares her disdain for homosexuals, following Farrakhan, Ms. Rain crit-icizes homophobia : "Ms Rain say homos not who rape me, not homos who let me sit up not learn for sixteen years, not homos who sell crack fuck Harlem. It's true. Ms. Rain the one who put chalk in my hand, make me queen of the ABCs" (81). Ms. Rain acknowledges the sexual and racial harm that has be-fallen Precious; she also, however, recognizes that same-gender sexuality was neither cause of nor factor in any of it. An exemplar of the novel's political vision, Ms. Rain demonstrates the power of self-generated and self-deter-mined communal supports to address social crises and alleviate poverty in marginalized communities. Advancing a vision similar to James Baldwin's, Sapphire contests the exclusionary components of black nationalist politics, and in so doing, she opens a space for sexual and familial diversity within the African American cultural context.

The central drama of Push is Precious's acquisition of literacy. Sapphire deploys multiple textual techniques to mark her protagonist's evolution from an illiterate teenager who barely recognizes or properly sounds the alphabet to the poet whose stirring verse concludes the novel. Using uneven grammar, irregular syntax, phonetic spelling, and parenthetical translation, Sapphire reveals the intelligence and sentience of a protagonist whose personhood is demarcated (and distorted) by extreme textual obscenity and grotesque racial embodiment. Multiply troped, Precious Jones incarnates the many excesses and exclusions of familial dysfunction and racial poverty. Sapphire makes Precious's experiences a narrative of progress by tying her growing literacy and attendant self-articulation to the overall improvement of her life circumstances. As Precious acquires access to the written word, she gains the power to narrate her experiences from her own vantage point. In a poignant scene, for example, Precious's mother, enraged that her rapist husband has abandoned the family, threatens to kill Precious. She holds Precious responsible for her husband's repeated sexual violations and for the family's impoverished state. A mother for the second time and fearing for her life, Precious decides to escape her mother's home. She narrates, "I got new baby boy in my arms 'n she callin me bitch hoe slut say she gonna kill me 'cause I ruin her life. Gonna kill me wif her 'BARE HANDS!' It's like a black wall gonna crush down on me, nuthin' to do but run. . . . Once I'm outside the door I stop at the top of the stairs, look hard at her. She still foaming at mouf, talking about her husband I spoze to steal. I do tell her one thing as I going down the stairs. I say, 'Nigger rape me. I not steal shit fat bitch your husband RAPE me RAPE ME!'" (74). Precious's fear of her abusive mother is palpable and reasonable. After being severely neglected, sexually abused, and repeatedly beaten by her mother, Precious takes seriously the woman's murder threat. Precious's first act of defiance, of self-defense, is to leave home. She quietly absorbs her mother's depraved harangue and waits until she has safely exited the front door before risking a single utterance. In that moment, the "one thing" that Precious tells her mother is what happened to her. Precious's father, her mother's husband, raped her.

While the acquisition of language and narrative authority clearly functions in the psychoanalytic sense to help a victim overcome the traumatic legacy of sexual abuse, a broader social empowerment is made possible by Precious's textual self-authoring. It is this broader social empowerment that, I would argue, drives the novel's emphasis on literacy and literary production. Precious's recovery is about overcoming not simply sexual abuse but also racist social exclusion. I am therefore a bit less concerned here with how Precious's narrativization of her experiences supports her recovery from incest, physical abuse, and parental neglect. Even as I do not wish to minimize the power of narrative recollection and reconstruction to alleviate the disaster of sexual assault and parental abuse, I take this observation, in the psychoanalytic sense, as self-evident. What I will highlight here instead is the triumph of Precious's narration as it attains primacy as the legitimate record of her existence.

As a novel, *Push* is structured dialogically, composed of two intersecting but competing narratives: Precious's autobiographical account of her life and its official documentation in her "file." Throughout the novel, particularly in scenes set in public-service sites, Precious's person, history, and projected outcomes are configured solely in terms of her file. Before expelling her from school, for instance, the school's guidance counselor blames the poor academic performance and prior pregnancy that are recorded in her file. At the hospital, the doctors and nurses review Precious's file before treating her. Finally, advocating her termination from welfare, the social worker refers to and records Precious's slow educational progress in her file. In sum, Precious's file has tracked, surveilled, and interpreted the facts of her life from birth, abstracting her particularized identity into a set of disparaging statistics and familiar stereotypes.

Precious's newfound literacy and literary capability allow her to produce an alternative to the "official," state-generated record of her life. In repossessing the details of her life and imbuing them with her own recollections and perceptions, Precious wrests from state agencies the power to define her solely in terms of marginalized identity categories and to (over)determine her outcomes based on them. In a novel that advocates the development of local, community-based alternatives that can replace government machinery and ultimately limit the state's institutional control of impoverished black lives, Precious's first-person narration may be understood itself as an act of individual empowerment and communal (re)appropriation and thus as a *textual enactment* of Sapphire's protest.

The Way Forward

I conclude this chapter by analyzing a most peculiar deployment of the incest narrative, one which does not emphasize black intra-familial traumas but that nevertheless builds on Sapphire's critique of structural imbalances, as well as problematic reactionary nationalism. In the literary genre of science fiction, Octavia Butler depicts human destruction as the inevitable result of hegemony. By representing incest, she issues an additional productive critique of (racial) authenticity and homogeneity in oppositional liberation philosophies and identity-based political activism.[49] The depiction of incest in *Imago*, the last book of Butler's Xenogenesis series, slips easily beneath the radar. Unlike other narratives in which incestuous events tend to consolidate and to calibrate the text's entire meaning, incestuous occurrences in *Imago* seem peripheral to its main focuses. Literary incest in *Imago* is thus peculiar when considered alongside the realist depictions that appear in the other texts under consideration in this chapter.

The psychic toll of incest and the familial damage it evinces, for instance, are altogether absent. There is, furthermore, no overt attempt to track the historical U.S. enterprise of nation building via racial enslavement and civic exclusion. The novel offers only an oblique examination of U.S. racial history in light of familial paradigms. Because Butler's depiction lacks so many standard features of incest narratives, critics have not treated incest as a thematic concern of the novel or of the trilogy. While it differs in these important respects from other incest narratives, it remains nonetheless central to my examination of the ways in which incest reflects and allegorizes the U.S. racial dilemma. In *Imago*, Butler uses incest as a meaningful political allegory to promote a progressive racial politics that values increased group diversity and wider social inclusivity.

Before proceeding in my analysis, it is necessary first to give a brief synopsis of the trilogy. The Xenogenesis series, collected and retitled *Lilith's Brood*, relates the apocalyptic destruction of Earth and its occupation by an extraterrestrial species called the Oankali. The Oankali are interplanetary space scavengers of a sort who search for new species for a regenerative and reproductive gene trade. They discover Earth after it has been destroyed by nuclear war, repair it, and rescue the few remaining human survivors. In the first book of the series, *Dawn*, the Oankali hold the humans captive, mostly in suspended animation, on their ship for nearly three centuries while Earth is regenerated and made safe for human habitation. Once Earth is repaired, the Oankali colonize it. They select Lilith, the black female protagonist of *Dawn*, to awaken the other humans from their state of suspended animation, to teach them how to survive on the artificially restored Earth, and to encourage cooperative mating with the Oankali. For their part, the Oankali sterilize human beings who refuse gene trade (or forced miscegenation) with them, interrupt the chemical and hormonal attractions between humans, and make human sexual activity and reproduction impossible without their intervention. Lilith eventually becomes the unwilling first mother of mixed human and Oankali—called "construct"—progeny. Xenogenesis designates the conception of this new alien and human mixed species.

The second book of the series, *Adulthood Rites*, finds Earth increasingly fractured by perpetual discord between the Oankali and resistant, now infertile humans. The story narrates the kidnapping of Lilith's humanoid son, Akin, by resisters who mistake him for a human child and, as such, the promise of uninterrupted human reproduction. As he matures, Akin's construct identity becomes evident. He nonetheless grows to sympathize with resistant humans who face extinction for their refusal of gene trade with the Oankali. Under his adult leadership, resistant humans are given a colony on Mars, now fit for human habitation, and have their reproductive powers restored. They may never return to Earth. The final book of the series, *Imago*, portrays the discovery of a colony of fertile humans that has escaped Oankali's detection for much of Earth's occupation. A single human female, referred to by her descendents as "the Mother," managed to escape sterilization by the Oankali during their initial rescue. After being gang raped by human males, the Mother is impregnated and gives birth to a fertile fully human son. Required by her community to procreate for the survival of the human species, she mates with her son to produce four additional fertile human children. Generations later, members of the colony face extinction because, after years of inbreeding in a limited and overly specialized gene pool, their members are stricken with severe genetic disorders. It is the depiction of incestuous inbreeding that claims my focus in the concluding section of this chapter. As I argue, the depiction of incestuous inbreeding in Butler's vision contains a warning for programs of racial uplift, such as black nationalism, which idealize racial purity and promote racial standardization and race loyalty as the exclusive remedies to social conquest.

In the Xenogenesis trilogy, Butler re-creates and recasts in the genre of science fiction the origin story of African Americans, narrating a history of racial and cultural hybridity brought about through technologies of captivity, bodily exploitation, and the colonization of a homeland by strangers. The survival of the Oankali species depends on the absorption and expansion of human traits. Particularly generative for them are human cancers, which give the Oanlaki powers of bio-regeneration. It is important to note that, even though cross-species reproduction and *not* labor exploitation is the main objective of the Oankali, they treat all humans as objects to be absorbed, domesticated, enjoyed—or as women, as slaves.

The specters of both slavery and incest haunt the coerced group matings. The reproductive process typically involves a human male and female, a sibling Oankali male-and-female pair, and a third-gendered Oankali ooloi, who is said to be at once neither and *more than* male or female. Although they are viewed by humans as "some kind of male-female combination," the ooloi "were no such thing. They were themselves, a different sex altogether."[50] Despite their other-gendered status, the ooloi usurp the masculine role in reproduction by penetrating and repeatedly injecting their "substance" repeatedly into their female *and* male mates during mating rituals. After collecting and fashioning genetic material from all mates into construct offspring, the third-gendered ooloi implant the "fetus" into either a human or an Oankali female for growth. Assuming, if not subsuming, the male contribution to the reproductive process, the ooloi gain mastery over both social outcome and the symbolic order. Much of the objection to gene trade is, in fact, proffered by human males who conceive of group mating as sexual enslavement by a dominant and masculinized super-species.

Butler sets up a complex situation of conquest. To address it, she adopts an integrationist political philosophy that supports cooperative survival over heroic death, separatism, or extinction. This philosophy is exemplified not by humans, who have nearly destoryed their species and their planet using nuclear death technology, but by the Oankali. The technologically advanced Oankali subject humans to coerced reproduction to prevent Oankali extinction. Their survival depends on intimate contact, entwined becoming, genetic and cultural hybridization. In a poignant scene in *Imago*, Jesusa and Tomas, two deformed human descendents of the Mother, meet Lilith and her female Oankali mate, Ahajas. Together, Lilith and Ahajas are the mothers of Jodahs, the first construct ooloi and the protagonist of *Imago*. Ahajas explains to Jesusa and Tomas the Oankali vision of life and death. "Nothing is more tenacious than the life we are made of," she says. "A world of life from apparent death, from dissolution. That's what we believe in" (663). This position runs counter to the racist domination and masculine heroism that typify U.S. national culture, as well as oppositional (nationalist) liberation philosophies and struggles. Butler's imaginative retelling of New World slavery interrogates received African American history and critiques contemporary racial politics by troubling the facile dichotomy between totalized group villainy and totalized group victimization. Butler furthermore offers a strident condemnation of gender subordination and sexual violence, which she demonstrates to be pervasive among humans across cultures. In Butler's narrative schema, the tendency to dominate and to destroy is a human flaw, not a racial one per se.

Imago presents cultural hybridization not as an element or extension of conquest but as a necessary corrective to it. Notably, Butler's vision of species (read: racial) cooperation via miscegenation and integration is not an idealist posture but a pragmatist one. Butler advances cultural cooperation and hybridization as the most viable opportunity for group survival after conquest and colonization. Her political vision makes literal Stuart Hall's prediction that "the future belongs to the impure. The future belongs to those who are ready to take in a bit of the other, as well as being what they themselves are."[51] Butler thus repudiates a purist or nationalist politics and presents group Oankali and human reproduction as a metaphor for an operational social relation, asymmetric but mutually sustaining nonetheless. To cite an example, as Jodahs attempts to convince Jesusa and her human brother Tomas to mate with him, he enumerates the lifesaving benefits to her people:

"Our bodies please one another and depend on one another. We keep one another well and make children together. We—"

"Have children with my brother!" [Jesusa questions.] "Jesusa . . ." I shook my head. "Your flesh is so like his that I could transplant some of it to his body, and with only a small adjustment, it would live and grow on him as well as it does on you. Your people have been breeding brother to sister and parent to child for generations."

"Not anymore! We don't have to do that anymore!"

"Because there are more of you now—all closely related.

Isn't that so?" . . . "People had to do what they did in the past. Like the children of Adam and Eve. There wasn't anyone else." (636–37)

Jodahs describes a situation of integrated, interdependent biological and cultural expansion. Cross-species reproduction enables Oankali survival and propagation. Healing human disease and deformity pleases and empowers the Oankali. Humans are tremendously attractive to them for their flaws. Likewise, cross-species mating saves the fertile human colony from extinction by expanding its gene pool—that is, by expanding the biological, cultural, technological, and spatial resources available to it.

The mating of Jodahs, Tomas, and Jesusa is a mediated incestuous occurrence. To reiterate an earlier observation, the specter of incest haunts Oankali and human group reproduction, as two of the Oankali mates are a male-and-female sibling pair. This scene presents the first instance of group mating with a human pair. Jodahs seduces the female sister and brother:

"You're with me now." [He tells them.] I lay down and moved close against Tomas so that all the sensory tentacles on his side of my body could reach him. Linking into his was such a sharp sweet shock for a moment, I could not see. When the shock had traveled through me, I became aware of Jesusa watching. I reached up and pulled her down with us. She grasped as the contact was completed. Then she groaned and twisted her body so that she could bring more of it into contact with me. Tomas, not really awake yet, did the same, and we lay utterly submerged in one another. (642)

As noted, once humans mate with the Oankali, they are repulsed by direct physical contact with their human lovers. In this way, the Oankali appropriate control of human attraction and reproduction. In particular, the ooloi—Jodahs, in this case—is a seducer who hijacks the role of administrator and orchestrator of human sexual and reproductive activity. Jodahs's claim that there would be no direct physiological contact between his human mates is correct. The same cannot be said for sensual contact. In all of the previous scenes of group mating, particularly those involving Lilith in *Dawn*, human mates are keenly aware of each other and experience an intensification of their lovemaking by virtue of the ooloi's presence and neurochemical manipulations. Jodahs's presence mediates but does nullify the lovemaking between Jesusa and her brother. In a later scene, Jodahs illustrates this point clearly: "I took their hands, rested each of them on one of my thighs so that I would not have to maintain a grip. I linked into their nervous systems and brought them together as though they were touching one another. It was not an illusion. They were in contact through me. Then I gave them a bit of an illusion. I 'vanished' for them. For a moment, they were together, holding one another. There was no one between them" (646). I call attention to the incestuous relation between human siblings to elaborate my claim about Butler's politics of survival and social integration.

I would like to suggest that sibling incest functions here as a trace. In other words, Butler preserves a somewhat—but not dangerously—narrowed gene pool among these fertile humans to enact cultural retention in the midst of participatory cultural hybridization. As a construct ooloi, Jodahs is more human than his ooloi ancestors and thus his progeny will have more human characteristics. While refuting any requirement of absolute species (or racial) purity, Butler does not call for the dissolution of all species (racial) cohesion or communal integrity. Notably, as I examined extensively in chapter 3, nationalism embeds and elaborates the fiction of normative family. Even this renegade fertile colony has a creation story that centralizes parental roles in social reproduction. Butler's depiction of mediated sibling incest—a corrective to deforming inbreeding—repudiates the patriarchal sovereignty embedded in both father–daughter incest and nationalism.

My analysis in this chapter sprawls across four novels to end with Butler in appreciation for her conciliatory deployment of sibling incest toward reparative ideological, aesthetic, and material ends. Butler negotiates black nationalism's separatist ideals to imagine an inclusive, egalitarian future. In *Imago*, racial cohesion is enacted not through patriarchal legitimation or the father's sovereignty but via the metaphor of sibling love. The sibling invocation of "Brother" and "Sister" commonly used in colloquial address among practitioners of black nationalism acquires meaningful resonance—the name for compatriots in the truest sense—in Butler's careful juxtaposition of cultural retention and meaningful integration. In her construction of sexual (always inevitably social) alliances that are both incestuous and cross-species, Butler offers a usable alternative societal model to one in which categories of difference—including race, ability, and gender—are exploited to sustain social hierarchies. In Butler's futuristic, fictive interpretation of the U.S. racial dilemma, both the conquerors and the victims of conquest work to evade the binds of history. In so doing, both manage to survive, and they nearly achieve democracy.

Complementing other depictions that I have explored in this chapter, Butler depicts incest to work through daunting contemporary social dilemmas. Toni Morrison, Gayl Jones, and Sapphire depict father–daughter incest to challenge reinvigorated heteropatriarchal imperatives, to interrogate black nationalism's legacy and utility in the post-civil rights era, and to demonstrate the tenacity of racial asymmetries in the putatively post-racial period. Notably, even at the moment of this writing, neither the new millennium nor the election of the nation's first black president has guaranteed the extension of ordinary protections or the basic entitlements of citizenship to black women and children in the United States. The decades since the legislative triumph of the Civil Rights Act of 1964 have been marked instead by a reinvigoration of racism, the popularization of white ethnocentrism, the increased militarization of urban spaces and national borders, the curtailment of the most basic civil liberties, disparate destitution, and the continuous denial of rights and resources to the most vulnerable members of the U.S. society—namely, poor women and children of color.

Literary incest powerfully critiques structural asymmetries that keep women and children of color at the economic and sociopolitical bottom. Literary incest, moreover, challenges the ideal of the heteropatriarchal family and its rhetorical, cultural, and political signification as the cornerstone of both U.S. nation building and black survival. Indicting family members as the simultaneous perpetuators of sexual harm and of a most transgressive mode of loving, incest bespeaks personal and social damage that is rooted insidiously in beginnings. Because desire dawns for those touched by incest in an originary moment of invasion from which neither identity nor desire can thereafter be wholly disengaged, incest figures the pained commingling of unpredictable and contradictory movement. In this way, and as demonstrated in my reading of Jones's *Corregidora*, incest becomes the striking but fitting metaphor for the psychic and social dynamics of American slavery—understood here as the systematic and maximal exploitation of black potentiality (by compatriots) for white subjective and national development via the *intimate* home space and *violent* home life of the slave plantation.

In all four novels discussed in this chapter, incest analogizes the devastating and very nearly deranging violences of American modernity on black subjects, hinting at the integral place of black subjecthood and black subjection in the project of New World formation. Contemporary literary incest, then, might be understood as the start-of-the-twenty-first-century literary counterpart to lynching in turn-of-the-twentieth-century black writing: as a way to narrate the misshapen world, as a way to name a certain mechanism for keeping specific people decidedly unfree in an environment of excessive license. In contemporary narratives of incest, however, unlike in the lynching narrative, black women and girls are made central to the narrative of raced existence.

Indeed, representations of incest in contemporary African American women's writing reveal ruinous failure on multiple levels of social life, marking in particular the continued effect of racism in an era in which race supposedly no longer matters. Portraying the sexual abuse of children in fiction, contemporary black women writers trace the frustration of convoluted, awful beginnings; the seeming impossibility of a way forward, or a way out; what can feel like the last days on Earth, or of Earth itself; and how so many things of (New World black) beauty come from an original period of horror from which the future must be crafted. By offering alternative models of self-conception and of humane social relations—through, for example, the entwined survival of hybrid human-aliens, Pecola's girlfriend narrators, the ethical imperatives of Ms. Rain's classroom, and Ursa's recollecting song—these contemporary incest novels also direct us to fragile but possible avenues of personal, political, ethical, and national repair.

Conclusion

Michael Jackson, 1958–2009

As I was in the final stages of completing the first draft of the manuscript for this book, the unthinkable happened—although I had not been aware of the unthinkability of this event until after its occurrence: Michael Jackson died. And so began for me an interesting process of mourning a celebrity(!) and a contemplation of the meaning of this mourning. This was not my first confrontation with the work of mourning the dead or of grappling with the inexorable finality of death itself. I have suffered the terrible loss of beloved family members. And one of my best friends died on my twenty-first birthday, an experience that so strained and obsessed me that I wrote my college senior thesis about death in American literature and submitted the essay as my writing sample for graduate school.

Michael Jackson's death was different from the death of a loved one, although to be sure, he was the beloved of many who had never laid eyes on him. Because I had never met him and could not even imagine his fleshed existence, his death did not reach me as the death of a *known* person. It was not, in other words, pronounced or plagued by an ensuing permanent absence. In fact, no bodily erasure marked Michael Jackson's passing. Rather, his departure was immediately followed by global fascination and a sensationalized spectralization of both his iconized self and his unexpected departure. There was, in fact, a marked proliferation in Michael Jackson's presence, as his countenance, music, voice, and famed dancing saturated visual media. With the exception of frequent updates about the coroner's findings and images of his sobbing relatives, associates, and fans, there was actually nothing to certify or to concretize in me that this man had left the world, in a way, never to return.

My own mourning fascinated me, particularly the element of anger. I was outraged by the circumstances of Jackson's death mere weeks before his comeback/final curtain call, and I was outraged by much reportage on his life after he died. Many people claimed to know *something* about this enigmatic man. I was enraged by nearly every biographical tidbit that was reported—his humble beginnings, his familial relationships, his physical and psychological ailments, the number of his plastic surgeries, his preferred drug cocktails, his musical ambitions, his sexual preferences, the "true" parentage of his children. It was all fallacious, I thought; it had to be. Most of us cannot speak authoritatively or resolutely about ourselves, our parents, our children, or the people who share our beds. Why were associates, reporters, and commentators so confident about the details they disclosed or the assumptions they, in fact, propagated? What about the inevitable privacy of each and every human? What about the mystery of a deliberate and consummate performer? And what can be known, in truth, about a person whose entire persona is constructed (at times by his own deliberate manufacturing) and *always* mediated by salacious, carnivorous media? What is it about celebrity, and perhaps about blackness itself, that creates such false and intrusive intimacy?

These questions led to others, more relevant here: How is Michael Jackson's embodied iconicity similar to or different from the general legibility of embodied blackness? Why and how does desire come to function as part and parcel of legible blackness and of racial fetish and as a welcome escape from both? Michael Jackson's death reminded me of the precarious, temporary inhabitance of any body versus the tenacity of racial fantasy, and it broke my heart. My upset as I reflected on the passing of (perhaps) the most famous human being of my lifetime, an African American, it turned out springs from the same sources that prompted the writing of this book. Thus, the conclusion that wraps up my study consciously wrestles with the death that interrupted, disrupted even, the wrapping up.

As an agent and as a product of (black) American expressive culture, Michael Jackson signified racial blackness importantly, if peculiarly. The ever changing and now forever absented landscape of his body bore some of my/our collective shadows and some of my/our collective fantasies. With his usual, remarkable acumen in U.S. cultural affairs, James Baldwin predicted the direction Michael Jackson's life would take, and in his last published essay he warned:

> The Michael Jackson cacophony is fascinating in that it is not about Jackson at all. I hope he has the good sense to know it and the good fortune to

snatch his life from the jaws of carnivorous success. He will not swiftly be forgiven for having turned so many tables, for he damn sure grabbed the brass ring, and the man who broke the bank at Monte Carlo has nothing on Michael. All that noise is about America, as the dishonest custodian of black life and wealth; the blacks, especially males, in America; and the burning, buried guilt; and sex and sexual roles and sexual panic; money, success and despair. . . .

Freaks are called freaks and are treated as they are treated—in the main, abominably—because they are human beings who cause to echo, deep within us, our most profound terrors and desires.[1]

Baldwin anticipated that Michael Jackson's outrageous success and celebrity (one element of his apparent "freakishness") would lead eventually to his demise.

Michael Jackson was, as Baldwin implies, a mediated and saturated repository of uniquely American longings and hopes and horrors and frailties. In an article for the *Huffington Post*, Rebecca Walker offers an astute consideration of Michael Jackson's utility as a culturally manufactured projection—or, as Greg Tate calls him, "our mirror."[2] Walker recalls:

[His] nose narrowed too much, and the ever-lightening skin grew hard to stomach. The lawsuits began to surface, one after another, and then the trial and the faces of the young boys with sorrowful tales of abuse. I sat transfixed before the television and trolled the Internet for sordid news. I watched, ridiculed, judged and tried to hold on to the unsullied image of the man I met. But the stage had been set. Michael's life was already one giant Rorschach. I sat on the sidelines with my popcorn, projecting hope and desire, fantasy and fear onto his increasingly frail body, waiting for the next set. . . .

Michael Jackson is dead? . . . Dead? I groped to put it in context, to read the moment, to see what it meant for him, but perhaps more importantly, what it meant for me. A part of me was dying, I decided. The part that hoped Michael could survive the tremendous burden he carried, that I carried. The part that held the memory of his precious innocence: my precious innocence.[3]

In Walker's description, Michael Jackson's "innocence" was hers. And it was ours. But of what was he *innocent*?

In his later years, Michael Jackson was often condemned for his body's morphing effects; he moved into and seemingly out of race, into and seemingly out of gender. Michael Jackson's corporeal mutations (whether the result of a degenerative autoimmune illness or the cosmetic surgeon's scalpel or both) were riveting because they revealed the seemingly intractable aptitude of bodily demarcation to make identity legible, and then they rendered *those same* anatomic markers null and void. Innocent of what, then? Whether in his mind-boggling pop-culture significance, his recordbreaking musical genius, or his Guinness World Record-noteworthy philanthropy, Michael Jackson defied limits and the logic of limits. Quite possibly, then, he made black people feel innocent of (or perhaps liberated from) the manifold failings that have been ascribed to our category of humans. He effectively, in Tate's brilliant summation, "erase[d] the erasure."[4]

One of the most effective erasures produced by Michael Jackson was a definitive link between his race and his sexuality. Twice married to women yet described alternately as homosexual, asexual, pre-sexual, and pedophiliac, Michael Jackson demonstrated none of the *commonly* referenced sexual excesses of black Americans. Or, to put it another way, he did not exemplify in the collective imaginary the brutish, hyperactive, degenerate, irresponsible sexuality so often attributed in discursive treatments and pop-culture portraits to African Americans. Nonetheless, even as Jackson's performance of black embodiment resisted and in moments refuted the sexual excesses of the black, it also contained and signified them.

Notably, to this day no attempt to bring Michael Jackson's sexuality into public purview—whether by virtue of his own provocative crotch-grabbing dance routines or a very public trial for child molestation of which he was exonerated—has succeeded in making scrutable, in making *known*, Michael Jackson's erotic life. Because of the fundamental elusiveness of sexuality (despite historical attempts to define and demarcate it), it is quite possible that the most famous human being in the world, the person onto whom entire nations have projected dreams, found privacy in the refuge of desire. This would seem to be the point then—and the most viable, achievable outcome. I am reminded here of Judith Butler's contention, "The task will be to consider this threat and disruption [of the abject] not as a permanent contestation of social norms condemned to the pathos of perpetual failure, but rather as a critical resource in the struggle to rearticulate the very terms of symbolic legitimacy and intelligibility."[5] The abject comprise those marginalized people who, by virtue of their perceived *essential* difference, have been relegated to the periphery of the normative sociality. Nonetheless, by occupying the space within and yet defining the boundaries of normative subjectivity and sociality, the abject embodies a threat to the established social schema and provides a rich source of sociopolitical, economic, national critique. Given the impossibility of totalized refutation, racialized subjects may productively undermine, obscure, and reroute what their existence has come to signify in the dominant imagination. This, it seems to me, is necessary not only to lessen the psychic injury of pathological ascription but also to resist the social, political, and material stratification that is enabled and sustained by virtue of it.

This brings me to my final comments on the study I have pursued throughout these pages. The spectacular, highly visible, and fantastical—that is, the public—character of embodied blackness grants it a level of iconicity. Because of the seeming immutability of racial difference, with its vexing tendencies to inspire desire and repulsion, exclusion and fixation, sexuality functions in African American literature and expressive culture, as I imagine it did in Michael Jackson's life: as a place of concealment and of imaginative (re)construction. Despite African Americans' history of sexualized racial conquest, and despite the ideations of moral and sexual debauchery that to this day accrue to blackness, sexuality constitutes a usable space for reflection and transformation. I am not thinking here of specific sexual acts; I am thinking instead of the exercise of individual will, the enactment of pleasure, the recovery from personal and collective trauma, the political refiguration of racialized identity, and the construction of a literary tradition.

Illuminating precisely how producers of African American expressive culture have mined the resources of transgressive erotic representation, this book offers an alternative reading of the black American literary tradition and makes a new case for its development. Representations of sexual divergence in black literary and cultural products do not simply mimic or reflect sexual practices and patterns among black people. Operating as the locus of desire and (often) of injury, sexuality functions now—and has always functioned—in black American literature as both optic and analogical tool for conjuring the manifold crises that plague black life and for imagining a way beyond them. During slavery, under a totalizing regime of domination, sadomasochism figures prominently in African American writing to represent the internal operations of slavery and its sadistic social and performative requirements. As such, sadomasochism both dramatizes the despair of stolen personhood and presents strategies for redefining agency and autonomy. During the post-Reconstruction era, lynching emerged as a powerful trope for figuring the solidification of whiteness through state-sanctioned racism and extralegal forms of racial terrorism. Lynching exposes, even as it perpetuates, the charade of black emancipation. During the civil rights era, literary representations of interracial romance presented idealized versions of interracial cooperation and anticipated the tranquil domestic space of a racially unified nation. The turn to black homocrotic love in the late era of black power, specifically in the work of James Baldwin, imagined a self-sustaining black community that could accommodate difference, an avowal of black humanity and political solidarity that did not require racial proscription. Finally, in the late twentieth century, incest appeared repeatedly in the writing of prominent black women authors. Literary depictions of incest speak to racism's profound and incessant injuries to black women and children, epitomizing the disintegration of the black family under the pressures of the legislative retrenchment of civil rights, reinvigorated black patriarchy, dwindling communal supports, negligible economic resources, and urban decay.

Looking closely at the main periods in African American experience—slavery, post-Reconstruction, civil rights and black power, and the post-civil rights era—this study demonstrates the ways in which specific tropes of sexual difference become dominant during specific periods to represent and redress the unique challenges of that moment. By traversing the entire history of black American literary production, I have endeavored to unearth the longstanding and deliberate use of the metaphorics of sexual transgressivity that, when read closely and particularly, reveal the psychodynamics of particular racial injuries, typify or transform generic conventions in black literary forms, and sketch the social crises and political aspirations of specific historical periods. This book presents a unique lens for reading the history of African American letters, one that radically centers sexual non-normativity as its predominant, driving mode of representation. In undertaking this work, I have sought to illuminate the potential of transgressive sexuality to create a representational structure that expresses the longings of African Americans to achieve individual and collective freedom. In so doing, I offer this book in the service of redirecting African American literary and cultural studies into more innovative and subtle examinations of race, transgression, subordination, abjection, and maneuvers of resistance.

Notes

Introduction

1. Foucault, *The History of Sexuality*, 103.
2. Ross and Rapp, "Sex and Society," 53.
3. Somerville, *Queering the Color Line*; Stoler, *Race and the Education of Desire*; and the monumental collection *Black Queer Studies: A Critical Anthology*, edited by E. Patrick Johnson and Mae G. Henderson, revise historical accounts and offer a new critical language for analyzing racialized sexualities and the place of sexuality in racial design. Harper, *Are We Not Men*; Holland, *Raising the Dead*; and Muñoz, *Disidentifications* centralize gender as they examine the interrelation of sexuality and race in light of the political aspirations and cultural productions of marginalized populations. Ferguson, *Aberrations in Black*; Reid-Pharr, *Once You Go Black*; and Stockton, *Beautiful Bottom, Beautiful Shame* offer some of the richest analyses of black identity, intellectual history, and cultural practice through the lens of abjection, drawing on methodologies derived from sociology, historiography, queer theory, and literary inquiry. Crossing a wide spectrum of disciplinary locales, these pathbreaking texts leave their imprint here. I place my study within this rich intellectual community to announce both its debt and what I hope will be its contribution.
4. Hortense Spillers, "All the Things You Could Be by Now, If Sigmund Freud's Wife Was Your Mother, 378, says it adroitly: "The individual in the collective traversed by 'race'—and there are no known exceptions, as far as I can tell—is covered by it before language and its differential laws take hold. It is the perfect affliction, if by that we mean an undeniable setup that not only shapes one's view of things but demands an endless response from him. Unscientific in the world of 'proofs,' governed by the inverted comma, unnatural and preponderant in its grotesque mandates on the socius, 'race' is destiny in the world we have made."
5. For readings on the continuing significance of race to making and preserving American identity, culture, and political economy, see Lubiano, *The House That Race Built*. Howard Winant writes, "Throughout U.S. history, racial conflicts con-

tinually shaped and reshaped the categories into which identities—all identities—
were classified": Winant, "Racial Dualism at Century's End," 87. Further, James
Baldwin, whose life work informs much of the work I do here, is quoted in Richard
Goldstein, "'Go the Way Your Blood Beats,'" saying something much to this effect. He asserts that the "sexual question comes after the question of color; it's
simply one more aspect of the danger in which all black people live" (180). I agree
wholeheartedly with both commentators.

6. Since the early 1990s, the term "queer" has been considered a more inclu-
sionary term by scholars of sexuality than the labels "homosexual," "gay," and
"lesbian," which designate more or less concrete identities based on specific sexual practices. This point is made quite clearly, for example, in the inaugural 1993
issue of the journal GLQ: A Journal of Lesbian and Gay Studies and by many leading
queer theorists, including Carolyn Dinshaw, Lisa Duggan, David Halperin, Anna-
marie Jagose, and Michael Warner. The term "queer," it is believed, undermines
the rigidity of a strict homosexual–heterosexual divide and couples analyses of
sexuality with considerations of race, class, ethnicity, religion, gender, and other
identity categories. For many, the deployment of the term "queer" is both an intellectual and a political exercise in eschewing boundaries, including disciplinary
ones.

7. Again, I invoke "queer" to represent the agential non-heteronormative, socially nonconformist subject in the celebratory sense of the usage "queer is by
definition *whatever* is at odds with the normal, the legitimate, the dominant. There
is nothing in particular to which it necessarily refers. It is an identity without
essence. 'Queer' then, demarcates not a positivity but a positionality *vis-à-vis* the
normative": Halperin, *Saint Foucault*, 62. I am cautious, though, to recall that in the
decade and a half since the term's adoption in academic and activist circles, its
political utility has come under question. As an umbrella term that articulates a
postmodern positionality, it has acquired a universalizing logic that, when used
haphazardly, may fail to account for the specific and varied experiences of the
oppressed. To deal with this, I generally locate queer more firmly on the outcast or
outsider side of the insider–outsider social divide, not always necessarily straddling or destabilizing it. Moreover, I link queerness explicitly with racialized identity, even when sexual desire and sexual practice are conspicuously heteronormative. As I argue later, there is always already something queer about blackness—and
something queer about desiring blackness. Thus, although not uncomplicatedly,
this study takes queer and black as mutually referencing, mutually reinforcing
terms.

8. A number of historical occurrences in the twenty-first century require us to
thoroughly reconsider racial experience. The election of the nation's first black
president is, of course, an unprecedented event that carries tremendous symbolic
significance. Regardless of the genuine political and material advancements that
marginalized peoples experience by virtue of this presidency, the psychic and cul-

tural implications of a black man's election to the presidency are powerful for the nation's inhabitants, regardless of color. In addition, the 2000 census included categories for biracial and multiracial citizens, effectively ending the one-drop rule. The increased presence of African-descended immigrants from the Caribbean and Africa is another consideration when thinking about twenty-first-century definitions of blackness in the U.S. context. No longer do expanding notions of blackness exclusively mean taking on a diasporic approach to conceiving and studying blackness. While I am aware of these contingencies and thus the diversity of experiences among black people in the United States, I am also highly attuned to continued social and material disparities that may be attributed to race, even to the residue of slavery, segregation, and Civil Rights retrenchment. Inadequate education, substandard housing, disproportionate incarceration, joblessness, malnutrition, inferior health care, and high morbidity rates continue to plague a large proportion of working-class and impoverished black Americans. For more on this point, see Kelley, Yo Mama's Disfunktional!; Roberts, Killing the Black Body; Wilson, Cities and Race; Wilson, The Truly Disadvantaged.

9. Gleason, "Voices at the Nadir," 27

10. Hale, Making Whiteness.

11. Two relevant books on racial definition and its relation to the visual and visibility are Seshadri-Crooks, Desiring Whiteness, and Wiegman, American Anatomies. Seshadri-Crooks writes, "The meanings we attach to racial identity, as stereotypes or as cultural history, [are] structurally contingent, culturally inconsistent, and ontologically incoherent. Racial identity seeks or locates its consistency on a different level—not meaning but visibility": Seshadri-Crooks, Desiring Whiteness, 27. For the uses of photography in black American liberation movements, including the resignification of lynching imagery, see Raiford, Imprisoned in a Luminous Glare.

12. Siobhan Somerville provides a useful genealogy of the development of discrete sexual categories in light of scientific racism and racial terrorism at the turn of the twentieth century. She argues convincingly that the obsession with racial difference and its rigid legislative regulation provided the ideological and legal framework for the emergence and taxonomy of (alternative) sexual identities. She asserts, "The formation of notions of heterosexuality and homosexuality emerged in the United States through (and not merely parallel to) a discourse saturated with assumptions about the racialization of bodies. These assumptions and the heightened surveillance of bodies demanded a specific kind of logic, which . . . gave coherence to the new concepts of homo- and heterosexuality": Somerville, Queering the Color Line, 4; emphasis added.

13. Ibid., 43. In The History of Sexuality, Michel Foucault gives an account of the transformation of aberrant sexual behavior into the constitutive basis for identity in the late nineteenth century.

14. I must note here that visualizations of the sexual outlaw do not reference

race exclusively. They rely also on gender and class. In the case of gender, sexual alterity is considered determinable also through the index of (maladapted, inappropriate) gender performance, as in the founding theory of the sexual invert, and through the register of class—in terms of upper-class debauchery or lower-class depravity.

15. Somerville, *Queering the Color Line*, 9.

16. Two essays that have been particularly instrumental to my thinking about the centrality of race, gender, and sexuality in eugenics discourse and imperialist efforts are Briggs, "The Race of Hysteria," and Stepan, "Race and Gender."

17. Duggan, *Sapphic Slashers*, is an extensive case study of the murder of Freda Ward by her former lover Alice Mitchell in Memphis, Tennessee, in 1892. Using newspaper accounts of the crime and trial, Duggan examines in depth how reportage of the crime helped to create a cultural narrative that marginalized and pathologized lesbians. She also demonstrates that the murder of Ward and other such case studies supported the burgeoning field of sexology. Duggan's book brilliantly connects the murder trial to Ida B. Wells's crusade against lynching.

18. I believe that feminist work in the academy has led to a general understanding of this principle. Nonetheless, excellent sources to review for in-depth treatment of the gendered implications of the mind–body divide include Butler, *Gender Trouble*; de Beauvoir, *The Second Sex*; Gallop, *The Daughter's Seduction*; and Irigaray, *This Sex Which Is Not One*.

19. Until recently, much scholarship on black familial patterns has tended to depict the matrifocal black family either as pathological for its divergence from the dominant cultural ideology and formation or as a viable alternative that nonetheless adhered to the ideological requirements of patriarchy. In other words, the household headed by a woman was presented as a necessary adaptation of the nuclear, patriarchal family as the result of enslavement and structural oppression, not as a preferred familial arrangement among some black women. Recent research, however, shows that since the post-Reconstruction era, black women have opted for matrifocal families that rely on extended kinship networks over possible poverty and gender subjugation in marriages to black men. For more on this point, see Frankel, *Freedom's Women*; Hill, *Black Intimacies*; Hine and Thompson, *A Shining Thread of Hope*. Shirley Hill argues, "Slavery had fostered a freedom from the strictures of gender and family conventions; moreover, it had disabused [black women] of idealized notions about the sanctity of marriage and womanhood and taught them that love, sexuality, childbearing, and family need not be tied to legally sanctioned contacts": Hill, *Black Intimacies*, 78.

20. Gilman, "Black Bodies, White Bodies," provides a useful record of medical journals that featured such studies. These theories were espoused by medical practitioners and sexologists such as Theodor Billroth, A. J. B. Parent-Duchatelet, and Cesare Lombroso.

21. Ibid., 248.

22. Ibid., 237.

23. Stember, *Sexual Racism*, 126–27.

24. Ibid., 127.

25. Ellis admits that there is no factual evidence of the preponderance of homosexuality within particular racial and ethnic groups. The absence of factual knowledge, however, is not taken as evidence against his claims about the preponderance of homosexuality among black people. Instead, he claims that it was due to the modesty and propriety of early European travelers and settlers who refused to document extensively perverse sexual practices as they encountered them during their centuries-long efforts at global conquest: Ellis, *Sexual Inversion*.

26. Freud, *Three Essays on the Theory of Sexuality*, 17. I must note that terms such as "primitive" and "savage" do not automatically or exclusively signal African or African-descended people. For centuries, however, these terms have designated people of color all over the world, including African people. Patricia Hill Collins contends that "European colonial powers redefined Africa as a 'primitive' space, filled with Black people and devoid of the accoutrements of the more civilized cultures. In this way, the broad ethnic diversity among the people of continental Africa became reduced to more generic terms such as 'primitive,' 'savage,' and 'native'": Collins, *Black Sexual Politics*, 98.

27. Ellis, *Sexual Inversion*, 8.

28. Ibid., 19, n.3.

29. Gilman describes Hegel's characterization of black people as childlike, an "infantile nation" of people generally incapable of abstract thought, moral development, self-government, or cultural advancement: Gilman, "The Figure of the Black in the Thought of Hegel and Nietzsche," 142. He traces the development of this concept and alludes to its lingering currency. It is useful to think of Freud in concert with other important European intellectuals, as these are the so-called architects of modern thought, and their various philosophies are still often regarded as truth in various academic disciplines.

30. There is a dearth of research on the particular significance of black women's asses in popular media culture. Many critics and spokespeople who deal with the bodily exploitation of black women in advertising, music, videos, and movies focus on their denigration, their objectification. Very little attention is paid to the implication of this ass-centricity on wider conceptions of black sexuality and identity, including for black men who are pathologized for desiring black women's purported excessive asses. Of notable exception is Hobson, "The 'Batty' Politic."

31. The Hottentot Venus is the popular name given to Sarah Baartmann, a woman who was taken from her native home in the Cape Colony in South Africa to London in 1810, where she was placed on display in the Piccadilly Circus. Of particular interest to voyeurs and scientists alike were her supposed genital anomalies, elongated labia, and steatopygia, or abnormally large butt. Baartmann was later exhibited in France. After her death at twenty-five, two autopsies were con-

ducted, the first by Henri Marie Ducrotay, and the other, more infamous and notable, by Georges Cuvier. Cuvier recorded his findings in *Memoires du Museum d'Histoire Naturelle* in 1817. Baartmann's brain, skeleton, and genitals were preserved and kept on display in France until 1974. Baartmann's story and legacy have been important to numerous scholars theorizing the intersection between race and sexuality, race and representation, and sexuality and slavery. For more on this, see Sharpley-Whiting, *Black Venus*. Many other scholars, including Donna Haraway, bell hooks, Anne McClintock, and Nancy Stepan, have written about Baartmann's enduring significance in the conception and visualization of racial, gendered, and sexual difference in the contemporary West.

32. Gilman, "Black Bodies, White Bodies," 238.

33. I refer to pivotal twentieth-century sociological studies of black life, such as Clark, *The Dark Ghetto*, and Frazier, *The Negro in the United States*. These studies share a main recognition of slavery's disfiguring legacy on black families and hold slavery responsible for purported deficits in character and behavior that result in multigenerational poverty and other self-perpetuating failures in black families and communities.

34. Patricia Hill Collins uses the terms "social blackness" and "socially blackened" to designate the marginalized group(s) of any society. Recognizing the fundamental role of New World slavery in establishing (imperial, transatlantic, technological) modernity, she treats black oppression as a powerful referent for experiences of labor exploitation, social denigration, pervasive sexual and reproductive violence, near ethnic extermination the world over: Collins, *Another Kind of Public Education*, 141.

35. Moynihan, *The Negro Family*, 30.

36. Ibid., 5; emphasis added.

37. Ferguson, *Aberrations in Black*, 119.

38. Moynihan, *The Negro Family*, 39.

39. Ibid., 42.

40. Ferguson, *Aberrations in Black*, 122.

41. Moynihan, *The Negro Family*, 42.

42. Ibid., 48.

43. Connolly, *Identity/Difference*, 64.

44. A number of recent texts treat the relationship between whiteness, white family structuration, and the consolidation of wealth in America. For capable, nuanced examinations, see Hale, *Making Whiteness*; Lipsitz, *The Possessive Investment in Whiteness*; Roediger, *The Wages of Whiteness*.

45. Loftus, "Speaking Silence," 29.

46. Reid-Pharr, "Tearing the Goat's Flesh," 373.

47. Lubiano, *The House That Race Built*, vii.

48. A strong example of the juxtaposition, and even opposition, of stereotypes can be found in the case of the mammy and the jezebel. As a supposedly unattractive and asexual female figure, the mammy is maternal while concealing not only

her agency as a sexual being but also the possibility of her desirability and, therefore, the history of her sexual abuse. Similarly, the rapacious sexuality of the jezebel unfits her for motherhood and therefore conceals her reproductive exploitation and the wrongful dispossession of her children.

1. "The Strangest Freaks of Despotism"

1. Hurston, *Their Eyes Were Watching God*, 16.

2. Orlando Patterson describes the disregard that masters had for slave unions and family units as a condition of slavery itself. The inability to determine or claim kinship networks was part and parcel of the condition of enslavement. He describes that in "slaveholding societies slave couples could be and were forcibly separated and the consensual wives of slaves were obliged to submit sexually to their masters; slaves had no custodial claims or powers over their children, and children inherited no claims or obligations to their parents": Patterson, *Slavery and Social Death*, 6.

3. A common feature of slave narratives is their depiction of the sexual depravity of slave masters. For example, despite grappling with their inability to fulfill nineteenth-century ideals of womanhood as a result of their sexual and reproductive exploitation, such well-known slave narrators as Mary Prince and Louisa Piquet allude to the rampant and violent sexual abuse on the plantation to decry the widespread moral corruption of slavery. In this chapter, I have chosen to read in depth specifically Douglass's and Jacobs's narratives to illustrate an early-nineteenth-century connection between enslavement, sexual criminality, and the later codification of homosexuality. I believe that Douglass's and Jacobs's narratives, more than others, embody and influence these constructions and connections.

4. Winthrop Jordan takes this quote from the travel narrative of an Englishman writing about Africa in the early seventeenth century: Jordan, *White over Black*, 33. Many European explorers recorded their impressions of Africans and commented on their skin complexions, their relative bodily exposure, and their marriage customs to suggest that Africans were lewd and libidinous. For additional textual references, see ibid.

5. Western attitudes about African sexuality in the seventeenth and eighteenth centuries are explored in Fredrickson's *The Black Image in the White Mind* and Jordan's *White over Black*.

6. A number of historians of sexuality have written thorough accounts of how scientific racism and the practice of comparative anatomy, specifically in studies of genitals and women's buttocks, helped to produce definitions of sexual difference according to a racial axis. Excellent additional sources for further examination, particularly in terms of the theoretical origins in polygenesis during slavery, are Stepan, *The Idea of Race in Science*, and Wiegman, *American Anatomies*.

7. Hartman, *Scenes of Subjection*, 23.

8. Much scholarship on slavery addresses its repressive statutes and the brutal measures by which they were enforced, particularly in terms of restrictions on slaves' speech and self-assertion. For more on this, see Bay, *The White Image in the Black Mind*; Blassingame, *The Slave Community*; Patterson, *Slavery and Social Death*; Stampp, *The Peculiar Institution*.

9. Andrews, "Slavery and Afro-American Realism," 65–66.

10. In *The Body in Pain*, a text I believe is of critical importance to understanding the operations and effects of embodied black slavery even though it does not take it up specifically, Elaine Scarry postulates, "Physical pain does not just resist language but actively destroys it." Pain is not only unrepresentable in language, but it also effectively nullifies its use. "Pain," she writes further, "centrally entail[s], require[s], this shattering of language": Scarry, *The Body in Pain*, 4–5.

11. Toni Morrison writes in *Beloved* that Ella's "puberty was spent in a house where she was shared by father and son, whom she called 'the lowest yet.' It was 'the lowest yet' who gave her a disgust for sex and against who she measured all atrocities. A killing, a kidnap, a rape—whatever, she listened and nodded. Nothing compared to 'the lowest yet'": Morrison, *Beloved*, 256.

12. This passage was taken from Dorothy Sterling's *We Are Your Sisters*, a compilation of slave women's testimonies taken from memoirs, slave narratives, and Works Progress Administration interviews. While the rendering of the slave's testimony in dialect is problematic and has the effect of minstrelizing slaves' experience and the slave herself, I have chosen not to "translate" the passage. I reproduce it as it was recorded in the original collection and later added to Sterling's book.

13. In her exposition on the gendered patterns of slavery in *Ar'n't I a Woman?*, Deborah Gray White explains that in the seventeenth century and early eighteenth century, slave women were purchased primarily for their field and domestic labor. The added emphasis on their reproductive labor developed in the mid-eighteenth century as slave owners increasingly saw the benefits of exploiting the womb functions of slave women to replenish and increase their slave property.

14. Foucault, *The History of Sexuality*, 27.

15. Ibid.

16. Ibid., 42–43.

17. Halperin, *One Hundred Years of Homosexuality*, 50.

18. By referencing the propagation of white generations, I refer to antimiscegenation laws that originated as slave codes meant to regulate the sexual intermingling of black men and white women and to ensure the safe transfer of wealth, citizenship, and property to whites only. Similarly, the ban on homosexuality originated in statutes against sodomy to prevent the proliferation of non-reproductive sexual practices in the eighteenth century and nineteenth century. Prohibitions on same-sex and interracial desire support the evolution and multiplication of the white family as both the basic unit of capitalist acquisition and a microcosm of the

U.S. nation. Both interracial sexuality and homosexuality were believed to be sexual deviations characterized by the choice of improper sexual objects, whether racial or gendered.

19. In writing that sexual violence is a main feature in the characterization of sexual deviance, I refer not only to the association of sexual difference as criminality as in, for example, Elisabeth Young-Bruehl's explanation that "homosexuals were, according to sexological consensus, abnormal beings, perverts, *deviants whose acts were criminal*": Young-Bruehl, *The Anatomy of Prejudices*, 29. But I also refer to the belief that sexual excesses (legible on the body in, for example, the oversize clitoris of the lesbian and the black woman or the large penis of the black male rapist) revealed a propensity for violent activities and social degeneracy. Sexual deviance did not come under the exclusive purview of medicine and psychology. It also came under the jurisdiction of the courts, where laws were made to prevent "sodomy" and "miscegenation," among other things, and to punish people who engaged in such practices.

20. Ibid., 34.

21. "Natal alienation" is a term coined by Orlando Patterson to describe the process by which slaves were barred from meaningful connections to both forebears and descendants. Slaves were thereby deprived of those essential connections and personal histories out of which identities are formed and individuals emerge as recognizable entities in the social body.

22. Carby, *Reconstructing Womanhood*, 31.

23. Hartman, *Scenes of Subjection*, 3; emphasis added.

24. Douglass, *Narrative of the Life of Frederick Douglass*, 397.

25. Ibid., 398.

26. Ibid.

27. Gwen Bergner makes the point that, despite the fragmenting effects of institutional slavery on the kinship structures of enslaved families, "Douglass's triad of master-aunt-self nonetheless composes a 'family' unit in slave society": Bergner, *Taboo Subjects*, 31. She postulates that the whipping scene is formative and instructive for the young Douglass, as it is by virtue of witnessing sexualized violence against his aunt that Douglass "learns his place" in the social order of the slave plantation: ibid.

28. Douglass, *Narrative of the Life of Frederick Douglass*, 396.

29. Spillers, *Black, White, and in Color*, 155.

30. For more on this, see Sundquist, *To Wake the Nations*; Wald, *Constituting Americans*. Eric Sundquist writes, "Douglass could not escape the conclusion that he was born of an act . . . that had no legal sanction, gave him no name or inheritance, and stripped him of the genealogical property of manhood": Sundquist, *To Wake the Nations*, 94. Although he does not go so far as to suggest that Douglass was born of an act of rape, Sundquist does agree that the circumstances of his birth in slavery sufficiently render him an unintelligible being, a non-person in effect.

31. Jordan, *White over Black*, 151–52; emphasis added.

32. Ibid., 155.

33. Katz, *Gay/Lesbian Almanac*, 146.

34. Halperin, *One Hundred Years of Homosexuality*, 15–16.

35. Spillers, "Mama's Baby, Papa's Maybe," 474.

36. Jordan, *White over Black*, 141.

37. JanMohamed, "Sexuality on/of the Racial Border," 109.

38. Jacobs first references the sexual abuse of male slaves by masters and overseers earlier in the narrative in her discussion of the rampant sexual abuse of young slave girls. She laments, "No pen can give adequate description to the all-pervading corruption produced by slavery": Jacobs, *Incidents in the Life of a Slave Girl*, 55. She also decries the absolute authority that masters and overseers claimed over the sexual and reproductive lives of enslaved women and girls and asserts that "in some cases they exercise the same authority over the men slaves": ibid.

39. The possibility of pleasure in pain is not precluded in the slave context, although to emphasize it is beyond the scope of my purpose in reading Jacobs's *Incidents* here. For more on the ways in which contractual sadomasochistic performance can relieve painful associations among the trauma of sexual violence, social practices of domination, and the resultant compromise of felt desire, see Hart, *Between the Body and the Flesh*.

40. Jacobs, *Incidents in the Life of a Slave Girl*, 1.

41. Ibid., 3.

42. Ibid., 1–2.

43. Sánchez-Eppler, *Touching Liberty*, 95.

44. Jacobs, *Incidents in the Life of a Slave Girl*, 33.

45. White, *Ar'n't I a Woman?*, 41.

46. Jacobs, *Incidents in the Life of a Slave Girl*, 34.

47. Karen Sánchez-Eppler notes that this scene is a moment of "erotic domination" that comes close to a representation of rape in Jacobs's narrative. However, by writing that Jacobs "identifies sexual oppression less with any physical act than with the representation of the act," she does not pursue the argument that Mrs. Flint is herself guilty of sexual abuse: Sánchez-Eppler, *Touching Liberty*, 97. Instead, her interest lies primarily with the extent to which disclosure re-enacts Linda's suffering and therefore fails to provide an adequate solution for it.

48. In what has become an indispensable study of Jacobs's narrative strategies, P. Gabrielle Foreman argues that Jacobs "undertells" her sexual victimization and "encodes types and agents of sexual abuse to preserve her own authority as she simultaneously evokes sympathy from her readers": Foreman, "Manifest in Signs," 79. Jacobs's strategy of narrative concealment and partial disclosure requires the reader to attend to both what is said and what is simply insinuated to arrive at a full narrative of her—and other enslaved women's—experiences in slavery.

49. Spillers, "Mama's Baby, Papa's Maybe," 474.

50. Foreman makes the point that Mrs. Flint is "the sexual aggressor" in the scene even as she is subject to Jacobs's "narrative control. She is stripped of her usually protected status as a true woman and 'curiosity' excited, ears exposed, she is sexualized": Foreman, "Manifest in Signs," 79. Foreman's point is important. Even as Jacobs is victimized by Mrs. Flint's predatory sexual curiosity, Jacobs is the agent of Mrs. Flint's sexualization by giving her what she wants—that is, the specific details of her husband's sexual harassment. In so doing, Jacobs transforms her position from one of disempowered sexual target to agential author.

51. Jacobs, *Incidents in the Life of a Slave Girl*, 215–16.

52. Ibid., 216.

53. In one of the few critical treatments of this scene, Maurice O. Wallace describes Jacobs's portrayal of the unnamed slave owner as "showing all of the worst symptoms of sexual deviancy according to certain popular discourses of illness and health current in the United States from the 1830's to Freud in the twentieth century, discourses in which euphemisms like 'vice,' 'excess,' and 'dissipation' connote a pathological aberration from cultural norms of the human sexual economy": Wallace, *Constructing the Black Masculine*, 89. He acknowledges the extent to which Jacobs self-censors in her allusion to Luke's sexual abuse by his master, and he suggests that both personal decorum and nineteenth-century limits on public speech prevented her full disclosure. Her insinuative descriptions of sexually aberrant behavior on the plantation are, nonetheless, fairly easy to decode.

54. Austin, *How to Do Things with Words*.

55. Jacobs, *Incidents in the Life of a Slave Girl*, 216.

56. For a cogent and detailed discussion of white men's fraternity and its relation to sexuality and the nineteenth-century homosocial order obtaining in white men's privilege, see Sedgwick, *Between Men*. For an analysis of the same in the colonial period, see Nelson, *National Manhood*.

57. Jacobs, *Incidents in the Life of a Slave Girl*, 216.

58. Benjamin, *The Bonds of Love*, 55.

59. Dayan, *Haiti, History, and the Gods*, 192; emphasis added.

2. *Iconographies of Gang Rape*

1. For excellent expositions of the entanglement of sexual ideologies and racial hierarchy invoked in lynching, see Davis, *Women, Race, and Class*; Harris, *Exorcising Blackness*; Patterson, *Rituals of Blood*; Stephens, "Racial Violence and Representation"; White, *Rope and Faggot*.

2. Stephens, "Racial Violence and Representation," 655.

3. Judith Berzon argues, for example, that nineteenth-century African American authors deployed the "mulatto character in order to emphasize his [or her] superiority, to show white America that some blacks could succeed within the framework

established by the dominant white majority, and to attack American society for not recognizing the worth of some members of the non-Caucasian group": Berzon, *Neither Black nor White*, 52. In *Reconstructing Womanhood*, Hazel Carby insists that, in addition to attributing the values of white bourgeois society to members of the black community, biracial characters in early black American fiction provoked meditations on the history and anticipated future of race relations.

4. Davis, *Faulkner's "Negro,"* 135.

5. Sullivan, "Persons in Pieces," 498.

6. Friday, "Miscegenated Time," 41.

7. Barkan and Bush, *Prehistories of the Future*, 6.

8. Torgovnick, *Gone Primitive*, 8.

9. Hale, *Making Whiteness*.

10. Lott, *Love and Theft*, 6.

11. Ibid., 51.

12. North, *The Dialect of Modernism*, 61.

13. Prominent twentieth-century African American authors have made this point. For example, James Baldwin argued this point in several of his prominent essays, including "Many Thousands Gone" and "In Search of a Majority," both of which are included in his final collection of essays, *The Price of the Ticket*. See also Morrison, *Playing in the Dark*, for a discussion of prominent twentieth-century novelists who use tropes of racial blackness to substantiate the development of white characters.

14. Davis, *Faulkner's "Negro,"* 135–36.

15. Kristeva, *Powers of Horror*, 4.

16. Faulkner, *Light in August*, 33, 114. Page numbers for direct quotes from *Light in August* in the rest of this chapter are cited in parentheses in the text.

17. Friday, "Miscegenated Time," 49.

18. For more on how the failure to extend patriarchal recognition to black men has hampered their masculine development, see Ferguson, *Aberrations in Black*; Harper, *Are We Not Men?*.

19. Wiegman, *American Anatomies*, 90.

20. Fowler, *Faulkner*, 9.

21. A crucial component of the character of whiteness is its reliance on serviceable raced "others" whose particularity enables its emergence and prominence as "race-less." For more on this, especially its manifestation in American literature, see Morrison, *Playing in the Dark*.

22. Minter, *Faulkner's Questioning Narratives*, 7.

23. Irwin, *Doubling and Incest / Repetition and Revenge*, 33.

24. Watson, Jay "Overdoing Masculinity in *Light in August*, or, Joe Christmas and the Gender Guard," 161.

25. Ibid.

26. Somerville, *Queering the Color Line*, 35.

27. Ibid.

28. Bederman, *Manliness and Civilization*, 22.

29. John Duvall smartly elucidates the homoeroticism and homosexual panic that subtend Joe Christmas's murder and dismemberment. He writes, "A clear portrait of homosexual panic emerges . . . in Grimm's killing and castration of Joe Christmas. . . . But a homoerotic subtext is also at play in this moment": Duvall, "Faulkner's Crying Game," 62.

30. Harris, *Exorcising Blackness*, 23.

31. Wiegman, *American Anatomies*, 99.

32. For more on the representation of the black eunuch as the comforting diminishment of black masculine prowess and authority, see the chapter "Psychopathologies of Black Envy" in Gubar, *Racechanges*.

33. Lisa Duggan powerfully characterizes lynching as a melodrama that both racializes and reproduces a popular narrative of men's heroism and women's docility and purity that circulated in other cultural venues—namely, fiction and sensational journalism. She describes the melodrama as a "kind of Alice in Wonderland mirror world where everything appeared upside down and backward. . . . Race and gender in this mirror world were aligned through the device of the sexual triangle, with the white woman positioned as the passive object of desire. The male rivals were morally polarized, the black villain versus the white hero": Duggan, *Sapphic Slashers*, 20.

34. As much research has proved, most black men who were lynched were neither guilty of nor even accused of rape. Wells-Barnett, for example, lists some of the crimes for which African American men were routinely lynched, including burglary, arson, larceny, assault, and incendiarism: Wells-Barnett, *The Red Record*, 70–71.

35. Ibid., 8.

36. Ibid., 10.

37. McCullough, "Slavery, Sexuality, and Genre," 25.

38. For more on Putzi's reading of gender in Hopkins's *Contending Forces*, see "Raising the Stigma."

39. For more on the pervasive rape of black women in the post-Emancipation period, see Clinton, "Bloody Terrain"; Edwards, *Gendered Strife and Confusion*; Hodes, *White Women, Black Men*.

40. It is important to note that, for all of its despicable physical brutality, lynching functions primarily through its symbolism. As Ralph Ellison succinctly describes it, the victim of lynching is "forced to undergo death for all his group": Ellison, "An Extravagance of Laughter," 17.

41. Given the strictures of nineteenth-century feminine codes adopted and advocated by mainstream black society, black women could enter the public arena only by means of an outrage so extraordinary as to warrant their intervention, such as lynching. Sandra Gunning makes this point about Wells-Barnett, saying that

her decision to join the anti-lynching campaign was motivated by "her own high sense of virtue and morality": Gunning, *Race, Rape, and Lynching*, 81.

42. Wells-Barnett, *The Red Record*, 9.

43. I refer to the common conception since slavery that, given their lascivious natures, black women could not be raped. Darlene Clark Hine asserts that the refusal to recognize and redress the pervasive sexual abuse of black women in and after slavery entails "the reduction of black women to something totally undeserving of human consideration": Hine, *A Shining Thread of Hope*, 174.

44. For substantial analyses of the use of sentiment by nineteenth-century African American writers, see Carby, *Reconstructing Womanhood*; duCille, *The Coupling Convention*; Gunning, *Race, Rape, and Lynching*; Tate, *Domestic Allegories of Political Desire*.

45. For more on this, see the instructive essay "To Allow No Tragic End," in which Lois Lamphere Brown argues convincingly that Hopkins traffics in the tropes of sentimental fiction but subverts them to accommodate and narrate black women's experiences—namely, rape, the loss of black men's protection and provision, and single motherhood.

46. Hopkins, *Contending Forces*, 37. Page numbers for direct quotes from *Contending Forces* in the rest of this chapter are cited in parentheses in the text.

47. There is a general consensus among scholars that lynching was used to reinvigorate white men's mastery over black people. The gendered subjugation entailed in rape had the same effect. As Laura Edwards clearly articulates it, "White men . . . used rape and other ritualized forms of sexual abuse to limit black women's freedom and reinscribe antebellum racial hierarchies": Edwards, *Gendered Strife and Confusion*, 199.

48. Carby, *Reconstructing Womanhood*, 132.

49. Spillers, *Black, White, and in Color*, 68.

50. Cardyn, "Sexualized Racism / Gendered Violence," 722.

51. Ibid., 730.

52. Many critical race theorists and historians expound on the consolidation of whiteness among native and immigrant European Americans. An excellent study of this is Roediger, *The Wages of Whiteness*. For a powerful and elucidating account of whiteness as property among the propertied and property-less white Americans, see the seminal Harris, "Whiteness as Property."

53. It is important to note that racially motivated acts of violence proliferated in Northern cities, as well, and they had some of the same motivations as lynching. An overarching desire to maintain the racial schema that originated in slavery, shifting immigration and migration patterns, political and economic competition, and perceived increases in African Americans' resources and opportunities, drove white people all over the country to try to annihilate black people. For an in-depth exploration, see Bennett, *The Party of Fear*.

54. Goldsby, *A Spectacular Secret*, 21.

55. Harris, *Exorcising Blackness*, 22.

56. Yarborough, "Introduction," xxxiii.

57. For more on the tropes of sentimental fiction and their subversive elements, see Tompkins, *Sensational Designs*; Baym, *Women's Fiction*; Cott, *The Bonds of Womanhood*; Douglas, *The Feminization of American Culture*; Kelley, *Private Woman, Public Stage*; Samuels, *The Culture of Sentiment*.

58. Baym, *Women's Fiction*, 19.

59. Claudia Tate adeptly summarizes the marriage function of the black heroine of post-Reconstruction domestic fiction. She describes the heroine as "the authority of her own ego reformation as well as the instigator of similar reform in her community. The heroine uses both reason and compassion to select the proper mate to assist her in achieving her personal and communal ambitions. And, finally, the heroine defines as well as manages an ideal household for an upwardly mobile family, mediating prosperity between the individual self and the collective black community": Tate, *Domestic Allegories of Political Desire*, 141. Sappho becomes an exemplar of a new socially sanctioned and viable black womanhood by virtue of her redemption after rape and unwed motherhood, demonstrated by her fulfillment of the mother function and her marriage to Will Smith.

3. Desire and Treason

1. My hypothesis does not reduce desire merely to longing or aspiration. It incorporates the important element of choice, which is inextricably tied to desire and its fulfillment. In suggesting that midcentury African American writing grapples with personal and political desire manifestly, I do not mean to suggest that desires, and the crucial element of choice, have been altogether absent from the African American context. In fact, it is useful to reproduce here Robert Reid-Pharr's stunning, incredibly smart claim that people "have the ability to choose, to move if you will, even if not within conditions of their own making": Reid-Pharr, *Once You Go Black*, 7. Reid-Pharr reminds us that even under repressive regimes, human desire, will, agency, and choice (must) remain operable.

2. For an extended meditation on the empowerment goals of the civil rights movement in terms of personal freedom and collective racial affirmation, see King, *Civil Rights and the Idea of Freedom*.

3. Patricia Hill Collins explores the nearly oppositional meaning of freedom for black women and men in matters of cross-racial sex. She writes, "African American men were forbidden to engage in sexual relations with white women, let alone marry them. In this context, any expansion of the pool of female sexual partners enhances African American men's standing within the existing system of hierarchical masculinities": Collins, *Black Sexual Politics*, 262.

4. King, *Letter from the Birmingham Jail*, 79.

5. Reid-Pharr provides a brilliant exposition of the symbology of the house in

American and African American thought and cultural production: see Reid-Pharr, *Conjugal Union*.

6. Jay Martin Favor argues, for example, that when it comes to the construction of black identity, there exist "rules for the expression of sexuality that determine one's standing as a racial being": Favor, *Authentic Blackness*, 96.

7. hooks, "Love as the Practice of Freedom," 243.

8. Foster, "How Dare a Black Woman Make Love to a White Man!," 107.

9. Barry, "Same Train Be Back Tomorrer," 151.

10. Petry, *The Narrows*, 68–69. Page numbers for direct quotes from *The Narrows* in the rest of this chapter are cited in parentheses in the text.

11. Martin Japtok picks up on Ann Petry's astute understanding of the concept and operation of whiteness. He writes, "'Whiteness' imagines not merely the ownership of oneself and one's own capacities, but the untrammeled freedom to infringe on the liberties of those who are not 'white,' specifically in terms of their property, whether it be their persons, their capacities or their assets. In U.S. history, 'whiteness' has come to mean not merely liberty of persecution from others, but the ownership of other people's property or, indeed, of other people": Japtok, "A Neglected Study in 'Whiteness,'" 357.

12. Jenkins, *Private Lives, Proper Relations*, 14.

13. Drawing on Nietzsche's concept of the transvaluation of values, Eddie Glaude Jr. argues that African Americans embrace a "politics of transvaluation . . . as a reassessment of the 'blackness' in terms of its value for black lives and black struggle." He explains that the celebratory transvaluation of blackness can function as an orienting philosophy that "is conducive to the preservation and enhancement of black individuals and communities throughout the United States": Glaude, "Introduction," 5.

14. I make an obvious, if subtle, reference to the double binds of black women's identification in the U.S. cultural and political context. This bind, this positionality and all of its attendant effects is examined in Petry's portrayal of two very different, central black female characters: Mamie Prowther and Abbie Crunch.

15. For more on the propertied features of whiteness, see the seminal Harris, "Whiteness as Property." See also Lipsitz, *The Possessive Investment in Whiteness*; Roediger, *The Wages of Whiteness*.

16. I refer here to economic disinvestment practices, such as redlining, rental of substandard residences, and discriminatory lending, that create stark disparities in wealth and support de facto segregation in Northern cities. Extended studies of these practices in mixed-race urban communities are in Massey and Denton, *American Apartheid*; Zegeye et al., *Exploitation and Exclusion*.

17. Higginbotham, "The Problem of Race in Women's History," 132.

18. Notably, black feminist scholars have long recognized the centrality of masculine bearing to African American uplift ideology. bell hooks, for example, writes,

"The discourse of black resistance has almost always equated freedom with manhood, the economic and material domination of black men with castration, emasculation. Accepting these sexual metaphors forged a bond between oppressed black men and their white male oppressors. They shared the patriarchal belief that revolutionary struggle was really about the erect phallus": hooks, "Reflections on Race and Sex," 58.

19. Walker, "*After the Fire Next Time*," 230.

20. Many recent studies investigate Baldwin's vision of social equality and democracy in the U.S. context via his fictive depictions of the intersections of racial and sexual difference. Prominent among them are Balfour, *Evidence of Things Not Said*; Clark, *Black Manhood in James Baldwin, Earnest J. Gaines, and August Wilson*; McBride, *James Baldwin Now*, and the excellent essays collected therein; Ohi, "I'm Not the Boy You Want"; Shin and Judson, "Beneath the Black Aesthetic."

21. Williams, "Living at the Crossroads," 140.

22. Ferguson, *Aberrations in Black*, 85.

23. Ibid., 86–87.

24. Marisa Chappell and her colleagues offer a cogent explanation of the civic and political utility of respectability, particularly in terms of how it functioned to allay whites' fears of integration. They suggest that respectability comprised "a whole range of tactics—from confrontation, through accommodation, to separatism—to resist the full brutality of southern racism": Chappell et al., "Dress Modestly, Neatly . . . as if You Were Going to Church," 71. Espoused by black leaders and educators, including Booker T. Washington, respectability was meant "to protect blacks from the worst manifestations of racism by insisting that they shared with all decent white folks a staunch belief in the value of religion, thrift, hardwork [sic], education, civic duty, temperance, matrimony, and family": ibid.

25. Quoted in duCille, *The Coupling Convention*, 14.

26. Ibid.

27. Gayle Wald argues, for instance, "To maintain and/or secure sexual and gender respectability [is] a means of racial self-assertion": Wald, *Crossing the Line*, 18.

28. Williams, "Living at the Crossroads," 141.

29. My main purpose here is to note how black nationalist concepts mobilized standardized models of gender identity and familial organization. Still, I must take care to avoid discussing black nationalism in the reductive terms that have become common in the academy. Often, black nationalism is understood as the most defiant articulation of black empowerment. It was a movement that encouraged black economic independence, racial preservation, communal self-defense, and black cultural value. Nonetheless, it is now generally critiqued as a failure for the eventual commodification of black subversion in forms of popular cultural and for the tendency of black nationalist ideology to obscure the varied interests, experiences, and political investments of African Americans. For astute histories and

analyses of the black nationalist movement, see Glaude, *Is It Nation Time?*; Reed, *Race, Politics, and Culture*; Van Deburg, *New Day in Babylon*.

30. Stephanie Dunning provides a skillful explanation of this, writing, "Black nationalism mobilizes around the question of reproduction and the threat of extinction (or death). The historical precedents for the threat to the perpetuation of the black race are the middle passage and slavery. By invoking pathos around the suffering black (mostly male) body as a kind of psychic, and in many cases, physical, death, black nationalism gives emotional and historical support to its claims about the threat of white supremacy. . . . The solution to the threat of extinction, then, is to exist and continue to exist. The call for the reproduction of the nation through heterosexual and mono-racial sex is one that is fundamental to black nationalist politics": Dunning, "Parallel Perversions," 97.

31. Harper, *Are We Not Men?*, 68.

32. James Dievler makes this point, citing Baldwin's claim that if he had not left the United States, he would have met the same tragic end as his friend Eugene, who killed himself in 1949 by jumping off the George Washington Bridge and on whom the character Rufus is based. He claims that Rufus "represents Baldwin before his departure for Paris . . . [while] Eric is the Baldwin who went to live in France": Dievler, "Sexual Exiles," 169.

33. Baldwin, *Another Country*, 20–21. Page numbers for direct quotes from *Another Country* in the rest of this chapter are cited in parentheses in the text.

34. My suggestion here is that music functions dually for Rufus as art and as connective tissue to his black cultural roots. For more on this point, see Moten, *In the Break*. In terms of the significance of black popular culture, including music, as a vehicle for inculcating black cultural values and expressing black longings, see Watkins, "Black Is Back."

35. Shin and Judson, "Beneath the Black Aesthetic," 251.

36. Glaude, *In a Shade of Blue*, 11.

37. For more detailed information about Baldwin's strong emotional and activist response to the upheaval in the United States during the Civil Rights and Black Power eras and to the assassination of some most prominent and formidable proponents, see Campbell, *Talking at the Gates*; Leeming, *James Baldwin*; Porter, *Stealing the Fire*; Weatherby, *James Baldwin*.

38. Scott, *James Baldwin's Later Fiction*, 132.

39. Ross Posnock writes that Baldwin's "homosexuality intensified his differential vision, making him acutely sensitive to the artifice of bounded identity": Posnock, *Color and Culture*, 231. Baldwin's felt sense of difference as a queer person within the black community heightened his awareness of individual existence beyond fixed identity categories, racial or otherwise. Although I maintain that Baldwin was committed to African American survival and was an avid celebrant of black American culture, his commitments to equality and inclusivity applied to the country as a whole, as well as to the black community within it.

40. Baldwin, *Just Above My Head*, 27–28.

41. For an in-depth exploration of this point, see Ross, "Beyond the Closet as a Raceless Paradigm."

42. Baldwin, *The Fire Next Time*, 7–8.

43. Walker, *After the Fire Next Time*, 220.

44. Lynn Orilla Scott deals expertly with this point in *James Baldwin's Later Fiction*. It is worth noting that the decline in Baldwin's popularity and (putatively) in the quality of his writing (particularly his fiction) is often attributed to his shift from an integrationist politics based on the redemptive capacity of human love and shared existence to a complete rejection of white supremacy characteristic of black nationalism. For his waning confidence in the promise of American democracy and for his increasing discursive alignment with a new generation of black activists in the 1960s and 1970s, Baldwin was criticized for his "pessimism." I would argue that Baldwin was not pessimistic, although he was increasingly concerned with the survival of African Americans who not only remained the targets of horrendous exclusionary policies but also lost their leading spokespeople to murder.

45. Baldwin, *The Fire Next Time*, 8.

4. Recovering the Little Black Girl

1. Als, *The Women*, 15.

2. Ibid.

3. Ibid., 16.

4. Ibid., 17.

5. Ibid., 15–16.

6. Candice Jenkins's postulation is illuminative here. "Jezebel reappears in contemporary American culture through such figures as the 'welfare queen,' the image of an unwed and unfit black mother feeding voraciously on white tax dollars and producing hordes of literally and figuratively 'dangerous' black children": Jenkins, *Private Lives, Proper Relations*, 11.

7. Barnes, *Incest and the Literary Imagination*, 3.

8. See Awkward, "The Evil of Fulfillment"; Breau, "Incest and Intertextuality in Carolivia Herron's *Thereafter Johnnie*"; Doane and Hodges, *Telling Incest*; Richardson, *Black Masculinity and the U.S. South*; Spillers " 'The Permanent Obliquity of an In-(pha)lliby Straight.' "

9. Froula, "The Daughter's Seduction," 622–23.

10. Hine, "Rape and the Inner Lives of Black Women in the Middle West," 912.

11. Hartman, *Scenes of Subjection*, 544.

12. Ibid., 543.

13. Saidiya Hartman presents an astute examination of the manifold "ruses of seduction" deployed by members of the slave-owning class to maneuver their enslaved subjects into positions of acquiescence and to co-opt their subversive

acts. Some of these ruses supported the system of concubinage that undergirded the institution: see ibid.

14. For more on how institutional slavery obliterated enslaved families, see Bay, *The White Image in the Black Mind*; Blassingame, *The Slave Community*; Patterson, *Slavery and Social Death*; Stampp, *The Peculiar Institution*; White, *Ar'n't I a Woman?*.

15. Spillers, "Mama's Baby, Papa's Maybe," 217.

16. Spillers, " 'The Permanent Obliquity of an In(pha)lliby Straight,' " 233.

17. Spillers, "Mama's Baby, Papa's Maybe," 218.

18. Doane and Hodges, *Telling Incest*, 5.

19. Jones, *Corregidora*, 59. Page numbers for direct quotes from *Corregidora* in the rest of this chapter are cited in parentheses in the text.

20. Hirsh, "Family Pictures," 8.

21. Rushdy, "Relate Sexual to Historical," 274.

22. Despite important distinctions between pedophilia and incest, I link the two terms here for their similar procedures and effects, noting that incest in many ways is an intensification of pedophilia in process and impact. Incest subordinates the child's need for parental adoration and affection to the adult's patently perverse sexual desire for the child or simply for someone smaller, weaker, and more vulnerable. In cases of both pedophilia and incest, once the child's desire for adult approval and appreciation has been perverted into a manifestly erotic excitation, the erotic element endures. I do not mean to suggest that the exploited child (or slave) is necessarily agential or collusive in her violation. In fact, Judith Lewis Herman and Lisa Hirschman argue, "Consent and choice are concepts that apply to the relationships of peers. They have no meaning in the relations of adults and children, any more than in the relations of freemen and slaves. . . . But just as, in those cases, the final decision rested with the master, the final choice in the matter of sexual relations between adults and children rests with the adult": Herman and Hirshman, *Father–Daughter Incest*, 27. I agree wholeheartedly with their claim. I also wish to emphasize here the persistence and proliferation of incestuous desire once it has been aroused.

23. Breau, "Incest and Intertextuality in Carolivia Herron's *Thereafter Johnnie*," 92.

24. A number of recent analyses of the novel treat its anachronistic narrative structure to show linkages between nineteenth-century slave life and contemporary cycles of abuse: see, e.g., Li, "Love and the Trauma of Resistance in Gayl Jones's *Corregidora*"; Rushdy, " 'Relate Sexual to Historical.' "

25. Rushdy, "Relate Sexual to Historical," 285.

26. For an extended study of Jones's engagement with black nationalism, including the writing conventions of the black nationalist aesthetic, see Dubey, *Black Women Novelists and the Nationalist Aesthetic*.

27. I refer to pivotal twentieth-century sociological studies of black life, such as Clark, *The Dark Ghetto*; Frazier, *The Negro in the United States*; and, of course, Moyni-

han, *The Negro Family*. These studies examine slavery's disfiguring legacy on black families and refer to the legacy of slavery to explain multigenerational poverty and other challenges faced by black families and communities. They all share the view that disasters of slavery have led to self-perpetuating cycles of pathological behavior in black communities.

28. Sielke, *Reading Rape*, 2.

29. Barnes, *Incest and the Literary Imagination*, 2.

30. Morrison, *The Bluest Eye*, 148. Page numbers for direct quotes from *The Bluest Eye* in the rest of this chapter are cited in parentheses in the text.

31. Gwin, "'Hereisthehouse,'" 318.

32. Ibid.

33. Awkward, "The Evil of Fulfillment," 193.

34. Willis, "Eruptions of Funk," 310.

35. Laura Mulvey observes, "The Lacanian 'symbolic order' rules by Name of the Father, defines the areas of circulation and exchange through which society expresses relations in conceptual, that is, symbolic, terms beyond the natural and experiential. Language, the universal, most sophisticate means of symbolic articulations, seals this process. Lacan mapped his concept of the symbolic on to Freud's concept of the Oedipal trajectory; access to the symbolic is achieved by crossing the frontier, out of the imaginary, the dyadic world of the mother and child into recognition of the Father's Name and Law. That is, out of body-based, maternal relationship into one created by social exchange, culture and legal taboos (of which the first, of course, is the incest taboo)": Mulvey, *Visual and Other Pleasures*, 165.

36. Ibid., 174.

37. My claim here contradicts that of a number of scholars who read Pecola's madness as a totalized psychological deterioration. In arguing that she has been restored to the realm of the imaginary, I am arguing that she has been reinstalled in the communion of (imagined) mother and beloved child, not relegated entirely to the space of social negation.

38. Sloooarov, *The Betrayal of the Urban Poor*, 10—11.

39. Kelley, *Yo Mama's Disfunktional!*, 95.

40. Helene Slessarev argues, "A true pledge to alleviate poverty would require a commitment to building structures of economic opportunity. Every economy has such structures, both formal and informal, designed to move each successive generation to a new level of economic security. In minority communities, these structures are often nonexistent or in acute disrepair, leaving the majority of residents without any real possibility of economic advancement. Given America's legacy of racial oppression, establishing structures of economic opportunity would entail more than just competent schools, career training, available employment, childcare and job referrals. It would require opening up the entire metropolitan labor market, which is now so geographically and occupationally stratified by race and class that poor minorities are confined to only a tiny fraction of the total job oppor-

tunities. It would include a commitment to eliminating all remaining forms of racial exclusion, even though they are not legally sanctioned": Slessarev, *The Betrayal of the Urban Poor*, 6.

41. Roberts, *Killing the Black Body*, 204.

42. See Fraser and Gordon, "A Genealogy of Dependency."

43. Sapphire, *Push*, 31. Page numbers for direct quotes from *Push* in the rest of this chapter are cited in parentheses in the text.

44. Doane and Hodges, *Telling Incest*, 125.

45. Shirley Hill makes the point that "black women are denigrated for their efforts to raise children without the help of the men who fathered them; moreover, the efforts to do so are seen as fostered by generous welfare policies. The controversy surrounding single mothers reveals our gendered assumptions about sexual morality, marriage, and family roles, and, when directed at black women, amplifies longstanding racial/sexual myths and stereotypes": Hill, *Black Intimacies*, 83.

46. The WEP program was a cornerstone in the transition from welfare to workfare. Purportedly designed to give welfare recipients work experience, it mandated full-time employment for workers who were compensated not with wages but with welfare stipends. Rather than alleviating poverty, WEP and other such reform initiatives further institutionalized it. For a more detailed description of welfare reform policies under Clinton, including the WEP program, see Kelley, *Yo Mama's Dysfunktional!*; Roberts, *Killing the Black Body*.

47. I must reiterate that some of the mandatory work programs do not ameliorate poverty but further institutionalize it. For example, as recipients of public assistance receive a stipend for full-time labor as janitors in recreational centers, parks, city department buildings, WEP jobs do not pay a living wage. They in fact save the city money by displacing sanitation workers. If the city hired these women as sanitation workers, the women would earn salaries in the tens of thousands of dollars annually. Such policies exploit destitute women who are often mothers, as well.

48. A new challenge for black feminist critique and work is to elucidate the complex relationship between individual agency and structural oppression. Revisionist historical and sociological research has tended to present a thriving, viable African American family structure to counter infamous claims of black cultural pathologies that perpetuate urban poverty, but these revisionist accounts may overemphasize the tenacity of race-based structural imbalances and unwittingly "camouflage human agency rather than revealing the fact that African Americans can and do make empowering effective, empowering individual choices": Hill, *Black Intimacies*, 14.

49. Wahneema Lubiano offers a deft explanation of the function of authenticity in black nationalist thought. "Authenticity functions within the terms of the economy as the way to counter what might otherwise be a possible destiny of cultural 'disappearance.' Claims of authenticity or criticism of its lack are the last defenses

against cultural imperialism. Cultural imperialism becomes the black nationalist cultural equivalent to actual imperialism (land seizure) because, lacking a homeland and sovereignty, culture is all we can call our 'own'": Lubiano, "Standing In for the State," 159. I am cautious to present an uncomplicated critique of authenticity in black nationalist thought. I do not in general support protocols of racial being and belonging for their potential exclusionary effects, but I stop far short of a wholesale condemnation of black nationalist politics and practice out of appreciation of their useful analysis of racism and their advocacy of African American independence.

50. Butler, *Imago*, 524. Page numbers for direct quotes from *Imago* in the rest of this chapter are cited in parentheses in the text.

51. Hall, "Subjects in History," 299.

Conclusion

1. Baldwin, "Here Be Dragons," 689.

2. Greg Tate, "Michael Jackson: The Man in Our Mirror," *Village Voice*, 30 June 2009.

3. Rebecca Walker, "The Untouchable Michael Jackson," *Huffington Post*, 11 July 2009.

4. Tate, "Michael Jackson."

5. Butler, *Gender Trouble*, 3.

Works Cited

Als, Hilton. *The Women*. New York: Farrar, Straus, and Giroux, 1996.

Andrews, William L. "The Representation of Slavery and the Rise of Afro-American Literary Realism, 1865–1920." *Slavery and the Literary Imagination*, ed. Deborah E. McDowell and William L. Andrews, 62–80. Baltimore: Johns Hopkins University Press, 1989.

Angelou, Maya. *I Know Why the Caged Bird Sings*. New York: Random House, 1969.

Austin, J. L. *How to Do Things with Words*. Cambridge: Harvard University Press, 1962.

Awkward, Michael. "'The Evil of Fulfillment': Scapegoating and Narrative in *The Bluest Eye*." *Toni Morrison: Critical Perspectives Past and Present*, ed. Henry Louis Gates Jr. and Kwame Anthony Appiah, 175–209. New York: Amistad, 1993.

Baldwin, James. *Another Country* (1962). New York: Dell, 1988.

——. *The Fire Next Time*. New York: Dial, 1963.

——. *Just Above My Head*. New York: Dial, 1979.

——. "Here Be Dragons." *The Price of the Ticket: Collected Nonfiction, 1948–1985*. New York: St. Martin's, 1985.

Balfour, Lawrie. *Evidence of Things Not Said: James Baldwin and the Promise of American Democracy*. Ithaca: Cornell University Press, 2001.

Barkan, Elazar, and Ronald Bush, eds. *Prehistories of the Future: The Primitivist Project and the Culture of Modernism*. Stanford: Stanford University Press, 1995.

Barnes, Elizabeth, ed. *Incest and the Literary Imagination*. Gainesville: University Press of Florida, 2002.

Barry, Michael. "'Same Train Be Back Tomorrer': Ann Petry's *The Narrows* and the Repetition of History." *MELUS* 24, no. 1 (Spring 1999): 141–59.

Barthes, Roland. *The Pleasure of the Text*, trans. Richard Miller. New York: Farrar, Straus, and Giroux, 1975.

Bay, Mia. *The White Image in the Black Mind: African-American Ideas about White People, 1830–1925*. New York: Oxford University Press, 2000.

Baym, Nina. *Women's Fiction: A Guide to Novels by and about Women in America, 1820–1870.* Ithaca: Cornell University Press, 1978.

Bederman, Gail. *Manliness and Civilization: A Cultural History of Gender and Race in the United States, 1880–1917.* Chicago: University of Chicago Press, 1995.

Benjamin, Jessica. *The Bonds of Love: Psychoanalysis, Feminism, and the Problem of Domination.* New York: Pantheon, 1988.

Bennett, David H. *The Party of Fear: From Nativist Movements to the New Right in American History.* New York: Vintage, 1990.

Bergner, Gwen. *Taboo Subjects: Race, Sex, and Psychoanalysis.* Minneapolis: University of Minnesota Press, 2005.

Berzon, Judith. *Neither Black nor White: The Mulatto Character in American Fiction.* New York: New York University Press, 1978.

Blassingame, John. *The Slave Community: Plantation Life in the Antebellum South.* New York: Oxford University Press, 1972.

Bondy, François. "The Negro Problem: A Conversation with James Baldwin." *Transition* 12 (1964): 1997.

Boykin, Keith. *One More River to Cross: Black and Gay in America.* New York: Anchor, 1996.

Breau, Elizabeth. "Incest and Intertextuality in Carolivia Herron's *Thereafter Johnnie.*" *African American Review* 31, no. 1 (1996): 91–103.

Briggs, Laura. "The Race of Hysteria: 'Overcivilization' and the 'Savage' in Late-Nineteenth-Century Obstetrics and Gynecology." *American Quarterly* 52, no. 2 (2000): 246–73.

Brown, Lois Lamphere. " 'To Allow No Tragic End': Defensive Postures in Pauline Hopkins's *Contending Forces.*" *The Unruly Voice: Rediscovering Pauline Elizabeth Hopkins,* ed. John Cullen Gruesser, 50–70. Urbana: University of Illinois Press, 1996.

Butler, Judith. *Gender Trouble: Feminism and the Subversion of Identity.* New York: Routledge, 1990.

——. *Bodies That Matter: On the Discursive Limits of Sex.* New York: Routledge, 1993.

Butler, Octavia. *Dawn.* Xenogenesis series. New York: Warner, 1987.

——. *Imago: Lilith's Brood.* New York: Warner, 2000.

Campbell, James. *Talking at the Gates: A Life of James Baldwin.* New York: Viking, 1991.

Carbado, Devon W., Dwight McBride, and Donald Weise, eds. *Black Like Us: A Century of Lesbian, Gay, and Bisexual African American Fiction.* San Francisco: Cleis, 2002.

Carby, Hazel. *Reconstructing Womanhood: The Emergence of the Afro-American Novelist.* New York: Oxford University Press, 1987.

Cardyn, Lisa. "Sexualized Racism / Gendered Violence: Outraging the Body Politic in the Reconstruction South." *Michigan Law Review* 100, no. 4 (February 2002): 675–867.

Carrigan, William, ed. *Lynching Reconsidered: New Perspectives in the Study of Mob Violence.* New York: Routledge, 2008.

Caruth, Cathy. *Unclaimed Experience: Trauma, Narrative, and History*. Baltimore: Johns Hopkins University Press, 1996.

Chappell, Marisa, Jenny Hutchinson, and Brian Ward. "'Dress Modestly, Neatly . . . as if You Were Going to Church': Respectability, Class, and Gender in the Montgomery Bus Boycott and Early Civil Rights Movement." *Gender in the Civil Rights Movement*, ed. Peter J. Ling and Sharon Monteith, 69–100. New York: Garland, 1999.

Chauncey, George. *Gay New York: Gender, Urban Culture, and the Making of the Gay Male World, 1890–1940*. New York: Basic, 1994.

Clark, Keith. *Black Manhood in James Baldwin, Earnest J. Gaines, and August Wilson*. Urbana: University of Illinois Press, 2002.

Clark, Kenneth B. *The Dark Ghetto: Dilemmas of Social Power* (1965). Middletown, Conn.: Wesleyan University Press, 1989.

Clinton, Catherine. "Bloody Terrain: Freedwomen, Sexuality and Violence during Reconstruction." *Georgia Historical Quarterly* (Summer 1992): 313–32.

Cohen, Cathy J. "Punks, Bulldaggers, and Welfare Queens: The Radical Potential of Queer Politics," *GLQ: A Journal of Lesbian and Gay Studies* 3, no. 4 (1997): 437–65.

Collins, Patricia Hill. *Black Sexual Politics: African Americans, Gender, and the New Racism*. New York: Routledge, 2004.

——. *Another Kind of Public Education: Race, Schools, the Media, and Democratic Possibilities*. Boston: Beacon Press, 2009.

Connolly, William E. *Identity/Difference: Democratic Negotiations of Political Paradox*. Ithaca: Cornell University Press, 1991.

Cott, Nancy. *The Bonds of Womanhood: Women's Sphere in New England, 1780–1835*. New Haven: Yale University Press, 1977.

Davis, Angela Y. *Women, Race, and Class*. New York: Random House, 1983.

Davis, Thadious M. *Faulkner's "Negro": Art and the Southern Context*. Baton Rouge: Louisiana State University Press, 1983.

Dayan, Joan. *Haiti, History, and the Gods*. Berkeley: University of California Press, 1995.

de Beauvoir, Simone. *The Second Sex* (1953), trans. H. M. Parshley. New York: Alfred A. Knopf, 1993.

Dent, Gina, ed. *Black Popular Culture: A Project by Michele Wallace*. Seattle: Bay Press, 1992.

Dievler, James A. "Sexual Exiles: James Baldwin and *Another Country*." *James Baldwin Now*, ed. Dwight A. McBride, 161–86. New York: New York University Press, 1999.

Doane, Janice, and Devon L. Hodges. *Telling Incest: Narratives of Dangerous Remembering from Stein to Sapphire*. Ann Arbor: University of Michigan Press, 2001.

Douglas, Ann. *The Feminization of American Culture*. New York: Alfred A. Knopf, 1977.

Douglass, Frederick. *Narrative of the Life of Frederick Douglass, an American Slave*. Reprinted in *Norton Anthology of African American Literature*, 2d ed., ed. Henry Louis Gates Jr. and Nelly W. McKay, 387–452. New York: W. W. Norton, 2004.

Doyle, Laura Anne. *Bordering on the Body: The Racial Matrix of Modern Fiction and Culture.* New York: Oxford University Press, 1994.

Dubey, Madhu. *Black Women Novelists and the Nationalist Aesthetic.* Bloomington: Indiana University Press, 1994.

duCille, Ann. *The Coupling Convention: Sex, Text, and Tradition in Black Women's Fiction.* New York: Oxford University Press, 1993.

Duggan, Lisa. *Sapphic Slashers: Sex, Violence, and American Modernity.* Durham: Duke University Press, 2000.

Dunning, Stefanie. "Parallel Perversions: Interracial and Same Sexuality in James Baldwin's *Another Country*." *MELUS* 26, no. 4 (Winter 2001): 95–112.

Duvall, John N. "Faulkner's Crying Game: Male Homosexual Panic." *Faulkner and Gender: Faulkner and Yoknapatwpha*, 1, ed. Donald M. Kartiganer and Ann J. Abadie, 48–72. Jackson: University Press of Mississippi, 1994.

Edwards, Laura. *Gendered Strife and Confusion: The Political Culture of Reconstruction.* Urbana: University of Illinois Press, 1997.

Ellis, Havelock. *Sexual Inversion.* Philadelphia: F. A. Davis, 1915.

Ellison, Ralph. *Invisible Man.* New York: Random House, 1952.

———. "An Extravagance of Laughter." *Going to the Territory*, 145–97. New York: Vintage, 1995.

Faulkner, William. *Go Down, Moses, and Other Stories.* New York: Random House, 1942.

———. *Absalom, Absalom!* New York: Random House, 1964.

———. *Light in August.* 1932. New York: Random House, 1972.

Favor, Jay Martin. *Authentic Blackness: The Folk in the New Negro Renaissance.* Durham: Duke University Press, 1999.

Ferguson, Roderick A. *Aberrations in Black: Toward a Queer Color of Critique.* Minneapolis: University of Minnesota Press, 2004.

Foreman, P. Gabrielle. "Manifest in Signs: The Politics of Sex and Representation in *Incidents in the Life of a Slave Girl*." *Harriet Jacobs and Incidents in the Life of a Slave Girl: New Critical Essays*, ed. Deborah M. Garfield and Rafia Zafar, 76–99. Cambridge: Cambridge University Press, 1996.

Foster, Guy Mark. "How Dare a Black Woman Make Love to a White Man! Black Women Romance Novelists and the Taboo of Interracial Desire." *Empowerment versus Oppression: Twenty First Century Views of Popular Romance Novels*, ed. Sally Goade, 103–28. Newcastle: Cambridge Scholars Publishing, 2007.

Foucault, Michel. *The History of Sexuality: An Introduction*, vol. 1., trans. Robert Hurley. New York: Pantheon, 1978.

Fowler, Doreen. *Faulkner: The Return of the Repressed.* Charlottesville: University of Virginia Press, 1997.

Frankel, Noralee. *Freedom's Women: Black Women and Families in Civil War Era Mississippi.* Bloomington: Indiana University Press, 1999.

Fraser, Nancy, and Linda Gordon. "A Genealogy of Dependency: Tracing a Keyword of the U.S. Welfare State." *Signs* 19, no. 2 (1994): 309–36.

Frazier, E. Franklin. *The Negro in the United States.* New York: Macmillan, 1957.

Fredrickson, George M. *The Black Image in the White Mind: The Debate on Afro-American Character and Destiny, 1817–1914.* Middletown, Conn.: Wesleyan University Press, 1987.

Freud, Sigmund. *Three Essays on the Theory of Sexuality*, trans. James Strachey. New York: Basic Books.

Friday, Krister. "Miscegenated Time: The Spectral Body, Race, and Temporality in *Light in August.*" *Faulkner Journal* 16, no. 3 (Fall 2000–Spring 2001): 41–64.

Froula, Christine. "The Daughter's Seduction: Sexual Violence and Literary History." *Signs* 11, no. 4 (Summer 1986): 621–44.

Gallop, Jane. *The Daughter's Seduction: Feminism and Psychoanalysis.* Ithaca: Cornell University Press, 1982.

Gilman, Sander L. "The Figure of the Black in the Thought of Hegel and Nietzsche." *German Quarterly* 53 (1980): 141–58.

——. "Black Bodies, White Bodies: Toward an Iconography of Female Sexuality in Late Nineteenth-Century Art, Medicine, and Literature." *"Race," Writing and Difference*, ed. Henry Louis Gates Jr., 233–61. Chicago: University of Chicago Press, 1986.

Glaude, Eddie S., Jr. "Introduction: Black Power Revisited." *Is It Nation Time? Contemporary Essays on Black Power and Black Nationalism*, ed. Eddie S. Glaude Jr., 1–21. Chicago: University of Chicago Press, 2002.

——. *In a Shade of Blue: Pragmatism and the Politics of Black America.* Chicago: University of Chicago Press, 2007.

Glaude, Eddie S., Jr., ed. *Is It Nation Time? Contemporary Essays on Black Power and Black Nationalism.* Chicago: University of Chicago Press, 2002.

Gleason, William. "Voices at the Nadir: Charles Chesnutt and David Bryant Fulton." *American Literary Realism* 24, no. 3 (Spring 1992): 22–41.

Goldberg, David Theo, ed. *Anatomy of Racism.* Minneapolis: University of Minnesota Press, 1990.

Goldsby, Jacqueline Denise. *A Spectacular Secret: Lynching in American Life and Literature.* Chicago: University of Chicago Press, 2006.

Goldstein, Richard. "'Go the Way Your Blood Beats': An Interview with James Baldwin." *James Baldwin: The Legacy*, ed. Quincy Troupe, 173–85. New York: Simon and Schuster, 1989.

Gordon, Linda. *Pitied but Not Entitled: Single Mothers and the Origins of Welfare.* Cambridge: Harvard University Press, 1995.

Gubar, Susan. *Racechanges: White Skin, Black Face in American Culture.* New York: Oxford University Press, 1997.

Gunning, Sandra. *Race, Rape, and Lynching: The Red Record of American Literature, 1890–1912.* New York: Oxford University Press, 1996.

Gwin, Minrose. "'Hereisthehouse': Cultural Spaces of Incest in *The Bluest Eye*." *Incest and the Literary Imagination*, ed. Elizabeth Barnes, 316–28. Gainesville: University Press of Florida, 2002.

Hale, Grace Elizabeth. *Making Whiteness: The Culture of Segregation in the South, 1890–1940*. New York: Pantheon, 1998.

Hall, Stuart. "Subjects in History: Making Diasporic Identities." *The House That Race Built: Black Americans, U.S. Terrain*, ed. Wahneema Lubiano, 289–300. New York: Pantheon, 1997.

Halperin, David. *One Hundred Years of Homosexuality, and Other Essays on Greek Love*. New York: Routledge, 1990.

——. *Saint Foucault: Towards a Gay Hagiography*. New York: Oxford University Press, 1995.

Harper, Phillip Brian. *Are We Not Men? Masculine Identity and the Problem of African-American Identity*. New York: Oxford University Press, 1996.

Harris, Cheryl I. "Whiteness as Property." *Harvard Law Review* 106, no. 8 (1993): 1709–91.

Harris, Susan K. *Nineteenth-Century American Women's Novels: Interpretive Strategies*. New York: Cambridge University Press, 1988.

Harris, Trudier. *Exorcising Blackness: Historical and Literary Lynching and Burning Rituals*. Bloomington: Indiana University Press, 1984.

Hart, Lynda. *Between the Body and the Flesh: Performing Sadomasochism*. New York: Columbia University Press, 1998.

Hartman, Saidiya V. *Scenes of Subjection: Slavery, Terror, and Self-Making in Nineteenth-Century America*. New York: Oxford University Press, 1997.

Herman, Judith Lewis, and Lisa Hirschman. *Father–Daughter Incest*. Cambridge: Harvard University Press, 1981.

Herron, Carolivia. *Thereafter Johnnie*. New York: Random House, 1991.

Higginbotham, Evelyn Brooks. "The Problem of Race in Women's History." *Coming to Terms: Feminism, Theory, Politics*, ed. Elizabeth Weed, 122–33. New York: Routledge, 1989.

Hill, Shirley. *Black Intimacies: A Gender Perspective on Families and Relationships*. Walnut Creek, Calif.: AltaMira, 2005.

Himes, Chester B. *If He Hollers Let Him Go*. Garden City, N.Y.: Doubleday, 1945.

Hine, Darlene. "Rape and the Inner Lives of Black Women in the Middle West." *Signs* 14, no. 4 (Summer 1989): 912–20.

Hine, Darlene C., and Kathleen Thompson. *A Shining Thread of Hope: The History of Black Women in America*. New York: Broadway, 1998.

Hirsh, Marianne. "Family Pictures: Maus, Mourning and Post-Memory," *Discourse: Theoretical Studies in Media and Culture* 15, no. 2 (1992–93): 3–29.

Hobson, Janelle. "The 'Batty' Politic: Toward an Aesthetics of the Black Female Body." *Hypatia* 18, no. 4 (Fall–Winter 2003): 87–105.

Hodes, Martha Elizabeth. *White Women, Black Men: Illicit Sex in the Nineteenth-Century South*. New Haven: Yale University Press, 1997.

Holland, Sharon Patricia. *Raising the Dead: Readings of Death and (Black) Subjectivity*. Durham: Duke University Press, 2000.

Holloway, Karla F. C. *Moorings and Metaphors: Figures of Culture and Gender in Black Women's Literature*. New Brunswick: Rutgers University Press, 1992.

hooks, bell. "Reflections on Race and Sex." *Yearning: Race, Gender, and Cultural Politics*, ed. Gloria Watkins. Boston: South End, 1990.

———. "Love as the Practice of Freedom." *Outlaw Culture: Resisting Representations*, 243–50. New York: Routledge, 1994.

Hopkins, Pauline E. *Contending Forces: A Romance Illustrative of Negro Life North and South* (1900). New York: Oxford University Press, 1988.

Hurston, Zora Neale. *Their Eyes Were Watching God* (1937). New York: Perennial Library, 1990.

Irigaray, Luce. *This Sex Which Is Not One*, trans. Catherine Porter and Carolyn Burke. Ithaca: Cornell University Press, 1990.

Irwin, John T. *Doubling and Incest/Repetition and Revenge: A Speculative Reading of Faulkner*. Baltimore: Johns Hopkins University Press, 1975.

Jacobs, Harriet. *Incidents in the Life of a Slave Girl* (1861). New York: Signet Classic, 2000.

JanMohamed, Abdul R. "Sexuality on/of the Racial Border: Foucault, Wright and the Articulation of 'Racialized Sexuality.'" *Discourses of Sexuality: From Aristotle to AIDS*, ed. Domna Stanton, 94–116. Ann Arbor: University of Michigan Press, 1992.

Japtok, Martin. "A Neglected Study in 'Whiteness'—Ann Petry's *Country Place*." *The Critical Response to Ann Petry*, ed. Hazel Arnett Ervin, 354–65. Westport, Conn.: Praeger, 2005.

Jenkins, Candice. *Private Lives, Proper Relations: Regulating Black Intimacy*. Minneapolis: University of Minnesota Press, 2007.

Jones, Gayl. *Corregidora*. New York: Random House, 1975.

Jordan, Winthrop D. *White over Black: American Attitudes toward the Negro, 1550–1812*. Chapel Hill: University of North Carolina Press, 1968.

Katz, Jonathan Ned. *Gay/Lesbian Almanac: A New Documentary*. New York: Harper and Row, 1983.

Kelley, Mary. *Private Woman, Public Stage: Literary Domesticity in Nineteenth-Century America*. New York: Oxford University Press, 1984.

Kelley, Robin D. G. *Yo Mama's Disfunktional!: Fighting the Culture Wars in Urban America*. Boston: Beacon, 1997.

King, Martin Luther, Jr. 1963. *Letter from the Birmingham Jail*. San Francisco: Harper San Francisco, 1994.

King, Richard. *Civil Rights and the Idea of Freedom*. New York: Oxford University Press, 1992.

Kristeva, Julia. *Powers of Horror: An Essay on Abjection*, trans. Leon S. Roudiez. New York: Columbia University Press, 1982.

Lacan, Jacques. *Écrits: A Selection*, trans. Alan Sheridan. New York: W. W. Norton, 1977.

Leeming, David. *James Baldwin: A Biography*. New York: Alfred A. Knopf, 1994.

Li, Stephanie. "Love and the Trauma of Resistance in Gayl Jones's *Corregidora*." *Callaloo* 29, no. 1 (Winter 2006): 131–50.

Lipsitz, George. *The Possessive Investment in Whiteness: How White People Benefit from Identity Politics*. Philadelphia: Temple University Press, 1998.

Loftus, Brian. "Speaking Silence: The Strategies and Structures of Queer Auto-biography." *College Literature* 24, no. 1 (1997): 28–45.

Lott, Eric. *Love and Theft: Blackface Minstrelsy and the American Working Class*. New York: Oxford University Press, 1993.

Lowenberg, Bert James, and Ruth Bogin, eds. *Black Women in Nineteenth-Century American Life: Their Words, Their Thoughts, Their Feelings*. University Park: Pennsylvania State University Press, 1976.

Lubiano, Wahneema, ed. *The House That Race Built: Black Americans, U.S. Terrain*. New York: Pantheon, 1997.

——. "Standing In for the State: Black Nationalism and 'Writing' the Black Subject." *Is It Nation Time?: Contemporary Essays on Black Power and Black Nationalism*, ed. Eddie S. Glaude Jr., 156–64. Chicago: University of Chicago Press, 2002.

Massey, Douglas, and Nancy Denton. *American Apartheid: Segregation and the Making of the Underclass*. Cambridge: Harvard University Press, 1993.

McBride, Dwight, ed. *James Baldwin Now*. New York: New York University Press, 1999.

McCullough, Kate. "Slavery, Sexuality, and Genre: Pauline E. Hopkins and the Representation of Female Desire." *The Unruly Voice: Rediscovering Pauline Elizabeth Hopkins*, ed, John Gruesser, 21–49. Champaign: University of Illinois Press, 1996.

Minter, David. *Faulkner's Questioning Narratives: Fictions of His Major Phase, 1929–1942*. Champaign: University of Illinois Press, 2001.

Morrison, Toni. *The Bluest Eye*. New York: Holt, 1970.

——. *Playing in the Dark: Whiteness and the Literary Imagination*. New York: Random House, 1993.

——. *Beloved*. New York: Plume, 1998.

Moten, Fred. *In the Break: The Aesthetics of the Black Radical Tradition*. Minneapolis: University of Minnesota Press, 2003.

Moynihan, Daniel Patrick. *The Negro Family: The Case for National Action*. Westport, Conn.: Greenwood Press, 1981.

Mulvey, Laura. *Visual and Other Pleasures*. Bloomington: Indiana University Press, 1989.

Muñoz, José E. *Disidentifications: Queers of Color and the Performance of Politics*. Minneapolis: University of Minnesota Press, 1999.

Nelson, Dana D. *National Manhood: Capitalist Citizenship and the Imagined Fraternity of White Men*. Durham: Duke University Press, 1998.

North, Michael. *The Dialect of Modernism: Race, Language, and Twentieth-Century Literature*. New York: Oxford University Press, 1994.

Ohi, Kevin. "'I'm Not the Boy You Want': Sexuality, 'Race,' and Thwarted Revelation in Baldwin's *Another Country*." *African American Review* 33, no. 2 (Summer 1999): 261–81.

Patterson, Orlando. *Slavery and Social Death: A Comparative Study*. Cambridge: Harvard University Press, 1982.

——. *Rituals of Blood: The Consequences of Slavery in Two Centuries*. Washington: Civitas/CounterPoint, 1998.

Petry, Ann. *The Narrows*. Boston: Houghton Mifflin, 1953.

Porter, Horace. *Stealing the Fire: The Art and Protest of James Baldwin*. Middletown, Conn.: Wesleyan University Press, 1989.

Posnock, Ross. *Color and Culture: Black Writers and the Making of the Modern Intellectual*. Cambridge: Harvard University Press, 1998.

Putzi, Jennifer. "Raising the Stigma: Black Womanhood and the Marked Body in Pauline Hopkins's *Contending Forces*." *College Literature* 31, no. 2 (2004): 1–21.

Raiford, Leigh. *Imprisoned in a Luminous Glare: Photography and the African American Freedom Struggle*. Chapel Hill: University of North Carolina Press, 2011.

Reed, Adolph, Jr., ed. *Race, Politics, and Culture: Critical Essays on the Radicalism of the 1960s*. Westport, Conn.: Greenwood, 1986.

Reid-Pharr, Robert F. "Tearing the Goat's Flesh: Homosexuality, Abjection, and the Production of a Late-Twentieth-Century Black Masculinity." *Studies in the Novel* 28, no. 3 (1996): 372–95.

——. *Conjugal Union: The Body, the House, and the Black American*. New York: Oxford University Press, 1999.

——. *Once You Go Black: Choice, Desire, and the Black American Intellectual*. New York: New York University Press, 2007.

Richardson, Riché. *Black Masculinity and the U.S. South: From Uncle Tom to Gangsta*. Athens: University of Georgia Press, 2001.

Roberts, Dorothy. *Killing the Black Body: Race, Reproduction, and the Meaning of Liberty*. New York: Random House, 1997.

Roediger, David R. *The Wages of Whiteness: Race and the Making of the American Working Class*. New York: Verso, 1991.

Ross, Ellen, and Rayna Rapp. "Sex and Society: A Research Note from Social History and Anthropology." *Powers of Desire: The Politics of Sexuality*, ed. Ann Snitow, Christine Stansell, and Sharon Thompson, 51–73. New York: New Feminist Library, 1983.

Ross, Marlon B. "Beyond the Closet as Raceless Paradigm." *Black Queer Studies: A Critical Anthology*, ed. E. Patrick Johnson and Mae G. Henderson, 161–89. Durham: Duke University Press, 2005.

Rushdy, Ashraf. "'Relate Sexual to Historical': Race, Resistance, and Desire in Gayl Jones's *Corregidora*." *African American Review* 34, no. 2 (Summer 2000): 273–97.

Samuels, Shirley, ed., *The Culture of Sentiment: Race, Gender, and Sentimentality in Nineteenth-Century America*. New York: Oxford University Press, 1992.

Sánchez-Eppler, Karen. *Touching Liberty: Abolition, Feminism, and the Politics of the Body*. Berkeley: University of California Press, 1993.

Sapphire. *Push*. New York: Alfred A. Knopf, 1996.

Scarry, Elaine. *The Body in Pain: The Making and Unmaking of the World*. New York: Oxford University Press, 1985.

Scott, Lynn Orilla. *James Baldwin's Later Fiction: Witness to the Journey*. East Lansing: Michigan State University Press, 2002.

Sedgwick, Eve Kosofsky. *Between Men: English Literature and Male Homosocial Desire*. New York: Columbia University Press, 1985.

Seshadri-Crooks, Kalpana. *Desiring Whiteness: A Lacanian Analysis of Race*. London: Routledge, 2000.

Sharpley-Whiting, T. Denean. *Black Venus: Sexualized Savages, Primal Fears, and Primitive Narratives in French*. Durham: Duke University Press, 1999.

Shin, Andrew, and Barbara Judson. "Beneath the Black Aesthetic: James Baldwin's Primer of Black American Masculinity." *African American Review* 32, no. 2 (Summer 1998): 247–61.

Sielke, Sabine. *Reading Rape: The Rhetoric of Sexual Violence in American Literature and Culture, 1790–1990*. Princeton: Princeton University Press, 2002.

Slessarev, Helene. *The Betrayal of the Urban Poor*. Philadelphia: Temple University Press, 1997.

Somerville, Siobhan. *Queering the Color Line: Race and the Invention of Homosexuality in American Culture*. Durham: Duke University Press, 2000.

Spillers, Hortense J. "Mama's Baby, Papa's Maybe: An American Grammar Book." *Within the Circle: An Anthology of African American Literary Criticism from the Harlem Renaissance to the Present*, ed. Angelyn Mitchell, 455–81. Durham: Duke University Press, 1994.

——. "All the Things You Could Be by Now, If Sigmund Freud's Wife Was Your Mother: Psychoanalysis and Race." *Black, White, and in Color: Essays on American Literature and Culture*, 376–427. Chicago: University of Chicago Press, 2003.

——. "'The Permanent Obliquity of an In(pha)lliby Straight': In the Time of the Daughters and the Fathers." *Black, White, and in Color: Essays on American Literature and Culture*, 230–50. Chicago: University of Chicago Press, 2003.

Stampp, Kenneth M. *The Peculiar Institution: Slavery in the Ante-bellum South*. New York: Alfred A. Knopf, 1956.

Stember, Charles Herbert. *Sexual Racism: The Emotional Barrier to an Integrated Society*. New York: Elsevier Scientific, 1976.

Stepan, Nancy Leys. *The Idea of Race in Science: Great Britain, 1800–1960*. Hamden, Conn.: Archon, 1982.

——. "Race and Gender: The Role of Analogy in Science." *The "Racial" Economy of Science: Toward a Democratic Future*, ed. Sandra Harding, 359–76. Bloomington: Indiana University Press, 1993.

Stephens, Judith. "Racial Violence and Representation: Performance Strategies in Lynching Dramas of the 1920's." *African American Review* 33, no. 4 (Winter 1999): 655–71.

Sterling, Dorothy. *We Are Your Sisters: Black Women in the Nineteenth Century*. New York: W. W. Norton, 1984.

Stockton, Kathryn. *Beautiful Bottom, Beautiful Shame: Where "Black" Meets "Queer."* Durham: Duke University Press, 2006.

Stoler, Ann Laura. *Race and the Education of Desire: Foucault's History of Sexuality and the Colonial Order of Things*. Durham: Duke University Press, 1995.

Sullivan, Nell. "Persons in Pieces: Race and Aphanisis in *Light in August*." *Mississippi Quarterly* 49, no. 3 (Summer 1996): 497–518.

Sundquist, Eric J. *To Wake the Nations: Race in the Making of American Literature*. Cambridge: Harvard University Press, 1993.

Tate, Claudia. *Domestic Allegories of Political Desire: The Black Heroine's Text at the Turn of the Century*. New York: Oxford University Press, 1992.

Tate, Greg. "Michael Jackson: The Man in Our Mirror." *The Village Voice*. 30 June 2009.

Tompkins, Jane P. *Sensational Designs: The Cultural Work of American Fiction, 1790–1860*. New York: Oxford University Press, 1985.

Torgovnick, Marianna. *Gone Primitive: Savage Intellects, Modern Lives*. Chicago: University of Chicago Press, 1990.

Van Deburg, William L. *New Day in Babylon: The Black Power Movement and American Culture, 1965–1975*. Chicago: University of Chicago Press, 1992.

Wald, Gayle. *Crossing the Line: Racial Passing in Twentieth-Century U.S. Literature and Culture*. Durham: Duke University Press, 2000.

Wald, Priscilla. *Constituting Americans: Cultural Anxiety and Narrative Form*. Durham: Duke University Press, 1995.

Walker, Alice. "The Child Who Favored Daughter." In *Love and in Trouble: Stories of Black Women*, 35–46. New York: Harcourt Brace Jovanovich, 1974.

——. *The Color Purple: A Novel*. New York: Harcourt Brace Jovanovich, 1982.

Walker, Rebecca. "The Untouchable Michael Jackson." *Huffington Post*. 11 July 2009.

Walker, Will. "*After the Fire Next Time*: James Baldwin's Postconcensus Double Bind." *Is It Nation Time? Contemporary Essays on Black Power and Black Nationalism*, ed. Eddie S. Glaude Jr., 215–33. Chicago: University of Chicago Press, 2002.

Wall, Cheryl, ed. *Changing Our Own Words: Essays on Criticism, Theory, and Writing by Black Women*. New Brunswick: Rutgers University Press, 1989.

Wallace, Maurice O. *Constructing the Black Masculine: Identity and Ideality in African American Men's Literature and Culture, 1775–1995.* Durham: Duke University Press, 2002.

Watkins, S. Craig. "Black Is Back, and It's Bound to Sell: Nationalist Desire and the Production of Black Popular Culture." *Is It Nation Time? Contemporary Essays on Black Power and Black Nationalism,* ed. Eddie S. Glaude Jr., 189–214. Chicago: University of Chicago Press, 1992.

Watson, Jay. "Overdoing Masculinity in *Light in August,* or, Joe Christmas and the Gender Guard." *The Faulkner Journal* 9, no. 1–2 (1993/1994): 149–77.

Weatherby, William J. *James Baldwin: Artist on Fire.* New York: Dell, 1989.

White, Deborah Gray. *Ar'n't I a Woman? Female Slaves in the Plantation South.* New York: W. W. Norton, 1985.

White, Walter. *Rope and Faggot: A Biography of Judge Lynch.* New York: Knopf, 1929.

Wiegman, Robyn. *American Anatomies: Theorizing Race and Gender.* Durham: Duke University Press, 1995.

Williams, Rhonda M. "Living at the Crossroads: Explorations in Race, Nationality, Sexuality, and Gender." *The House That Race Built: Black Americans, U.S. Terrain,* ed. Wahneema Lubiano, 136–56. New York: Pantheon, 1997.

Willis, Susan. "Eruptions of Funk: Historicizing Toni Morrison." *Toni Morrison: Critical Perspectives Past and Present,* ed. Henry Louis Gates Jr. and Kwame Anthony Appiah, 308–29. New York: Amistad, 1993.

Wilson, David. *Cities and Race: America's New Black Ghetto.* New York: Routledge, 2007.

Wilson, William J. *The Truly Disadvantaged: The Inner City, the Underclass, and Public Policy.* Chicago: University of Chicago Press, 1987.

Winant, Howard. "Racial Dualism at Century's End." *The House That Race Built: Black Americans, U.S. Terrain,* ed. Wahneema Lubiano, 87–115. New York: Pantheon, 1997.

Yarborough, Richard. "Introduction." *Contending Forces: A Romance Illustrative of Negro Life North and South* (1900), by Pauline E. Hopkins. New York: Oxford University Press, 1988.

Young-Bruehl, Elisabeth. *The Anatomy of Prejudices.* Cambridge: Harvard University Press, 1996.

Zegeye, Abebe, Leonard Harris, and Julia Maxted, eds. *Exploitation and Exclusion: Race and Class in Contemporary U.S. Society.* New York: H. Zell, 1991.

Index

Benjamin, Jessica, 49

Biraciality. See Mulattos

Black cultural production. See Cultural production

Black nationalism: authenticity in, 178–79 n. 40; black patriarchy in, 140–41; critique of, 126, 173–74 n. 30; on heterosexuality, 99, 140; on integration, 99; recontextualization of, 108

Blackness: coded references to, 114–15; as delimiter of whiteness, 59; homosexuality and, 1, 27; identity and, 1–2, 19; invention of, 7; mulattos and, 56–57; non-heternormativity and, 98–99; as normative, 91; post-Emancipation, 53; primitivity and, 55–56; public character of, 155; in racist discourse, 97; sexual perversions and, 9; transvaluation of, 172 n. 14

Black Panthers, 95

Black poor. See Poverty among African Americans

Black Power: black nationalism and, 99; fist as emblem, 125; on homo-erotic love, 4, 156; on masculine identity, 95, 100; viability of, 86

Bluest Eye, The (Morrison), 117, 127–32; birthing in, 130; derangement in, 131–32; incest in, 127–28, 129, 131, 132; white voyeurism in, 128

Breau, Elizabeth, 123

Brown v. Board of Education, 94, 95

Bush, George W., 134

Bush, Ronald, 55

Butler, Judith, 154

Butler, Octavia, 117, 118, 143–50; science fiction origin story, 145; Xenogenesis series, 144–46. See also Imago

Carby, Hazel, 4, 35, 73

Cardyn, Lynn, 75

Castration, 39, 66, 79

Chivalry, 71–72

Citizenship: African American, 4, 8, 51, 53, 98, 149; ethical, 85; illegality and, 92

Civil rights: legislation, 8, 116, 136, 156; movement, 95; retrenchment of, 134, 156; whiteness and, 93–94

Civil Rights Act (1875), 8

Civil Rights Act (1964), 116

Clinton, Bill, 135, 137

Closet, notions of, 9

Cohen, Cathy J., 1

Collins, Patricia Hill, 15, 161 n. 26, 162 n. 34, 171 n. 3

Connolly, William, 18

Contending Forces (Hopkins), 52–53, 69–76; on black poor, 76–77; domestic sphere in, 76; gang rape in, 72–76; interracial sexuality in, 72–73; lynching in, 70–71, 72, 77–78; miscegenation in, 69; racial terrorism in, 70, 77–78; rape in, 72; reconstructed family in, 81; as subversive literary form, 79

Corregidora (Jones), 117, 119–26; desire in, 122–25; on incestuous slave past, 121–22; postmemory in, 122; sexual invasion in, 123–24

Cultural production, 3, 6, 15, 20, 33

Davis, Thadious, 57

Dawn (Butler), 144

Dayan, Joan, 49

Dent, Gina, 1

Desire: in African American writing, 83–84, 122; circuits of, 15; coercion and, 42; collective, 71, 72, 83, 108; cross-racial, 9, 39, 63, 83–84, 90; denial of, 100; economies of, 39;

erotics and, 3, 4; incest and, 122–23; intra-gender, 86, 124; lesbian, 124–25; narcissism and, 63; nationalism and, 82; privacy and, 154; racial, 83; representations of, 83; sexual, 9, 10, 14, 24, 27, 31, 39, 83, 176 n. 22; white masculinity and, 54. *See also* Interracial sexuality; Sexuality

Difference: anatomy and, 11; identity and, 58–59; political practice and, 6; sexuality and, 2, 7; signals of, 9; sociological accounts of, 11–12; tenacity of, 94

Doane, Janice, 120–21, 136

Douglass, Frederick, 26, 35–38. See also *Narrative of the Life of Frederick Douglass*

Doyle, Laura, 114

duCille, Ann, 4, 99

Duggan, Lisa, 10, 160 n. 17, 169 n. 33

Dunning, Stephanie, 174 n. 31

Ellis, Havelock, 11, 13–14

Ellison, Ralph, 85, 118

Endogamy, 61, 99

Erotics: power of, 1; race and, 3. *See also* Sexuality

Faces and genitalia, 13

Family institution, 16–18, 23, 81, 117

Farrakhan, Louis, 140

Faulkner, William, 52–53, 54–60; on miscegenation, 54, 55. See also *Light in August*

Feminization: of black males, 40, 67, 75; racial exclusion and, 18

Ferguson, Roderick, 16, 18, 97–98

Fire Next Time, The (Baldwin), 111–12

Foster, Frances Smith, 4

Foster, Guy Mark, 86

Foucault, Michel, 2, 9, 32, 45, 159 n. 13

Fowler, Doreen, 58–59

Frederickson, George, 27

Freedmen's Bureau, 98

Freud, Sigmund, 13–14

Friday, Krister, 54, 58

Froula, Christine, 118–19

Fugitive Slave Law, 49

Gang rape, 51, 52, 67, 72–76, 73

Gayness. *See* Homosexuality

Gender: noncompliance, 15; normativity, 18; race and, 15–19; studies, 5, 23

Genitalia: of black men, 8, 10, 27; of black women, 8, 10–11, 12–13, 14, 27, 36, 161–62 n. 31; faces and, 13; prostitutes and, 11

Gilman, Sander, 11, 14, 161 n. 29

Glaude, Eddie, Jr., 108–9, 172 n. 14

Gleason, William, 8

Gordon, Linda, 135

Great Migration, 84

Gwin, Minrose, 128–29

Hale, Grace Elizabeth, 8, 56

Hall, Stuart, 146

Halperin, David, 33–34, 40

Harper, Phillip Brian, 100

Harris, Trudier, 67

Hartman, Saidiya, 25, 28, 30–31, 35, 119

Heteronormativity: bourgeois, 137; endogamy and, 61; exclusion/inclusion and, 2, 97–99; interracial sexuality and, 35; model of family, 23, 117; respectability and, 5; sexuality and, 33; whiteness and, 34

Heterosexuality: anality and, 14; black nationalism on, 99, 140; compulsory, 34, 61, 98–99; domination and, 28; endogamous, 61, 99; master class and, 38; promiscuous, 27;

Lacan, Jacques, 79
Lesbianism. *See* Homosexuality
Letter from the Birmingham Jail (King), 84
Liberation: black, 73, 80, 95, 109; marriage rights and, 99; oppositional philosophies, 143, 146; politics of, 6; sexuality and, 2, 3
Light in August (Faulkner), 52–53, 54–60; abject in, 57; homoeroticism in, 55, 64; lynching in, 66–68; miscegenation in, 54, 55; sexual assault in, 65–66; white womanhood in, 52–53; willing whiteness in, 60–68
Lilith's Brood (Butler), 144–46
Locke, John, 93
Lott, Eric, 56
Lubiano, Wahneema, 19, 82, 178–79 n. 49
Lynching: in African American writing, 3, 4, 72, 94; black emancipation and, 4, 53, 155; as communal spectacle, 48; as gang rape, 51, 52, 67, 73; as homoerotic act, 53; interracial sexuality and, 34; in literature, 66–68; pleasure and, 82–83; sexual sadism of, 53, 78; stereotyping and, 69, 78, 94; as white racial terrorism, 69; white supremacy and, 52

Malcolm X, 95
Marriage: black heroines and, 171 n. 59; blacks' right to, 58, 98–99; heteronormative ideal of, 35, 38, 97–98; interracial, 34, 84, 91, 92; patriarchy and, 11; patronym in, 91; polygamous, 27
McCullough, Kate, 69–70
Meillassoux, Claude, 120
Minstrelsy, 7, 8, 56
Minter, David, 60
Miscegenation: defined, 54; Faulkner on, 54, 55; legislation, 7, 8, 53, 64,

82, 164 n. 18, 165 n. 19; slavery and, 68; source of, 69; species cooperation and, 146
Mitchell, Alice, 9
Mixed-race. *See* Mulattos
Morrison, Toni, 117, 127–32. See also *Bluest Eye, The*
Moynihan, Daniel Patrick, 16–18
Mulattos, 56–58, 71, 167–68 n. 3
Mulvey, Laura, 131

Narrative of the Life of Frederick Douglass (Douglass), 26, 28, 35–38; beating in, 36–37; blood-stained gate in, 35–36
Narrows, The (Petry), 85, 86–95; cross-racial desire in, 90–93; lynching in, 94; on racial caste, 87–88; on racial difference, 94–95; storyline, 86–87, 88–90
Natal alienation, 34
Nationalism, defined, 82, 97
Nation of Islam, 99
Negro Family, The (Moynihan), 16–18
Non-heteronormativity, 16, 19, 26, 38, 49, 96, 98–99, 158 n. 2
North, Michael, 56

Oedipal drama, 131
One-drop rule, 53
Otherness, 18

Pedophilia, 117–18, 176 n. 22
Personal Responsibility and Work Opportunity Reconciliation Act (1996), 135
Perversity. *See* Sexual perversity
Petry, Ann, 85, 86–95
Plessy v. Ferguson, 8, 64
Politics: power and, 1; race and, 3; sexuality and, 3

1, 2, 6; race and, 3, 6, 7–15, 20, 34; racial terrorism and, 69; slavery and, 2, 4, 26, 30, 31, 33–38; studies, 14, 33; transformation and, 155. *See also* Erotics; Genitalia; Interracial sexuality

Sexual perversity: black family and, 16; blackness and, 9, 11; classification of, 33; metaphorics of, 3–4, 156; racial inequality and, 5; sexuality studies and, 14, 33; social exclusion and, 10

Shame, 44, 76, 91, 130, 131, 132

Sielke, Sabine, 127

Silence: incest and, 119; as resistance, 33; in slave narratives, 28–33

Slave narratives, 27; omissions in, 28; on oppression, 50; performativity in, 47; rationality in, 29; sadomasochism in, 41–42, 47, 155, 163 n. 3; silence in, 28–33. *See also under specific narratives*

Slavery: cultural constructions and, 26–27; feminization of black men and, 40, 67; incest rooted in, 119–20; as matrilineal, 37–38, 42–43; miscegenation and, 68; moral depravity of, 43, 50; as paternalistic institution, 49, 120–21, 124; as peculiar institution, 38–39; racist attitudes and, 34; rape during, 10, 31–32, 36, 37, 38–41; same-sex abuse and, 41; sexuality and, 2, 4, 26, 30, 31, 33–38; social status and, 7; survival strategies during, 42

Slessarev, Helene, 134, 177–78 n. 40

Somerville, Siobhan, 9–10, 63, 159 n. 12

Spectatorship, 8–9

Spillers, Hortense, 37, 40, 45, 73, 120

Stember, Charles Herbert, 11–13

Stephens, Judith, 51–52

Stereotypes: of black male rapist, 39, 69; of black women, 22, 116, 162–63 n. 48; enabling, 8–9, 56; lynching and, 94; racial identity and, 159 n. 11; welfare and, 136

Subjectivity, 6, 39, 41, 67, 86, 122–23, 131, 154

Tate, Claudia, 4, 98–99, 171 n. 59

Tate, Greg, 153, 154

Their Eyes Were Watching God (Hurston), 25

Till, Emmett, 95

Tompkins, Jane, 79

Torgovnick, Marianna, 55

Trauma: of black female embodiment, 130; cultural, 122, 127, 155; legacy of, 142; silence and, 115; slave diaries and, 31, 50; from slavery, 68. *See also* Incest; Lynching; Rape; Sadomasochism

Visual and Other Pleasures (Mulvey), 131

Walker, Rebecca, 153

Walker, Will, 95–96

Wall, Cheryl, 114

Wallace, Maurice O., 167 n. 53

Watson, Jay, 62

Weber, Max, 97

Welfare. *See* Public assistance

Wells-Barnett, Ida B., 68–69, 71, 80

WEP. *See* Work Experience Program

White, Deborah, 44

Whiteness: attractiveness and, 12–13; black identity and, 7, 18–19; capitalist accumulation and, 34, 135, 172 n. 11; civil rights and, 93–94; delimited by blackness, 59; heteronormativity and, 34; heterosexuality and, 34, 49; manhood and, 57; post-Reconstruction, 55; racial terrorism and, 4, 53,

Aliyyah I. Abdur-Rahman is an assistant professor
of English at Brandeis University.

Library of Congress Cataloging-in-Publication Data
Abdur-Rahman, Aliyyah I.
Against the closet : black political longing and the erotics
of race / Aliyyah I. Abdur-Rahman.
p. cm.
Includes bibliographical references and index.
ISBN 978-0-8223-5224-2 (cloth : alk. paper)
ISBN 978-0-8223-5241-9 (pbk. : alk. paper)
1. African Americans—Race identity. 2. African
Americans—Sexual behavior. 3. United States—Race
relations—History. 4. Queer theory. 5. Identity
(Psychology) I. Title.
E185.625.A333 2012
305.896′073—dc23
2011053089